# Imagining Death in Spenser and Milton

*Other books by the editors include:*

*Elizabeth Jane Bellamy*

TRANSLATIONS OF POWER: Narcissism and the Unconscious in Epic History

AFFECTIVE GENEALOGIES: Psychoanalysis, Postmodernism and the 'Jewish Question' After Auschwitz

*Patrick Cheney*

MARLOWE'S COUNTERFEIT PROFESSION: Ovid, Spenser, Counter-Nationhood

SPENSER'S FAMOUS FLIGHT: A Renaissance Idea of a Literary Career

*Michael Schoenfeldt*

BODIES AND SELVES IN EARLY MODERN ENGLAND: Physiology and Inwardness in Spenser, Shakespeare, Herbert and Milton

PRAYER AND POWER: George Herbert and Renaissance Courtship

# Imagining Death in Spenser and Milton

Edited by

**Elizabeth Jane Bellamy**
*Professor of English*
*University of New Hampshire*

**Patrick Cheney**
*Professor of English and Comparative Literature*
*Pennsylvania State University*

**Michael Schoenfeldt**
*Professor of English*
*University of Michigan*

palgrave
macmillan

First published 2003 by
PALGRAVE MACMILLAN
Houndmills, Basingstoke, Hampshire RG21 6XS and 175 Fifth Avenue,
New York, N. Y. 10010
Companies and representatives throughout the world

PALGRAVE MACMILLAN is the global academic imprint of the Palgrave
Macmillan division of St. Martin's Press, LLC and of Palgrave Macmillan
Ltd. Macmillan® is a registered trademark in the United States, United
Kingdom and other countries. Palgrave is a registered trademark in the
European Union and other countries.

ISBN 0–333–98398–X

This book is printed on paper suitable for recycling and made from fully
managed and sustained forest sources.

A catalogue record for this book is available from the British Library.

Library of Congress Cataloging-in-Publication Data

Imagining death in Spenser and Milton/co-edited by Elizabeth Jane
    Bellamy, Patrick Cheney, Michael Schoenfeldt.
        p.    cm.
    Includes bibliographical references and index.
    ISBN 0–333–98398–X
    1. Spenser, Edmund, 1552?–1599 – Criticism and interpretation.
2. Death in literature.    3. English poetry – Early modern, 1500–1700 –
History and criticism.    4. Spenser, Edmund, 1552?–1599 – Knowledge
– Manners and customs.    5. Milton, John, 1608–1674 – Knowledge –
Manners and customs.    6. Milton, John, 1608–1674 – Criticism and
interpretation.    I. Bellamy, Elizabeth J. (Elizabeth Jane)    II. Cheney,
Patrick Gerard, 1949–    III. Schoenfeldt, Michael Carl.

PR2367.D4.I43  2003
821'.3093548—dc21

                                                                    2003042944

10    9    8    7    6    5    4    3    2    1
12    11    10    09    08    07    06    05    04    03

Printed and bound in Great Britain by
Antony Rowe Ltd, Chippenham and Eastbourne

# Contents

*List of Illustrations*                                    vii

*Acknowledgements*                                         viii

*Notes on Contributors*                                    ix

1 Introduction: Towards Defining a Poetics of Death in
  Spenser and Milton                                         1
  *Elizabeth Jane Bellamy, Patrick Cheney and*
  *Michael Schoenfeldt*

2 Spenser and the Death of the Queen                        28
  *Andrew Hadfield*

3 Psychic Deadness in Allegory: Spenser's House of
  Mammon and Attacks on Linking                             46
  *Theresa M. Krier*

4 Death in an Allegory                                      65
  *Gordon Teskey*

5 'After the First Death, There is No Other': Spenser,
  Milton, and (Our) Death                                   78
  *Roger Kuin and Anne Lake Prescott*

6 Anatomizing Death                                         95
  *Linda Gregerson*

7 Reading Death and the Ethics of Enjoyment in Spenser
  and Milton                                                116
  *Marshall Grossman*

8 Sublime/Pauline: Denying Death in *Paradise Lost*        131
  *Rachel Trubowitz*

9 Imagining the Death of the King: Milton, Charles I, and
  Anamorphic Art                                            151
  *Laura L. Knoppers*

10 Milton's Nationalism and the Rights of Memory            171
   *Paul Stevens*

**11 Death's Afterword**                                              185
    *David Lee Miller*

*Bibliography*                                                       200

*Index*                                                             212

# List of Illustrations

*Figure 6.1* *Paradise Lost* 1 1–16                                                          104

*Figure 9.1* Anamorphic Portrait of Charles I (ca. 1660). By
            courtesy of the National Swedish Art Museums.                 152

*Figure 9.2* Hans Holbein, *The Ambassadors* (1533). By courtesy
            of the National Gallery, London.                             154

*Figure 9.3* Corrected image of anamorphic skull, Holbein,
            *The Ambassadors* (1533). By courtesy of the National
            Gallery, London.                                             155

*Figure 9.4* Anamorphosis of a Skull (1615) from Lucas Brunn,
            *Praxis Perspectivae* (Nürnberg, 1615). By permission
            of the Houghton Library, Harvard University.                 156

*Figure 9.5* Anamorphic Engraving of Charles I (ca. 1649). By
            courtesy of the National Portrait Gallery, London.           157

*Figure 9.6* Charles I at prayer, frontispiece to *Eikon Basilike*
            (1649). Reproduced by permission of Rare Books
            and Manuscripts, Special Collections Library, The
            Pennsylvania State University Libraries.                     162

*Figure 9.7* Anamorphic Portrait of Charles II (ca. 1660). By
            courtesy of the National Swedish Art Museums.                167

# Acknowledgements

The editors of this volume wish to thank Ann Marangos, Emily Rosser and Paula Kennedy of Palgrave Macmillan for their editorial guidance and patience; and we thank the anonymous reader of our manuscript for offering such a generous and enthusiastic reading. We wish also to thank the many people who attended the 1999 evening panel, 'Spenser and Death', sponsored by Spenser at Kalamazoo and the Thirty-fourth International Congress on Medieval Studies at Western Michigan University. The question-and-answer session was lively (despite the 'deadly topic') and thought-provoking, giving the editors of this volume the impetus to assemble a collection of essays on the larger topic of death in Spenser and Milton.

Finally, the editors owe an enormous debt of gratitude to our editorial assistants, Freda Hauser and Keith Botelho, doctoral students in English at the University of New Hampshire. Their organizational skills, energy, and indeed, prophetic vision averted many disasters and were major factors in bringing this volume to completion. It could not have happened without them.

# Notes on the Contributors

**Elizabeth Jane Bellamy** is Professor of English at the University of New Hampshire. She is the author of *Translations of Power: Narcissism and the Unconscious in Epic History* (1992) and *Affective Genealogies: Psychoanalysis, Postmodernism, and the 'Jewish Question' After Auschwitz* (1997). She has published numerous articles on early modern literature and the relevance of psychoanalysis for cultural critique.

**Patrick Cheney** is a Professor of English and Comparative Literature at Penn State University. He is the author of *Spenser's Famous Flight: A Renaissance Idea of a Literary Career* (1993) and *Marlowe's Counterfeit Profession: Ovid, Spenser, Counter-Nationhood* (1997). He has co-edited *Worldmaking Spenser: Explorations in the Early Modern Age* (1999); *Approaches to Teaching Shorter Elizabethan Poetry* (2000); and *European Literary Careers: The Author from Antiquity through the Renaissance* (2002). A past President of the International Spenser Society, he is now co-editing *The Collected Works of Edmund Spenser*.

**Linda Gregerson** is the author of *The Reformation of the Subject: Spenser, Milton, and the English Protestant Epic; Negative Capability: Contemporary American Poetry*; and three volumes of poetry, the most recent of which is *Waterbourne*. She teaches at the University of Michigan and is currently at work on *The Commonwealth of the Word*, a study of collective identity in Reformation England.

**Marshall Grossman** is Professor of English at the University of Maryland. He is the author of *The Story of All Things: Writing the Self in English Renaissance Narrative Poetry* and *'Authors to themselves': Milton and the Revelation of History*, and editor of *Aemelia Lanyer: Gender, Genre and the Canon*. He is currently at work on *The Seventeenth Century* for Guide to Literature series.

**Andrew Hadfield** is Professor of English at the University of Sussex, and visiting Professor at Columbia University. He is the author of a number of studies of Renaissance literature and culture including *Spenser's Irish Experience: Wilde Fruit and Salvage Soyl* (1997); *Literature, Travel and Colo-*

*nial Writing in the English Renaissance, 1545–1630* (1998); and *Shakespeare and Renaissance Political Culture* (2003).

**Laura L. Knoppers** is Professor of English and Director of the Institute for the Arts and Humanities at Penn State University. She is the author of *Historicizing Milton: Spectacle, Power, and Poetry in Restoration England* (1994) and *Constructing Cromwell: Ceremony, Portrait, and Print, 1645–1661* (2000), as well as various articles and essays on seventeenth-century British literature, politics, and religion.

**Theresa M. Krier**, until recently Associate Professor at the University of Notre Dame, is Professor of English at Macalester College. She is the author of *Gazing on Secret Sights: Spenser, Classical Imitation, and the Decorums of Vision* (1990) and *Birth Passages: Maternity and Nostalgia, Antiquity to Shakespeare* (2001), and editor of *Refiguring Chaucer in the Renaissance* (1998). She is also editor of *The Spenser Review*.

**Roger Kuin** is Professor of English Literature at York University in Toronto, Canada. He has published an edition of Robert Langham's *Letter* on the Kenilworth festivities, and more recently *Chamber Music*, an experimental study in Elizabethan sonnet-sequences and modern criticism. Numerous articles include 'Querre-Muhau: Sir Philip Sidney and the New World' (*Renaissance Quarterly* LI:2, summer 1998), and 'The Double Helix: Public and Private in Spenser's *Faerie Queene*' (*Spenser Studies* XVI, 2002). He is currently editing the correspondence of Sir Philip Sidney, and is Secretary of the International Sidney Society as well as a member of the *Sidney Journal*'s editorial board.

**Anne Lake Prescott** teaches at Barnard and Columbia. The author of *French Poets and the English Renaissance* and *Imagining Rabelais in Renaissance England*, she is editor, with William Oram and Thomas P. Roche, of *Spenser Studies* and, with Hugh Maclean, of *The Norton Critical Edition of Spenser*. With Betty Travitsky she is co-editor of a series of early modern works by or relevant to women.

**David Lee Miller** is Professor of English at the University of Kentucky. He is the author of *The Poem's Two Bodies: The Poetics of the 1590* Faerie Queene (1988) and *Dreams of the Burning Child: Sacrificial Sons and the Father's Witness* (2003); he is also co-editor of *Approaches to Teaching Spenser's* Faerie Queene (1994) and *The Production of English Renaissance Culture* (1994).

**Michael Schoenfeldt** is Professor of English at the University of Michigan, and Director of the Program in Medieval and Early Modern Studies. He is the author of *Prayer and Power: George Herbert and Renaissance Courtship* (1991), *Bodies and Selves in Early Modern England: Physiology and Inwardness in Spenser, Shakespeare, Herbert, and Milton* (1999), and of published essays on Spenser, Shakespeare, Jonson, Donne, Herrick, Lanyer, and Milton.

**Paul Stevens** is Professor of English and Comparative Literature at the University of Toronto. He is the author of *Imagination and the Presence of Shakespeare in 'Paradise Lost'* (1985) and co-editor of *Discontinuities: New Essays on Renaissance Literature and Criticism* (1998). He is currently working on a book provisionally entitled *Nationalist Milton*.

**Gordon Teskey**, Harvard University, is author of *Allegory and Violence* (1996). He is in the process of completing *Delirious Milton*.

**Rachel Trubowitz** is Associate Professor of English at the University of New Hampshire, Durham. She has written articles on a variety of early modern topics. Her most recent publication is 'Crossed Dressed Women and Natural Mothers: "Boundary Panic" in *Hic Mulier*', in *Debating Gender in Early Modern England* (Palgrave Macmillan, 2002).

# 1
## Introduction: Toward Defining a Poetics of Death in Spenser and Milton

*Elizabeth Jane Bellamy, Patrick Cheney and Michael Schoenfeldt*

In his groundbreaking study of changing Western attitudes towards death since antiquity, the social historian Philippe Ariès has argued that death is not a fixed concept but rather a cultural construct reimagined through time.[1] The cultural practice of 'imagining' death assumes distinctive changes from one era to the next. The early modern era is especially compelling for how it imagined death. In contrast to the early Middle Ages, when Western Christianity could take comfort in assurances of personal salvation, Ariès argues that the macabre iconography of the fourteenth century – its increasing fixations on the partially decomposed corpse – 'betrayed the bitter feeling of failure, mingled with mortality: a passion for being, an anxiety at not sufficiently being' (105). By the late sixteenth and seventeenth centuries, Ariès contends, the heightened sense of personal identity that shaped the early modern 'self' also gave rise to a more intense anxiety about death (138). In the past few years Ariès's comprehensive book has paved the way for a number of important studies of death in early modern England – and, in particular, in early modern English literature.[2] To cite one such study, Robert N. Watson, in his *The Rest is Silence*, asserts that Jacobean culture 'struggled with the suspicion that death was a complete and permanent annihilation of the self, not merely some latency of the body awaiting Last Judgment' (3).

In a seemingly unrelated arena, one of the larger and more enduring questions within the literary history of early modern England has been: what, precisely, does it mean to trace a literary continuum between the two giants of the early modern English canon, Edmund Spenser and John Milton? In his *Preface to Fables Ancient and Modern*, John Dryden writes that Milton 'has acknowledged to me that Spenser was his original' (247).[3] At stake in Milton's acknowledgement is nothing less than shaping the core of a literary history for early modern England; and over the last thirty years or so, various scholars (including two contributors to this volume, Linda Gregerson and Gordon Teskey) have sought to undertake the challenging task of articulating the complexities of Milton's intellectual debt to Spenser.[4] But, incredibly, no collection of essays on Spenser and Milton has, to date, been published – let alone a collection on the provocative topic of how death is taken into a Spenserian and Miltonic consciousness. As Marshall Grossman cogently argues in his essay for this volume, 'Whatever else it might entail, thinking about Spenser, Milton, and death is a literary historical exercise.' (See Chapter 7 by Grossman.)

This volume draws its impetus from the conviction that death is a central, yet curiously understudied preoccupation for Spenser and Milton. We contend that death – in all its early modern reformations and deformations – is an indispensable backdrop for any attempt to articulate the relationship between Spenser and Milton, as well as for ongoing attempts to trace, echoing Ariès, early modern writers' 'anxiety at not sufficiently being'.

The title of our volume, *Imagining Death in Spenser and Milton*, poses an implicit question: is death in Spenser and Milton 'real', or can it only be displaced, that is, *imagined*? Spenser's and Milton's attempts to imagine the unknowable experience of death result in death's being both everywhere and nowhere throughout their works. Our volume will explore such overarching questions as: who dies in Spenser's and Milton's work, and why? What is the relationship between death and desire in Spenser and Milton? To what extent should death in Spenser and Milton be equated with 'loss' as opposed to 'real' death? What is the relationship between death and Spenserian and Miltonic poetic form? Do Spenser's characters have *time* to die in the 'endlesse worke' of *The Faerie Queene*? Does *Paradise Lost* hold us in a 'death grip' such that there is no way to write epic in its wake? To what extent are Spenserian and Miltonic representations of death intrinsic to allegory? How is death memorialized, or how does death fail to be memorialized in Spenser and Milton? What are the erotics of Spenserian and Miltonic death? To what extent do Spenser's and Milton's treatment of death inhabit the divide between public and private domains? What are the political, ideological, and national implications of death in Spenser and Milton?[5]

This introduction attempts, in exploratory fashion, to trace some of the general parameters of what is entailed in reading Spenserian and Miltonic epic under the sign of death. Before turning to Spenserian and

Miltonic epic, it is necessary to glance briefly at tragedy as the genre most intimately defined by death.

Michael Neill's *Issues of Death* argues that tragedy 'was among the principal instruments by which the culture of early modern England reinvented death' (3). Neill's thesis achieves two provocative goals. Not only does he argue that literature was a powerful tool for 'reinventing' death in early modernity, but his specific focus on tragedy also forges an intrinsic link between literary genre and death. For Neill, Renaissance tragic drama, at its core, is about 'the discovery of death and the mapping of its meanings' (1). Death is constitutive of tragedy, with the inevitable death of the tragic progatonist determining, in an Aristotelian vision, tragedy's very structure. As the privileged emblem of early modern tragedy's preoccupation with death, Neill offers *Hamlet*'s graveyard 'with its anonymous pit of clay [as] the play's most brutal sign of mortal ending' (87).[6]

The success of Neill's study for early modern English tragedy and its mappings of the meanings of death prompts the question of whether early modern English epic can serve as a similarly powerful genre for interrogating death in the Renaissance. If, as Neill argues, early modern tragedy served as 'an instrument for probing the painful mystery of ending' (31), can we speak of a 'poetics' of death in early modern English epic? Is there any sense in which death is *intrinsic* to early modern epic? Can Spenser's and Milton's epics offer the kinds of fundamental insights into early modern representations of death that, say, tragedy does? What is there in *The Faerie Queene* and in *Paradise Lost* that can link us to death as powerfully as the icon of *Hamlet*'s graveyard?

Further complicating any attempt to answer these questions is that the general topic of death in Spenser and Milton must also negotiate the vexed question, alluded to earlier, of what it means to trace a literary continuum between Spenserian and Miltonic epic. Milton's declaration of poetic filiation to Spenser – his claim that Spenser was his 'original' – makes it imperative that readers of *Paradise Lost* listen to the echoes of *The Faerie Queene* throughout Milton's epic. But where do we begin this process of listening? At one point, Maureen Quilligan, in her *Milton's Spenser*, urges a well-perceived focus on the concept of error as a means of reading *Paradise Lost* against the grain of *The Faerie Queene*: in *Paradise Lost*, Adam and Eve's 'easy binary either/or choice' to obey and abstain 'is quite simple compared with the potential for error' that pervades *The Faerie Queene* (76). But, error being the errant concept it is, the implications here are that the differences between the two major

Renaissance epic poets in English may be more fundamental than the similarities. And Milton's claim that Spenser was his 'original' can begin to seem a red herring.[7]

Three years later, Gordon Teskey (See Chapter 4) confronted the many significant generic differences between Spenser's and Milton's epic modalities. Picking up, in a sense, where Northrop Frye's *Secular Scripture* and its claim that *The Faerie Queene* is a romance not comparable to Milton's epic leaves off, Teskey argues, 'It is strange that the poet whom Milton acknowledged as his "original" should be a master of all the techniques of narrative romance that are scornfully dismissed in *Paradise Lost* as "the skill of Artifice or Office mean"' (9.39, qtd on 9).[8] Because Milton so pointedly rejects the fanciful 'artifices' of narrative romance, Teskey is moved to suggest Homer, Virgil, and Tasso as epic precursors more central to Milton's preoccupations; and he puts much-needed pressure on Dryden's claim: 'In what sense, then, was Spenser Milton's original'? (9).

Nevertheless, at the same time, the allegorical figure of Death has often been seen as Milton's most Spenserian episode. As John King has recently argued, 'Satan's encounter with Sin and Death has troubled modern readers as a problematic intrusion of Spenserian allegory in *Paradise Lost*' (69).[9] As King points out in a chapter aptly entitled 'Milton's Den of Error', both Addison and Dr Johnson found the allegory of Sin and Death to manifest 'one of the greatest faults of the poem', in Dr Johnson's unambiguous judgment. King attempts to rescue Milton's allegory by comprehending it amid the vituperative language of religious controversy. A different set of generic expectations are required, he suggests, to appreciate just what Milton is getting at in the allegory of Sin and Death. According to King, Milton follows Spenser by injecting into epic material imagery developed in religious polemic to depict doctrinal error.

From widely differing critical presuppositions, then, Quilligan, Teskey, and King each view the concept of error as intrinsic to reading the two epics together. Error, as a principle of wandering, delay, and deferral, inhabits an entirely different register from the finality of death. Nevertheless, a brief glance at the marked contrasts between Spenserian and Miltonic narratives of error can also be a useful first step in pondering the differences in how Spenser and Milton represent death.

Spenser's notorious dragoness Errour is an allegory for the dilatoriness of narrative romance itself (most vividly embodied in her 'endlesse traine'), signalling that Spenser's wandering narrative is literally and figuratively *errant*.[10] Milton's narrative, on the other hand, is structured on deliberate choice. Thus, in the prelapsarian world of *Paradise Lost*, error is confined or, in Teskey's words, 'set apart from existence and restricted to a category of things that are *not* – perversity, paradox, and negation – so that the narrative will remain uninfected' (9, italics in original). In *Paradise Lost*, where error is limited to one simple (and fatal) decision by Adam and Eve, we could say that death 'lives' with greater vitality (and finality?). Milton's well-known figure of Death, Satan's son by his own daughter Sin, is one of the few allegorical tropes in *Paradise Lost*, but he is a true and unmistakable antagonist: 'with delight he snuffed the smell / Of mortal change on earth' (10.272–3).[11] Put another way, he is an allegory openly inviting a literal reading: in *Paradise Lost*, Death is truly a negation of life. But Milton's Death is also alive, dangerously alive, a predatory creature of infinite appetite, drooling at the prospect of devouring all of creation.

However, any focus on error in *The Faerie Queene* presents a serious challenge for posing death as a useful rubric for understanding Spenser's epic. If Miltonic narrative leaves little room for the ambiguities of error, Spenserian narrative is error's thriving terrain, where the finality of death is often deferred indefinitely. In the next few pages, we turn to a consideration of some of the ways in which Spenserian error actually works to evade and avoid death in *The Faerie Queene*.

For his part, Spenser seems attracted to narratives in which characters miraculously survive death, but not through heroic performance, since they tend to fall into unconsciousness, as Redcrosse does in Orgoglio's dungeon (1.7–8), Guyon outside Mammon's cave (2.7–8), or Timias in the dark forest near Belphoebe's glade (3.5). Spenser does not confer distinction on his titular heroes, nor on the psychologically deep resources of individual subjectivity, but rather on external agents of divine grace sent directly by God, as represented through Arthur in the stories of Redcrosse and Guyon or Belphoebe in the story of Timias. Thus, Spenser confers distinction not on the dying but on the saving, not on interior but on exterior power, not on humankind but on the deity.

In *The Faerie Queene*, the figure of Death ('Vnbodied, vnsoul'd, vnheard, vnseene') appears briefly in the pageant of Time that concludes the 'Mutabilitie Cantos' (7.7.46). But he is pointedly paired with Life, '[f]ull of delightful and liuely joy' (7.7.46); and it is Life, not the figure of Death, that concludes Time's pageant.[12] Spenser's inconsequential Death makes his brief and largely forgettable appearance not as Life's mighty opposite, but as a kind of passing shadow. And it is surely significant that he appears in a fragmented book concerned with investigating not mortality but change and mutability as ordering principles for the universe. In *The Faerie Queene*, it is not 'vnsouled' Death, but the 'haughty' Mutabilitie that, to echo Milton, more resolutely, 'snuff[s] the smell / Of mortal change on earth'. Thus, far more than the finality of death, the 'infecting' concepts of wandering and error, of fragmentation and anticipation, structure the 'endlesse worke' of *The Faerie Queene.* When it comes to representations of death, can we truly claim that Spenser was Milton's 'original'? If Milton's change is mortal, Spenser's mortality appears to be highly changeable.

The overarching, (dis)ordering principle of Spenser's epic as a whole is Errour, perhaps the primary obstacle to imagining death in *The Faerie Queene.* The figure of Errour has, of course, been the subject of much scholarly attention for decades. But it is worth lingering awhile on the precise moment of her death. Errour dies early in Book 1 – but it is a death strangely lacking in 'deadly' finality. In his battle with Errour (the first of his many tests in Book 1), Redcrosse finally manages to hack off the dragoness's head – the moment of her death, to be sure. But her resulting bloodshed has a curiously sustaining quality. Errour's monstrous, hermaphroditic 'scattred brood', so used to nourishing themselves by '[s]ucking vpon her poisonous dugs' and taking shelter by creeping into her mouth, suffer 'troublous feare' when they see their slain mother. But they then resourcefully 'flocked all about her bleeding wound, / And svcked vp their dying mothers blood, / Making her death their life [. . .]' (*FQ* 1.1.25). Errour's gory death is less a death than, however perversely, an ongoing, nurturing 'life' for her brood. Redcrosse watches 'amazde' as Errour's brood, having satisfied their thirst, 'with fulnesse burst, / And bowels gushing forth: well worthy end / Of such as drunke her life, the which them nurst' (*FQ* 1.1.26). Though Errour's death offers a momentary 'drink' of life for her offspring, they too eventually die. But should we say that Errour's brood are 'dead' – or rather, have their engorged, bursting bowels propelled the narrative into an allegorical 'life' of Errour, as if the pieces of their exploded, gushing innards offer a nurturing life for *The Faerie Queene's* wandering narrative? By briefly '[m]aking her [Errour's] death their life', Errour's 'deformed monsters' constitute a kind of bizarre life force that unleashes Errour throughout Faerie land, nourishing the 'endlesse traine' of moral error in the epic as a whole.

If Teskey is right in claiming that, in *Paradise Lost*, error is 'restricted to a category of things that are *not*', in *The Faerie Queene* error – even (especially?) in death – is very much a thing that *is*. Thus, among other considerations, our volume's introduction is under some constraints to address the question: to what extent does death in Spenser's epic elude representation in a narrative world entangled in error, delay, and defer-ral? How successfully does death challenge and terminate the power-fully punning force of Errour as it drives the 'endlesse worke' of *The Faerie Queene*? To what extent does the finality of death inevitably cede place to a deferring Errour?[13]

For every image of a swift or certain death in *The Faerie Queene* (from Book 2's Mordant and Amavia to Book 6's Old Melibee and his wife) numerous counter-examples can be cited of (one struggles for wording here) deaths that will not die. One of Spenser's most vivid examples of a resistance to death is Maleger, who, as his troops besiege Alma's Castle, emerges as one of Arthur's most formidable antagonists. The cadaver-ous Maleger seemingly represents the diseased body on the brink of death; but he is strangely resistant to crossing that threshold, and he persistently forces Arthur to struggle with the physical and existential dilemma of '[h]ow to take life from that dead-liuing swaine' (2.9.44). Engaging Arthur in intensely prolonged combat, Maleger at one point falls 'groueling to the ground' (2.11.34). But, nourished by his mother earth, he '[o]ut of his swowne arose, fresh to contend, [. . .] / As hurt he had not beene' (*FQ* 2.11.34–5). With his sword, Arthur then succeeds in cutting '[a]n open passage through his riuen brest', triumphantly step-ping back to survey the bloodshed from 'the wounde so wide and won-derous' and to witness his antagonist's impending death (*FQ* 2.11.37–8). But, again, Maleger weirdly evades death:

> . . . he [Arthur] looked euermore
> When the hart bloud should gush out of his chest,
> Or his dead corse should fall vpon the flore;
> But his dead corse vpon the flore fell nathemore.

> (*FQ* 2.11.37)

Though a 'dead corse', Maleger does not die: he is a carcass '[t]hat could doe harme, yet could not harmed bee, / That could not die, yet seem'd a mortall wight, / That was most strong in most infirmitee' (*FQ* 2.11.40). Tossing his useless armor aside, Arthur crushes Maleger's body, picking him up in a bear hug and dashing '[t]he lumpish corse' to the ground – but 'back againe it did aloft rebownd' (*FQ* 2.9.42). Remembering that earth is Maleger's mother, Arthur again 'scruzed out of his carrion corse / The lothfull life', this time tossing the body into a stagnant lake where Maleger's body finally stirs no more. As has been widely noted, the combat between Arthur and Maleger is based on the myth of Hercules's overcoming of Antaeus. But identifying Spenser's source for the episode

should not excuse us from pondering the sheer metaphysical strange-
ness of Maleger's evasions of death: Maleger does eventually die – but
not until the narrative of Book 2, Canto 11 has engorged itself with the
tale of his several extended lives. Indeed, James Nohrnberg has teased
out some disturbing implications of the Maleger episode: 'The whole
question of what constitutes an allegorical agent's "death" is raised
here [. . .]' (298).[14]

Nohrnberg's observation that Spenser's allegory often struggles to represent death can prompt us to consider *The Faerie Queene*'s many other
curious deaths that will not die. In Book 1, Redcrosse slays Sansfoy and
later seemingly mortally wounds the Saracen's brother Sansjoy. But
Sansjoy, lying in a field as 'the pray of fowles', is rescued from the brink
of death by Duessa and Night, who convey his bleeding body to the
healer Aesculapius in the underworld (*FQ* 1.5.23). The argument to
Book 3.5 narrates that Belphoebe discovers the wounded body of Timias
'almost dead', who survives to engage in further narrative entangle-
ments. Malbecco, cuckolded by Hellenore, banishes himself to a cliff-
side cave, perpetually threatened by deadly falling rock. At this point,
Malbecco is less a man than an allegory of *Gealosie*: 'Yet can he neuer
dye, but dying liues' (*FQ* 3.10.60) – another vivid illustration of
Nohrnberg's contention that *The Faerie Queene* can be viewed as an
ongoing probing of 'the whole question of what constitutes an allegorical agent's death'.

Also in Book 3, we can be reminded of Amoret's abduction by the
wicked enchanter Busyrane. Amoret, her side '[e]ntrenched deepe with
knife accursed keene', her disembowelled heart dripping blood in
Busyrane's silver basin (*FQ* 3.12.20), is a particularly vivid icon of a death
that will not die, again prompting Nohrnberg to suggest wryly: 'though
Amoret was absent from her own wedding, she may be present at her
own funeral' (488).[15] In Book 4, the slain Priamond's soul enters his
brother Diamond. When Diamond is beheaded, both souls are absorbed
into the third brother Triamond, who then loses one soul through a
throat-wound, and a second from a wound in the arm-pit. Though he
'fell dead vpon the field', Triamond then arises 'breathing now another
spright' (*FQ* 4.3.34–4). Once again, the notion of Spenser's allegorical
deaths is rendered problematic. Given that Triamond dies (lives?) twice
symbolically in his two brothers, in the final analysis how different is he
from Maleger as *The Faerie Queene*'s paradigmatic 'dead-liuing swaine'?

Many critics have identified Spenser's mythopoetic Garden of Adonis
as *The Faerie Queene*'s existential and metaphysical axis, a key moment
where the poet confronts the reality of death. Many critics have under-

taken the difficult task of analysing the cyclic rhythms of the Garden of Adonis, where the perpetual generations trace a genealogical circle, constituting 'the first seminairie / Of all things, that are borne to live and die, / According to their kinds' (*FQ* 3.6.30). But, in its broadest scope, it is a paradoxical locus where life dies and death lives; and it is as much a celebration of origins as a meditation on death. In the Garden of Adonis, death is not *dead*; rather, the finality of death is recuperated as 'retirement' back into the Garden – which is why the Garden's namesake Adonis, as *The Faerie Queene*'s prototypical dying god, resides 'eterne in mutabilitie' (*FQ* 3.6.47).[16]

One might be tempted, then, to conclude that the wanderings of Spenserian epic romance are not the most favorable terrain for examining early modern literary representations of death. For Neill, as we have seen, early modern tragedy is about 'the discovery of death and the mapping of its meanings'. But the map of Spenser's Faerie land is traversed by deaths that will not die, deaths aborted, deaths deferred, death-in-life, life-in-death – as if Spenser prefers a metaphysical suspension 'eterne in mutabilitie' (3.6.47) to the heavy aesthetic and philosophical charge of representing the meaning of death.

But if, generically speaking, *The Faerie Queene* is categorized as an epic romance, it is also a *dynastic* epic; and it is worth exploring the ways in which death, every bit as much as error, lurks within a dynastic framework that otherwise constitutes such a purposeful establishing of the House of Tudor as the *imperium sine fine* – or empire *without end*.

Any consideration of the deep structure of dynastic epic narrative, in general, can benefit from Peter Brooks's compelling insistence that '[a]ll narrative is obituary' (284).[17] Brooks's claim for narrative as harboring a death drive has an uncanny resonance for the prophecies that structure dynastic epic narrative. In Book 6 of the *Aeneid*, for example, Aeneas, descending to the underworld, sees the shade of his father Anchises who foretells, among other future Roman glories, the advent of Augustus. During the ensuing pageant of Rome's future heroes, however, Aeneas also glimpses the sad shade of Marcellus, Augustus's nephew and successor, who is destined to die prematurely (885ff). Even as Anchises unfolds his otherwise celebratory prophecy of a glorious Roman future, the Marcellus passage injects into the grand sweep of this prophetic vision an unavoidable moment of tragic pathos.[18]

But how do we evaluate epic prophecy when, as part of its often eulogistic vision, it encodes the more particular and brutal instance of murder? In light of the venerable epic binary of force and fraud, how do we evaluate epic prophecy when it shifts its focus from the heroism of epic 'force' to the fatal treacheries of epic 'fraud'? We now turn to a consideration of how the embeddedness of fatal treachery in *The Faerie Queene*'s epic prophecy may be Spenser's way of inviting us to imagine our own deaths as we engage in the very process of reading his work.

In *The Faerie Queene*'s concluding 'Mutabilitie Cantos', the figure of Death, as we have seen, makes a brief appearance with 'grim and griesly visage' (7.7.46). But more relevant to the death drives of epic prophecy is the similarly 'griesly grim aspect' of 'Abhorred *Murder*', who makes an appearance at Mercilla's Palace to testify against Duessa (as Mary Queen of Scots) at her trial (*FQ* 5.9.48). Among other things, Murder's appearance, along with Sedition and Ate, confirms the poet's fears, expressed early in Book 5, that the heroism of the 'antique world' has 'runne quite out of square' (Proem.1). Death within epic narrative is one thing – but it is 'Abhorred *Murder*' (in conjunction with such figures as Envy, Slander, Detraction, and the backbiting Blatant Beast itself – in short, all of *The Faerie Queene*'s avatars of epic 'fraud') that is the more dreaded signifier of the decline and fall of epic heroism that preoccupies so much of Spenser's turbulent Book 5. Here, more is at stake than the sadly premature death of the *Aeneid*'s Marcellus: in a 'degendered' world of decaying heroism, Spenser's 'Abhorred *Murder*' powerfully encodes death-by-treachery as the unexpectedly insidious *telos* of epic destiny.

For a specific instance of how epic prophecy encodes 'Abhorred *Murder*' into dynastic narrative, let us glance at the prophetic structure of Ariosto's *Orlando furioso*, a major source for the narrative structure of *The Faerie Queene*. A vestige of the Marcellus episode can be detected in the depths of Merlin's cave, where the fulfillment of Ferrara's epic destiny is explicitly linked with the onset of death – this time, with the death of an epic protagonist. In this cave, Merlin's assistant Melissa reveals to Bradamante the ancestry of the dynastic House of Este. But even as the warrior maiden happily anticipates her union with her dynastic spouse-to-be Ruggiero, Melissa slips into the narrative a disturbing foretelling of his future doom: Ruggiero is slated for brutal murder by the Pontieri of the treacherous Maganza clan (3.24).[19] Melissa's prophecy, the point at which the specter of 'Abhorred *Murder*' is perhaps most haunting in the *Orlando furioso*, does not dwell on this dire future event. But the sorceror Atlante, himself eventually entombed in a funeral *cipresso* (for Tasso's Clorinda, also, the tree of death), is all too aware that the 'masterplot' of the movement of the *translatio imperii* to Ferrara will write his ward's obituary; and thus crucial sections of the *Orlando furioso*'s otherwise meandering narrative can be directly traced to Atlante's futile determination to keep Ruggiero sequestered in the safe haven of his enchanted magic palace.[20] Phrased broadly, the fore-knowledge of treachery that Merlin's epic prophecy strives to keep safely circumscribed in a distant future is the object of Atlante's obsession in the present tense of the *Orlando furioso* itself.

Ariosto's choice of Merlin as his vehicle for epic prophecy is further evidence of the death drive that structures dynastic epic narrative. Unlike Virgil's Anchises who, even in death, appears before his son with poignant paternal benevolence, Merlin, having been tricked by the Lady of the Lake, is a far more ambiguous prophet-mage. Like Atlante entombed in the *cipresso*, Merlin himself inhabits an obscure threshold between life and death. As Melissa informs Bradamante:

> This is the ancient memorable cave
> Which Merlin, that enchanter sage, did make:
> Thou may'st have heard how that magician brave
> Was cheated by the Lady of the Lake.
> Below, beneath the cavern is the grave
> Which holds his bones; where, for that lady's sake,
> His limbs (for such her will) the wizard spread.
> Living he laid him there, and lies there dead.

> (3.11)

In this strange passage, the grave matter of the founding of epic dynasty originates quite literally in Merlin's own grave (*tomba*) of scattered bones from a body hovering ambiguously between life and death.

Impelling much of the narrative of the *Orlando furioso* is Charlemagne's heavy reliance on the heroic feats of Ruggiero to defeat the enemy forces of Agramante, whose downfall is complete when Ruggiero slays the formidable Rodomonte. But Atlante's frantic (counter) efforts to protect Ruggiero and stave off his ward's inevitable brutal murder – the sorceror's efforts, in effect, to sequester Ruggiero from the larger forces of epic destiny – persistently remind any forgetful readers that beyond the bounds of the immediate epic narrative, the simple fact of death awaits the hero. Merlin also knows what Atlante knows: Ruggiero's epic heroism will be rewarded, in the end, by fatal treachery. Thus, when the 'matter' of Arthur (that is, Merlin as Ariosto's chosen prophet-mage) intersects with the 'matter' of Charlemagne, a wedge of dissonance, a taint of doom, cuts an oblique and deadly angle into the prophecy's celebration of genealogical continuity.

Tricked by the Lady of the Lake, Merlin has, of course, experienced treachery first hand, rendering him a highly appropriate prophet of

Ruggiero's particular doom. But that same appropriateness, that is, Merlin's own legendary entanglement in webs of deceit, renders him a 'tricky' voice of prophecy, indeed. In *The Faerie Queene*, Spenser, exploiting the 'tricky', folkloric potential of Ariosto's Merlin, appropriates the mage as his own mouthpiece for Tudor epic destiny; and as Britomart and Glauce discover, Spenser's Merlin, entrapped by 'the false Ladies traine', also suffers a living death 'buried vnder beare' (3.3.8–11). Significantly, as in the *Orlando furioso*, imperial prophecy in *The Faerie Queene* also predicts 'Abhorred *Murder*'. Thus, one of Spenser's more explicit borrowings from Ariosto occurs in Merlin's prophecy to Britomart in Book 3 in his underworld cave, where the mage hints darkly at her dynastic spouse-to-be Arthegall's 'last fate': even as Britomart is told of the happy genealogy of '[r]enowmed kings, and sacred Emperours, / Thy fruitfull Ofspring, [that] shall from thee descend' (3.3.23), she learns that Arthegall, like Ruggiero, will be 'too rathe cut off by practise criminall / Of secret foes that him shall make in mischiefe fall' (3.3.28). It is worth noting that Merlin, himself a victim of the Lady of the Lake's treachery, may be particularly attuned to Arthegall's 'too rathe' (too early) demise from 'practise criminall'.

Unlike Ruggiero, Arthegall has no protective, Atlante-like ward to periodically remind the reader of the hero's future doom that will occur (will have occurred?) beyond the bounds of *The Faerie Queene* itself. Thus, we could say that Spenser's readers are freer to focus on Arthegall's many Herculean heroic feats that will eventually pave the way for a Tudor *imperium sine fine* (such as his rescue of Irena from Grantorto). It is as if the seductions of Spenser's wandering narrative virtually *require* readers to forget his horrible doom. For that matter, one could even argue that in the strictest generic sense, Arthegall traces a 'comic' trajectory, insofar as he is destined to be a major protagonist in Spenser's 'divine comedy' of Tudor imperial marriage. Nevertheless, for the particularly vigilant reader (the reader-as-Atlante), the melancholic fact of Arthegall's impending death by 'practise criminall' forever lurks in the narrative. And no investigation of death in *The Faerie Queene* can be complete without continually keeping this fact in mind. Thus, *The Faerie Queene*'s 'Galfridian matrix' (to borrow Angus Fletcher's term) – that is, the fact that Arthegall's doom is foreseen by Merlin and conveyed to Britomart – has the mortal effect of writing the knight's obituary.[21]

Arthegall's future 'Abhorred *Murder*' is as curiously underplayed as it is intractable and inescapable. Merlin does not dwell on Arthegall's 'last fate' (nor, strangely, does the text record any display of affect from

Britomart). But Arthegall's impending death subtly intrudes on the hero's narrative. His very life as an epic hero becomes its own *memento mori*: despite (because of?) his heroic deeds, he always already hurtles towards a death that will have occurred at some future moment. Because of Merlin's prophecy, Arthegall's death in a future anterior gives rise to an unrelieved tension, a kind of agitating background static that inserts his heroic activity into an oddly different register from other heroes in *The Faerie Queene*.

Every other hero, that is, except Arthur. The etymology of Arthegall's name (as 'Arthur's equall') points to Arthur as the main coordinate in *The Faerie Queene*'s Galfridian matrix, the 'once and future king' who is the overarching hero of Spenser's epic. The death drive that *is* Spenser's Galfridian matrix is, of course, even more powerfully represented by Arthur. Spenser never refers to Arthur's own impending death, but informed readers of the poet's source, Geoffrey of Monmouth, read Arthur's feats with the full knowledge that the hero will eventually be fatally betrayed by his nephew Mordred.

*The Faerie Queene* frequently indulges in sly, quirky moments that toy with readers as they struggle to assess Spenser's tone. A prime example is the poet's teasing challenge to his readers to locate the elusive Faerie lond: 'Of Faerie lond yet if he more inquire, / By certain signes here set in sundry place / He may it find' (*FQ* 2.Proem.4). But surely one of the strangest of these teasing moments involves Arthur's future death. Midway through Book 1, the poet informs his readers that Arthur was given a suit of armor by Merlin as a 'young Prince, when first to armes he fell' (*FQ* 7.36.7). Then, in an odd parenthesis, he adds, 'But when he dyde, the Faerie Queene it brought / To Faerie lond, where yet it may be seene, if sought' (*FQ* 36.8–9). In this digression, we are presented with a brief and evanescent foreshadowing of the deadly termination of Arthur's 'prophetic moment' – a moment reduced to a memorializing fetish of his enervate armour.

Nothing in the literary history of dynastic epic can help us properly assess Spenser's tone here. Arthur's future death is swiftly rewritten as a *past* event. And the treachery of his death is curiously elided, almost casually taken for granted: the poet displays no affect, as if he suspects that Ruggiero's, Arthegall's, and Arthur's deaths by treachery are an epic *topos* that may have long since deteriorated into cliché. Evidently, the poet is telling his readers that if we so choose (and if we are fortunate enough to locate the 'certain signes' of Faerie land), we can view Arthur's enervate armour. But then . . . do what? Remember how he died? Ruminate on the waning of epic glory and its displacement by fatal treachery? Perhaps ruminate on the death of the Faerie Queene herself? Though she is the one who brings Arthur's armour to Faerie land, we can reflect that, after all, she too will die, as will Redcrosse, Una, Florimell, Satyrane, Braggadocchio – in short, all of *The Faerie Queene*'s characters who are alive within the bounds of Spenser's narrative, but who, like Arthegall and Arthur, also await their deaths.

In sum, the generic fact that *The Faerie Queene* is a dynastic epic may be precisely the point at which Spenser most intimately and profoundly 'imagines' death within romance error and deferral. By pressuring us to keep Arthur's and Arthegall's impending deaths in mind as we read his poem, Spenser may also be pressuring us to ponder our own deaths.

Milton likewise intends us to become aware of our own impending deaths. As many critics have observed, death assumes a dynamic presence in *Paradise Lost*.[22] If death is a powerful but understated subtext in *The Faerie Queene*, in *Paradise Lost* it is the announced outcome of the poem's central action. If *The Faerie Queene* is about nationalist dynasty, *Paradise Lost* resolutely resists any nationalistic proclamations in order to focus on the fate of humanity. The narrative voice famously proclaims the subject of the epic:

> Of Mans First Disobedience, and the Fruit
> Of that Forbidden Tree, whose mortal tast
> Brought Death into the World, and all our woe . . .

The epic is explicitly designed to explain the existence of death and its attendant miseries in a world ruled by an omnipotent, omniscient, and benevolent deity. It is the terrible fact of death, furthermore, that makes Milton's appointed task – 'to justify the ways of God to men' – so difficult. Milton does so by dealing with death in three distinct but related ways – as an allegorical character, as a state of psychological misery akin to Spenser's Despair, and as a physiological phenomenon attendant on the inevitable corruption of mortal flesh at the Fall. In each case, Milton works to distance the fact of Death from the actions of his God, so that we forget that the ultimate author of Death is God. Indeed the story of the birth of Death is so delightfully strange that we overlook the role that an omnipotent and omniscient deity must have had in its creation. Sin describes to Satan vividly the birth of Death:

> Long I sat not, till my womb
> Pregnant by thee, and now excessive grown
> Prodigious motion felt and rueful throes.

Thine own begotten, breaking violent way
Tore through my entrails, that with fear and pain
Distorted, all my nether shape thus grew
Transform'd: but he my inbred enemy
Forth issu'd, brandishing his fatal Dart
Made to Destroy: I fled and cri'd out Death;
Hell trembl'd at the hideous Name, and sigh'd
From all her Caves, and back resounded Death.

(PL 2.778–89)

The love-child of Satan and Sin, Death immediately rapes his mother, engendering in the process the 'Hell Hounds' that 'never ceasing bark'd [. . .] yet when they list, would creep, / If aught disturb'd their noyse, into her womb, / And kennel there' (PL 2.654–8). This profoundly Spenserian scenario – Sin and her brood emerge almost unchanged from the portrait of Errour and her children in Book 1 of The Faerie Queene – nevertheless demonstrates that Milton overtly characterizes what Spenser only infers. Milton's Death has no direct Spenserian analogue in Book 1 of The Faerie Queene.

Milton's Death is paradoxically distinguished by its complete lack of physical distinction:

the other shape,
If shape it might be call'd that shape had none
Distinguishable in member, joint or limb,
Of substance might be call'd, that shadow seem'd
For each seem'd either; black it stood as Night,
Fierce as ten Furies, terrible as Hell,
And shook a dreadful Dart; what seem'd his head
The likeness of a Kingly Crown had on.

(PL 2.666–70)

The only defining feature of Death is its colour – black – and even this causes it to blend with its shadow. Milton has perhaps learned this trait of distinct indistinction from 'our sage and serious poet Spencer, whom I dare be known to think a better teacher then Scotus or Aquinas' (Areopagitica, qtd in Flanagan 1006). Not in Book 1 of The Faerie Queene but rather in the 'Mutabilitie Cantos', Spenser emphasizes a similar formlessness in his figure of Death: 'Death with most grim and grisly visage seene [. . .] like a shade to weene, / Unbodied, unsoul'd, unheard, unseene' (*FQ* 7.7.46). Milton's Death does carry a dreadful dart and wear a kingly crown, elements borrowed from traditional iconography, but the crown may also hint at Milton's decidedly antimonarchical attitudes. Because of his shapelessness, no one knows quite what to make of the allegorical figure of Death: Satan calls Death an 'execrable shape [. . .] grim and terrible' (*PL* 2.681), although after paternity is acknowledged, Death becomes Satan's 'fair Son [. . .] the dear pledge / Of dalliance had with [Sin] in Heav'n' (*PL* 2.818–19). The narrator calls Death a 'Goblin full of wrauth' (*PL* 2.687). Death will ultimately describe himself as 'this Maw, this vast unhide-bound Corps' (*PL* 10.601), emphasizing his rapacious appetite. The Father also sees Death in terms of his appetite, but to the Father Sin and Death are not ferocious predators, but rather necessary scavengers who fulfil a critical part of God's larger plan; they are 'these Dogs of Hell' (*PL* 10.616), 'these wastful Furies' (*PL* 10.620), 'Hell-hounds' who 'lick up the draff and filth / Which mans polluting Sin with taint hath shed / On what was pure' (*PL* 10.630–3).

In fact, Sin and Death supply a critical role in the ecology of God's universe; Sin and Death, that is, solve the problem of waste-disposal that was beginning to trouble Adam and Eve in paradise even before the Fall. If nothing decays, and everything grows, what is to keep creation from suffocating on its own plenitude? As literal Hell hounds, Sin and Death possess insatiable appetites that dispose of the waste that would otherwise pile up from a continually proliferating but geographically limited world. All of creation becomes a banquet for Death carefully prepared by his mother, Sin:

> Thou therefore on these Herbs, and Fruits, and Flours
> Feed first, on each Beast next, and Fish, and Fowle,
> No homely morsels, and whatever thing
> The Sithe of Time mowes down, devour unspar'd,
> Till I in Man residing through the race,
> His thoughts his looks, words actions all infect
> And season him thy last and sweetest prey.

> (*PL* 10.603–9)

A true *alma mater*, Sin offers a multi-course meal to her son, beginning with a salad and ending with a meat dish. Sin and Death, moreover, also play a critical role in the end of Time. A well-stuffed Death will be used to shut up the mouth of Hell:

> At one sling
> Of thy victorious Arm, well-pleasing Son
> Both Sin, and Death, and yawning Grave at last
> Through Chaos hurld, obstruct the mouth of Hell
> For ever, and seal up his ravenous Jawes.
> Then Heav'n and Earh renewd shall be made pure
> To sanctitie that shall receive no staine.

(*PL* 10.633–40)

Allegorical Death, then, plays a critical role in the larger patterns of Milton's universe.

But what is the relationship of this allegorical figure to the moral and physiological phenomena that humans experience at the Fall? This allegorical figure, in other words, must in some way be coordinated with physiological death, or Dr Johnson's censures will remain unchallenged. Physiological Death is introduced as something of an epistemological blind spot for Adam and Eve before the Fall. Discussing with Eve the prohibition against eating from the Tree of Knowledge, Adam remembers that 'God hath pronounc't it death to taste that Tree,' but knows not what form that punishment will take: 'What ere Death is, / Some dreadful thing no doubt' (*PL* 4.425–7). Even after the Fall, Adam can't figure out just what the sentence of death means:

> Why delayes
> His hand to execute what his Decree
> Fixd on this day? Why do I overlive,
> Why am I mockt with death, and length'nd out
> To deathless pain?

(*PL* 10.771–5)

It is as if death's shapelessness is manifested in the protracted entry of death into mortal experience. The suspense is murderous; Adam indeed feels as if he would welcome death if only it would come:

> How gladly would I meet
> Mortalitie my sentence, and be Earth
> Insensible, how glad would lay me down
> As in my Mothers lap? There I should rest
> And sleep secure . . .

(*PL* 10.775–9)

As he continues, though, Adam, like Shakespeare's Hamlet, ponders the prospect of death not as insensibility but rather as a state of eternal punishement:

> Yet one doubt
> Pursues me still, least all I cannot die,
> Least that pure breath of Life, the Spirit of Man
> Which God inspir'd, cannot together perish
> With this corporeal Clod; then in the Grave,
> Or in some other dismal place, who knows
> But I shall die a living Death? O thought
> Horrid, if true!
>
> (*PL* 10.782–9)

Adam then wonders if death is a particularly miserable state of life rather than the extinction of it:

> But say
> That Death be not one stroak, as I suppos'd,
> Bereaving sense, but endless miserie
> From this day onward, which I feel begun
> Both in me, and without me, and so last
> To perpetuitie.
>
> (*PL* 10.808–13)

As a psychological state of mind, Death is here linked with Spenser's despair. Adam's soliloquy concludes with the realization of the torturous uncertainty of this thing called death: 'O Conscience, into what Abyss of fears / And horrors hast thou driv'n me; out of which / I find no way, from deep to deeper plung'd!' (*PL* 10.843–5). As he later realizes, death is for fallen humanity not a 'sudden, but a slow-pac't evill, / A long days dying to augment our paine' (*PL* 10. 962–6).

In the vision of the future that Michael grants Adam, though, death assumes a physiological correlative even more gruelling than its initial psychological ineffability. Adam is forced to watch one of his sons beat the life out of another – Abel 'fell, and deadly pale / Groand out his Soul with gushing bloud effus'd' (*PL* 11.446–7). Here the standard epic death is given a particularly grisly and unglamorous incarnation. Adam asks, 'But have I now seen death? Is this the way / I must return to native dust? O sight / Of terrour, foul and ugly to behold.' Adam, that is, wonders if the epistemological uncertainty of his punishment has finally achieved visual resolution. Michael responds by telling Adam that 'Death thou hast seen / In his first shape on man; but many shapes / Of Death, and many are the wayes that lead / To his grim Cave, all dismal' (*PL* 11.465–8). Michael's desire to exhibit for Adam the multiple ways in which death will exercise his cruel power over humanity issues in the nightmarish vision of the lazar-house, filled with 'a monstrous crew' suffering 'Diseases dire', which attempts to represent death in all its horrible incarnations:

> Immediately a place
> Before his eyes appeard, sad, noisome, dark,
> A Lazar-house it seemd, wherein were laid
> Numbers of all diseas'd, all maladies
> Of gastly Spasm, or racking torture, qualms
> Of heart-sick Agonie, all feavorous kinds,
> Convulsions, Epilepsies, fierce Catarrhs,
> Intestin Stone and Ulcer, Colic pangs,
> Daemoniac Phrenzie, moaping Melancholie
> And Moon-struck madness, pining Atrophie,
> Marasmus, and wide-wasting Pestilence,
> Dropsies, and Asthma's, and Joint-racking Rheums.
> Dire was the tossing, deep the groans, despair
> Tended the sick busiest from Couch to Couch;
> And over them triumphant Death his Dart
> Shook, but delaid to strike, though oft invok't
> With vows, as thir chief good, and final hope.

(PL 11.477–93)

Here physiological death merges seamlessly with psychological despair and allegorical Death. This exhaustive catalogue of mortal affliction, which Milton actually bothered to expand by three lines (485–7) in 1674, describes the infinite bounty of corporeal and psychological suffering that awaits Adam and his progeny. Perhaps the decided shapelessness of the allegorical figure of Death derives from the fact that no single shape could encompass the myriad horrors that Death brings, horrors that include, perversely, the prolongation of a miserable life. Physiological Death does not so much lack form as it possesses an infinite multitude of forms for the imposition of suffering and decay on mortal flesh. Adam is stunned not just at the physical suffering but also at the aesthetic degradation of humanity:

> Can thus
> Th'Image of God in man created once
> So goodly and erect, though faultie since,
> To such unsightly sufferings be debas't
> Under inhuman pains? Why should not Man,
> Retaining still Divine similitude
> In part, from such deformities be free,
> And for his Makers Image sake exempt?
>
> (*PL* 11.507–13)

Michael answers Adam by suggesting that the afflicted 'villifi'd' themselves:

> To serve ungovern'd appetite, and took
> His Image whome they serv'd, a brutish vice,
> Inductive mainly to the sin of Eve.
> Therefore so abject is thir punishment,
> Disfiguring not Gods likeness, but thir own,
> Or if his likeness, by themselves defac't
> While they pervert pure Natures healthful rules
> To loathsome sickness, worthily, since they
> Gods Image did not reverence in themselves.
>
> (*PL* 11.514–25)

This is a profoundly Spenserean moment, where the lessons of Book 2 of *The Faerie Queene*, devoted to the virtue of Temperance, provide the ethical machinery. Just as Acrasia's devotees are turned into 'figures hideous, / According to their mindes like monstruous' by their beastly surrender to 'intemperate' lust (2.12.85), so does Milton imagine that the physical degradation attendant on mortality signifies inner moral decay. Milton, then, uses the physiological doctrine of temperance to attempt to render just the tortuous physiological entropy that inevitably obtains after the Fall.[23]

Indeed, Milton has his Adam reluctantly concede the justice of such rampant suffering – 'I yield it just, said Adam, and submit' (*PL* 11.526) – just as Milton hopes his reader will ultimately apprehend the justice of the ways of God to humans. But to Milton's credit, disease and death remain phenomena highly resistant to the fictional blandishments of moral posturing. Indeed, Michael promises Adam that if he lives well and temperately he will not die one of the horrible deaths he has just witnessed, but will instead drop 'like ripe Fruit [ . . . ] / Into thy

Mothers lap, or be with ease / Gatherd, not harshly pluckt, for death mature' (*PL* 11.535–7). This comparatively gentle, even comforting vision is nonetheless tempered by the quotidian physical discomforts and spiritual depressions of old age to which Milton devotes lavish detail:

> But then thou must outlive
> Thy youth, thy strength, thy beauty, which will change
> To witherd weak and gray; thy Senses then
> Obtuse, all taste of pleasure must forgoe,
> To what thou hast, and for the Aire of youth
> Hopeful and cheerful, in thy blood will reigne
> A melancholy dampe of cold and dry
> To weigh thy Spirits down, and last consume
> The Balme of Life.
>
> (*PL* 11. 538–46)

This slow procession into insensibility and depression is seen as the death most devoutly to be wished for after the Fall.

But because of the Son's willingness to endure 'a reproachful life and cursed death', a heroic and gratuitous act which makes possible the Redemption of fallen humanity, 'temporal death' will be for the blessed 'like sleep / A gentle wafting to immortal Life' (*PL* 12.406, 433–5). The death of the Son, that is, will 'bruise the head of Satan, crush his strength / Defeating Sin and Death, his two maine armes' (*PL* 12.430–1). Death is thus rendered not just the tortuous if deserved punishment for Adam and Eve's sin; it also becomes 'to the faithful [. . .] the Gate of Life' (*PL* 12.571). In *Paradise Lost*, then, we see Death move from ferocious predatory monster to a necessary scavenger, and from a physical and psychological torture to a rite of passage to eternal life. Throughout the epic, Milton prosecutes the transformation of Death with imaginative force and persuasive eloquence, perhaps best convincing us of the justice of God's ways in the ultimately benign portrait of Death's role in God's larger plans.

Death haunted Milton's life even as it blessed his literary production; the deaths of acquaintances, friends, and family members provide a perpetual if painful spur to his muse of his youth. One needs only look at the titles of Milton's poems to see how fully his work wrestles with the angel of death: 'An Epitaph on the Marchioness of Winchester', 'On Shakespeare' (his first published poem), two poems 'On the University Carrier, who sickn'd in the time of his vacancy', Elegy 2 'On the Death of the Beadle of the University of Cambridge', Elegy 3 'On the Death of the Bishop of Winchester', 'On the death of Vice-Chancellor, a physician', 'On the death of the Bishop of Ely', 'On the Late Massacher in Piemont', 'Epitaphium Damonis', 'On the Death of a Fair Infant dying of a Cough', the incomplete poem on 'The Passion' as well as two of the most accomplished poems of mourning in the English language, the pastoral elegy 'Lycidas' and the sonnet 'Methought I saw my late exposed saint'. If 'Building up a culture also means, amongst other things: finding a standpoint from which to spread lies about death,' as the anthropologist Franz Baermann Steiner has argued, then Milton is to be admired for his heroic attempt to locate death amid larger patterns that would render it less devastating, perhaps even meaningful.[24] In *Paradise Lost* in particular, Milton struggles to redefine the meaning of epic death, from what he terms the 'long and tedious havoc [of] fabl'd knights / In Battels feign'd' to 'the better fortitude / Of Patience and Heroic Martyrdom / Unsung' (9.30–3). As he works to merge the patterns of epic with the arguments of theology, Milton brilliantly participates in a kind of eternal agon between the cultural fictions of comfort and the brutal facts of mortality. Although the fictions may have less pull on us today than they did in the seventeenth century, the compelling eloquence and imaginative brilliance in which they were encased has the capacity, as Milton suggests in his poem 'On Shakespeare', to 'make us Marble with too much conceiving'. Perhaps Spenser's and Milton's ultimate engagement with death occurs in the capacity of their poetry to transform each reader into a kind of marmoreal monument, even for a short time, against the ineluctable ravages of death.

In his essay, Andrew Hadfield catalogues the plentitude and especially the variety of spectacular deaths in *The Faerie Queene*, asserting that the 'real deaths' framing the narrative were those of Queen Elizabeth and Mary, Queen of Scots. Spenser anxiously anticipated Elizabeth's barren legacy, worrying that her death would leave England to the civil war of Arthurian legend. Reading the narrative in light of literary tradition and historical context, Hadfield focuses on the 'Two Cantos of Mutabilitie', which Spenser wrote, he argues, to 'dramatize the conflict between Nature and order ranged against the forces of chaos; Jove against the Titans; Elizabeth against Mary Queen of Scots; the Tudors against the Stuarts'.

Critics searching for allegorical unity have long imposed a coherence on disparate fragments of Guyon's descent to the underworld in Book 2 of *The Faerie Queene*. Focusing in particular on Spenser's Tantalus ('daily dy[ing]') and on his Garden of Proserpina ('direfull deadly blacke both leafe and bloom'), Theresa M. Krier's essay, 'Psychic Deadness in Allegory: Spenser's House of Mammon and Attacks on Linking', argues that Spenserian allegory undermines readerly efforts at 'linking' and signals nothing less than a death drive for Guyon.

In his essay, 'Death in an Allegory', Gordon Teskey, also focusing on Spenser's allegorical method, argues that the event of death cannot be represented in an allegory. Rather, the death of an allegorical character is the precise moment when that character 'is most alive as meaning'. Focusing on the deaths of the brothers Cymocles and Pyrocles in *The Faerie Queene*, Book 2, Teskey argues that death in an allegory is actually 'the moment of the revelation of meaning'.

Several of the essays offer a comparative perspective on the ways that Milton assimilated or rejected the example of Spenser. Roger Kuin and Anne Lake Prescott, for example, emphasize the relationship between death and holiness, a virtue that was of central importance to both Spenser and Milton, but one for which we in the skeptical twenty-first century have less respect. Arguing that sequential reading is an ethical – even heroic – experience, Kuin and Prescott battle the murderous despair that parades as facile cynicism in much contemporary criticism, by way of gauging the pressures that death exerts on the moral convictions of Spenser and Milton. Linda Gregerson likewise explores the impact of Spenser on Milton, and looks to the developing science of anatomy for a clue to the various representations of death in Spenser and Milton. Where Kuin and Prescott explore how Spenser and Milton turn to religion as a response to death, Gregerson explores how Spenser and Milton turn to poetic form as a bulwark against the inevitable ravages of death. Blending historical contextualization with formal analysis, Gregerson shows how Spenser and Milton found solace against death in the parallel acts of reproduction that are the begetting of children and the creation of literature. Gregerson parses the curious nexus of death and consumption, whereby eating for Milton is a sin that brings death into the world, and not eating is for Spenser a torture that invites death into the body.

Like Gregerson, Marshall Grossman focuses on questions of historical process and literary form. Grossman, though, is interested not so much in exploring what Milton learns from Spenser as in articulating the immense differences between the two poets. Like Kuin and Prescott, Grossman emphasizes the process of reading. But for Grossman, this process issues in a profound contrast between Spenser's processes of infinite unfolding and Milton's relentlessly predetermined dialectic. Grossman ambitiously maps the different narrations of death in Spenser and

Milton against some of the central transformations of early modern literary history – the movement from allegory to historical causation, and the turn from mimesis to expression.

In 'Sublime/Pauline: Denying Death in *Paradise Lost*,' Rachel Trubowitz argues that Adam's lament in Book 10 of Milton's epic encapsulates the poet's complex, politically inflected response to Reformation culture's disavowal of death as a public and ceremonial experience. By abstracting and internalizing death, the reformers aimed to dispel the old religion's 'vulgar errors' concerning the after life, especially the doctrine of Purgatory. But if these radical acts of disenchantment rendered death meaningless in customary, ceremonial terms, they also left the newly individualized psyche without sufficient means to come to terms with death. Through Adam's tortured meditations on death, Milton both represents this Reformation 'mortality crisis' and offers a remedy to it – a remedy that reflects his anti-monarchical and anti-theatrical politics and aesthetics. Fusing his radical Paulinism with a republican application of Longinus's theory of the sublime, Milton rewrites 'death' in anti-dynastic and 'post-natural' terms.

Because Milton was such a relentlessly engaged partisan about issues that actually led people on both sides to kill each other, the essays that focus on Milton attend, perhaps inevitably, to the implicit politics of the representation of death. Laura Knoppers uses the artistic technique of shifting perspective called anamorphosis to explore the differences between the portrait of the suffering king in the *Eikon Basilike* and Milton's attitude to the death of Charles I in the *Eikonoklastes*. Knoppers shows how Milton uses optical imagery to challenge the Christ-like spectacle of Charles I in prison that Bishop Gauden, the ghost-writer of the *Eikon*, had produced. Knoppers views these two texts in a pitched battle over the meaning of the death of the king – a battle which Milton, for all his rhetorical expertise, loses, as the fact of the Restoration makes clear.

Paul Stevens likewise explores the politics of death in Milton. But where Knoppers analyses Milton's attempt to undo a royalist martyrology which prompts the nation to grief, Stevens looks at the relationship between Milton's personal expressions of grief and his longstanding commitment to English nationalism. Using Stephen Greenblatt's recent work on remembering and forgetting, Stevens demonstrates how Milton was involved in assimilating the act of remembering the dead to the task of forging a national consciousness. The dead hold us in their power with a grip as precise as it is ineffable, Stevens argues; challenging the political fiction of national identity – a fiction allied to death through the violence done in its name – can feel like closing our ears to the purgatorial sufferings of our ancestors. Where death would seem to be the ultimate leveler of all distinctions, including those based on the fiction of national identity, Stevens shows how the articulation of grief can be both a way of uttering political grievance and of buttressing national identity.

No single volume can possibly do justice to the topic of representations of death in Spenser and Milton. Thus, we offer this collection of essays not as a comprehensive treatment but rather as a kind of preliminary probing of the topic and, we hope, a stimulus for future investigations that can help construct a larger picture of how Spenser and Milton represent death. In short, the essays in this volume demonstrate the myriad ways in which death is very much 'alive' in Spenser and Milton. Each essay breaks new critical ground on death as a central preoccupation in Spenser's and Milton's work. In their broadest scope, we hope that these insights into Spenser's and Milton's struggles to represent death will provide readers with rich new perspectives on the religious, cultural, ideological, and psychic anxieties of early modern England itself.

## Notes

1. See Philippe Ariès, *Western Attitudes Toward Death: From the Middle Ages to the Present* (1974). More recent cultural and social histories of death in the West include Jonathan Dollimore, *Death, Desire, and Loss in Western Culture* (1998), and Bruce Gordon and Peter Marshall, *The Place of the Dead: Death and Remembrance in Late Medieval and Early Modern Europe* (2000).

2. For studies of death in early modern England, see, for example, Clare Gittings, *Death, Burial and the Individual in Early Modern England* (1984); Michael MacDonald and Terence R. Murphy, *Sleepless Souls: Suicide in Early Modern England* (1990); Julian Litten, *The English Way of Death: The Common Funeral since 1450* (1991); Nigel Llewellyn, *The Art of Death: Visual Culture in the English Death Ritual C. 1500–C. 1800* (1991); David Cressy, *Birth, Marriage, and Death: Ritual, Religion, and the Life-Cycle in Tudor and Stuart England* (1997); and Clare Gittings and Peter Jupp (ed.), *Death in England: An Illustrated History* (2000).

   A sampling of studies of death in early modern English literature includes: Peter Sacks's *The English Elegy: Studies in the Genre from Spenser to Yeats* (1985); Dennis Kay, *Melodious Tears: The English Funeral Elegy from Spenser to Milton* (1990); Robert N. Watson, *The Rest Is Silence: Death as Annihilation in the English Renaissance* (1994); and Michael Neill, *Issues of Death: Mortality and Identity in English Tragedy* (1997).

3. *Essays* (1900; rpt 961) II.

4. Important attempts to link Spenser and Milton include: Patrick Cullen, *Infernal Triad: The Flesh, the World, and the Devil in Spenser and Milton* (1974); A. Kent Hieatt, *Chaucer, Spenser, Milton* (1975); Kathleen Williams, 'Milton, Greatest Spenserian', in *Milton and the Line of Vision* (1975); Richard Neuse, 'The Virgilian Triad Revisited' (1978); Joseph A. Wittreich, Jr, *Visionary*

*Poetics: Milton's Tradition and His Legacy* (1979); Maureen Quilligan, *Milton's Spenser: The Politics of Reading* (1983); John Guillory, *Poetic Authority: Spenser, Milton, and Literary History* (1983); Gordon Teskey, 'From Allegory to Dialectic: Imagining Error in Spenser and Milton' (1986); and Linda Gregerson, *The Reformation of the Subject: Spenser, Milton, and the English Protestant Epic* (1995).

5. For example, given that *The Faerie Queene* was written in the shadows of Elizabeth's death, and given that Milton first conceived of the idea of writing *Paradise Lost* not long after the execution of Charles I, one can reasonably claim that the materiality of royal death was a major backdrop for both poets, but with vastly different results.

6. Stephen Greenblatt's recent study of Shakespeare's *Hamlet* amid available conflicting ideas of the afterlife explores the spiritual costs and benefits of the Reformation abolition of Purgatory as a fiction (*Hamlet in Purgatory* [2002]). Greenblatt discovers a lingering wish to commune with the dead in the ghosts that haunt Shakespeare's plays and protagonists, and views the fictions performed on the early modern stage as cultural forms that absorbed the human longings to which the doctrine of Purgatory was designed to appeal. See also Bettie Anne Doebler, *Rooted Sorrow: Dying in Early Modern England* (1994).

7. A number of years ago, Angus Fletcher wrote, 'Although much has been made in literary histories of the link between Milton and Spenser, we need to insist on the relative unimportance of this link. Milton was not unduly perturbed, surely, by the example of *The Faerie Queen*' (*The Transcendental Masque: An Essay on Milton's 'Comus'* [1971], 142–3).

8. Northrop Frye, *Secular Scripture: A Study of the Structure of Romance* (1976); Gordon Teskey, 'From Allegory to Dialectic: Imagining Error in Spenser and Milton, (1986)'.

9. John King, *Milton and Religious Controversy: Satire and Polemic in Paradise Lost* (2000).

10. For more on the errancies of epic romance, see Patricia Parker, *Inescapable Romance: Studies in the Poetics of a Mode* (1978), and David Quint, *Epic and Empire: Politics and Generic Form from Virgil to Milton* (1993).

11. All references to Milton's works are taken from Roy Flannagan, *The Riverside Milton* (1998).

12. All references to *The Faerie Queene* are taken from *Edmund Spenser: The Faerie Queene*, ed. A. C. Hamilton (1977).

13. To pose these questions is certainly not to ignore the obvious fact that death occurs everywhere in *The Faerie Queene*. Moreover, in Spenser's shorter poems, death performs a variety of contradictory roles: the figure of death is at once a dancer (the *November* eclogue of *The Shepheardes Calender* 15); a warrior (*November* 123); a judge (*Virgils Gnat* 447); a thief (*Daphnaida* 303); and a devouring eater (*The Ruines of Time* 52). Most intriguingly, death appears as a fine-chiselling artist and writer – nowhere finer than when fashioning the beautifully laid out corpse of the 19-year-old Douglas Howard: 'those pallid cheekes and ashy hew, / In which sad death his pourtraicture had writ' (*Daphnaida* 302–3). Here, death assumes a face, acquires a physiology and an interiority, an allegorical villain grimly inscribing his textualizing hand deeply on the bodies of those we learn to love most. The real life

deaths of Spenser's patrons and friends are, of course, at issue here – for example, Robert Dudley, earl of Leicester, in *The Ruines of Time* and *Virgils Gnat*, and Sir Philip Sidney in *Astrophel*.

14. *The Analogy of 'The Faerie Queene'* (1976).
15. Of Amoret's non-death, Harry Berger argues, 'The erotic and sadistic fascination of the [Busyrane's] game depends on her continuing existence and resistance; therefore she cannot be literally or finally killed' (*Revisionary Play: Studies in the Spenserian Dynamics* [1988], 182).
16. For a reading of Spenser's Garden of Adonis episode against the grain of Freud's *Beyond the Pleasure Principle* and its analysis of the death drive, see Elizabeth J. Bellamy, *Translations of Power: Narcissism and the Unconscious in Epic History* (1992), 239–45.
17. Peter Brooks, 'Freud's Masterplot', in *Literature and Psychoanalysis: The Question of Reading: Otherwise* (1982).
18. For more on the Marcellus passage as confirming 'the tragic nature of history that the prophet has so far seemed to struggle to deny', see Andrew Fichter, *Poets Historical: Dynastic Epic in the Renaissance* (1982), 36.
19. In Ariosto's cynical *Cinque Canti*, a depiction of the origins of the Roland saga, the Maganzan Gano (or Ganelon), goaded by l'Invidia, becomes 'the father of treacheries and betrayals' (2.32).
20. For a discussion of Atlante's actions as a 'stay of execution' for the doomed Ruggiero, see David Quint, 'The Figure of Atlante: Ariosto and Boiardo's Poem' (1979).
21. Fletcher's identifies the Galfridian matrix as one of five key 'typological' narrative strands in *The Faerie Queene* (*The Prophetic Moment: An Essay on Spenser* [1971]). The epic's Galfridian matrix is constituted by Geoffrey of Monmouth's Arthurian writings, particularly the *Prophecies of Merlin* and the *History of the Kings of Britain*, as the confluence of Arthurian myth and British history.
22. Critics who have discussed Milton's attitude to death include Mary Adams, 'Fallen Wombs: The Origin of Death in Miltonic Sexuality'(1993); A. E. B. Coldiron, 'Milton in parvo: Mortalism and Genre Transformation in "Sonnet 14" (1994); Clay Daniel, *Death in Milton's Poetry* (1994); Roland Mushat Frye, *Milton's Imagery and the Visual Arts: Iconographic Tradition in the Epic Poems* (1978); Cherrell Guilfoyle, '"If Shape It Might Be Call'd That Shape Had None": Aspects of Death in Milton,' (1978); Dennis Kezar, *Guilty Creatures: Renaissance Poetry and the Ethics of Authorship* (2001); John N. King, *Milton and Religious Controversy* (2000); Arnold Stein, 'Imagining Death: The Ways of Milton' (1993); Robert B. White, 'Milton's Allegory of Sin and Death: A Commentary on Backgrounds' (1972–3). Michael Schoenfeldt would like to acknowledge the bibliographical expertise of Aaron McCollough, who aided in the preparation of the section of the introduction dealing with Milton.
23. On the importance of temperance to Spenser and Milton, see Michael C. Schoenfeldt, *Bodies and Selves in Early Modern England: Physiology and Inwardness in Spenser, Shakespeare, Herbert, and Milton* (1999).
24. Franz Baermann Steiner, *Selected Writings*, vol. 1, *Taboo, Truth and Religion*, edited by Jeremy Adler and Richard Fardon Berghahn (2001): cited in *TLS*, 2 March 2001, in a review by Henning Ritter 31.

# 2
# Spenser and the Death of the Queen

*Andrew Hadfield*

Few Renaissance poems contain more examples of different types of spectacular death than Spenser's *The Faerie Queene.*[1] We witness numerous monsters, dragons, giants and other villains coming to justly sticky ends; Christian and pagan knights falling in battle; as well as some deaths which appear to be more natural, such as the strange deaths of Mortdant and Amavia (2.2).[2] The poem is also full of near death experiences such as the Red-Cross Knight's planned suicide when tempted by Despair (1.9), the sufferings of Marinell and Timias (3.4–5), and the rescue of Serena and then Pastorella (6.8; 11). And there are deaths of numerous kings and mythological figures (such as Adonis, represented in a tapestry on the walls of Castle Joyous (3, 1, 34)) in the chronicles and embedded narratives. The rate of deaths and executions increases as the poem becomes more violent in Books 5 and 6, where it is a rare canto that does not contain a killing of some sort, although the first four books are not without their bellicose moments. In *The Faerie Queene* we witness the deaths of Error (1.1); Sansfoy (1.2); Fradubio (1.2); Orgoglio (1.8); the old Dragon (1.9); Mortdant and Amavia (2.1); Pyrochles and Cymochles (2.8); Maleger (although he may already be dead) (2.11); Corflambo (4.8); the headless lady killed by Sanglier (5.1); Pollente and Munera (5.2); the Giant with the Scales (5.2); the sons of Dolon (5.6); Radigund (5.7); the Souldan (5.8); Malengin (5.9); Geryoneo's seneschal (5.11); Geryoneo (5.11); Grantorto (5.12); Malefort (6.1); an anonymous knight slain by Tristram (6.2); the savages who kidnap Serena (6.8); and Meliboee, the shepherds and the brigands (6.11).

It is the variety of deaths as well as their sheer number that is important. On one obvious level, these grisly incidents help to distinguish *The Faerie Queene* from Italian romances such as the *Orlando Furioso* or native chivalric works such as *Le Morte D'Arthur*.[3] But as well as performing this task they also point to the deaths *not* actually represented in the poem, ones which no reader could possibly have failed to miss or ignore. The death that everyone was waiting for in the 1590s was that of the aged Elizabeth, who was 57 in 1590 when the first edition of *The Faerie Queene* was published, not only well beyond the life expectancy of an aristocratic woman in the sixteenth century, but also beyond the age that any Tudor monarch had survived before her reign (Henry VIII had lived to 56; Henry VII to 52). And, as Spenser's poem makes absolutely clear, the Faerie Queene herself was Elizabeth: 'in that Faery Queene I meane glory in my generall intention, but in my particular I conceiue the most excellent and glorious person of our soueraine the Queene, and her kingdome in Faery land' (716).

Nevertheless, when the Faerie Queene does appear, she presents an image of life – albeit an insubstantial one. She enraptures the weary Prince Arthur when he falls asleep in a passage that is as tantalising as the evidence of her presence she leaves behind ('nought but pressed grass, where she had lyen' (1.9.15)) that:

> Most goodly glee and louely blandishment
> She to me made, and bad me loue her deare,
> For dearly sure her loue was to me bent,
> As when iust time expired should appeare.
> But whether dreames delude, or true it were,
> Was neuer hart so rauisht with delight,
> Ne liuing man like words did euer heare,
> As she to me deliuered all that night;
> And at her parting said, She Queene of Faeries hight.

> (1.9.14)

This verse exploits numerous ambiguities, most obviously the tradition of knights serving and loving ladies in chivalric romance. The most famous example of such ambiguity was the relationship of Lancelot and Guinevere, one of the key stories of the romance tradition. Lancelot was able to serve his king with apparent honesty because he could declare that he loved the queen as her knight, and so could hide the fact that he had embarked on an adulterous affair with her.[4] Spenser has recast this story in proposing an ambiguous relationship between the young Arthur, later to be the cuckolded husband of Guinevere, and the Faerie Queene. The potentially sexual nature of the encounter is manifest: the queen may only deliver words in the night but they ravish Arthur, and the pressed grass she leaves behind more than hints at a roll in the hay. Moreover, the encounter recalls the vividly real dream that separates the Red-Cross knight from Una (1.2), and looks forward to the al fresco love-making that Calidore disturbs later (6.3).

However, reading the episode correctly, I think, involves juxtaposing knowledge of a literary tradition with a basic knowledge of contemporary events in England. As a reader of Caxton's edition of Malory (1485) – or any other version of the Arthurian legends – would have known, the union of Arthur and Guinevere failed to produce any children and so plunged Britain into a devastating civil war which destroyed the legacy of the greatest dynasty the island had produced. The last book of Caxton's edition contains the author's famous address to the English people in which he berates them for deserting their true king and siding with the usurper, Mordred:

> Lo ye all Englishmen, see ye not what a mischief here was? For he that was the most king and knight of the world, and most loved the fellowship of noble knights, and by him they were all upholden, now might, now might not these Englishmen hold them content with him. Lo thus was the old custom and usage of this land; and also men say that we of this land have not yet lost ne forgotten that custom and usage. Alas, this is a great default of us Englishmen, for there may nothing please us no term.          (II, p. 507)

A few pages later we are given a graphic description of the effects of the resulting civil war. As the 'grievously wounded' Sir Lucan leaves the battle field where the final confrontation has taken place he turns round and sees in the moonlight that 'pillers [plunderers] and robbers were comen into the field, to pill and to rob many a full noble knight of brooches, and beads, of many a good ring, and of many a rich jewel; and who that were not dead all out, there they slew them for their harness and their riches' (II, p. 515).

The virgin queen Elizabeth was now far too old to have children and so her people, Spenser implies, will be plunged into uncertainty, chaos and gloom when she dies because she has not secured the succession. The civil war that destroyed Arthur's Britain may be visited on the island after the Tudor dynasty expires. It was not beyond the bounds of possibility that England would be plunged into a major war when Elizabeth died, similar to the Wars of the Roses which are the subject of Malory's heartfelt address to the English people, only along religious lines.[5] Arthur's barren union is mirrored in Elizabeth's barren virginity: she has led suitors nowhere, content to flirt and play off one against another without delivering the goods, oblivious of the historical precedent, just as the Faerie Queene leads Arthur on. *The Faerie Queene* signals the death of the neochivalric cult of the last years of her reign: as in Malory, the knights turn out to be victims of the failings of the monarch.[6] An encounter that looks as though it promises union and procreation only serves to remind readers of the missed opportunities of the past and the impending death of both queen and regime.

The picture is more starkly drawn in the 'Two Cantos of Mutabilitie', which contain a pointed *memento mori* aimed at Elizabeth, one that is all the more powerful for being easily detachable from its context in the poem:

> And first, concerning her that is the first,
> Euen you, faire *Cynthia*, whom so much ye make
> *Ioues* dearest darling, she was bred and nurst
> On *Cynthus* hill, whence she her name did take:
> Then is she mortall borne, how-so ye crake;
> Besides, her face and countenance euery day
> We changed see, and sundry forms partake,
> Now hornd, now round, now bright, now brown and gray;
> So that *as changefull as the Moone* men vse to say.

> (7.7, 50)

It is not surprising that these lines were only published in 1609 after Elizabeth's death, as they are scarcely allegorical. Elizabeth as Cynthia is reminded that she is mortal and will soon die: the changes referred to describe her ageing, but also her fickle policies which, Spenser indicates, seem ridiculous in an old woman. The glamorous Faerie Queene who enraptures Arthur has been transformed into a hideous and foolish old crone blind to her mortality.

*The Faerie Queene*, praised long ago by C. S. Lewis as a work full of 'images of life', has to be read more carefully and sceptically as a work that lives in the shadow of death and contains numerous reminders of impending death and extinction.[7] In Book 2 Spenser follows an Aristotelian definition of chastity as a mean between extremes of lust and abstinence. In *The Nichomachean Ethics* Aristotle does not define chastity as such, but includes a chapter, 'Continence and Incontinence: Pleasure', in which he explains that pleasure – including sexual pleasure – is good so long as it is controlled and that the 'study of pleasure and plain belongs to the political philosopher; for he is the architect of the end, with a view to which we call one thing bad and another good without qualification' (183). Aristotle makes a distinction between the temperate and continent man which is clearly relevant to Spenser's narrative representation of the virtues of temperance and chastity in *The Faerie Queene*:

> both the continent man and the temperate man are such as to do nothing contrary to the rule for the sake of bodily pleasures, | but the former has and the latter has not bad appetites, and the latter is such as not to feel pleasure contrary to the rule, while the former is such as to feel pleasure but not to be led by it.                    (181)[8]

In adopting a definition of chastity in line with Aristotle's philosophical principles, Spenser deliberately avoids defining chastity as virginity, a more usual Christian definition.[9] Instead, we have a classically defined virtue – as the 'Letter to Raleigh' indicates – which supports the Protestant view of companionable marriage as the truly chaste, virtuous mode of living.[10] The point to be made is that the queen's social state is quite deliberately excluded from the good ways of living represented in the poem: the virgins we see, Florimell, Belphoebe and the Faerie Queene herself, are far from wholly admirable characters who cause a great deal of harm through their behaviour.[11]

Florimell very nearly causes the death of her intended partner, Marinell, who pines away after his defeat by Britomart when she flees in fear (3.4; 4.12), and is only properly healed when the pair are united and married (5.3). His ills stem from a prophecy delivered by Proteus to his mother, Cymoent, when she is warned that 'of a woman he should have much ill, / A virgin strange and stout him should dismay, or kill' (3.4.25). Cymoent's response is to keep him from the presence of women:

> For thy she gaue him warning euery day,
> The loue of women not to entertaine;
> A lesson too too hard for liuing clay,
> From loue in course of nature to refraine:
> Yet he his mothers lore did well retaine,
> And euer from faire Ladies loue did fly;
> Yet many Ladies faire did oft complaine,
> That they for loue of him would algates dy:
> Dy, who so list for him, he was loues enimy.

> (3.4, 26)

The ironies in this stanza are numerous and writ large, nicely placing the episode on the border between comedy and tragedy. The repetition of 'dy' as the link word in the final couplet emphasises the deathly state of virginity and the refusal to procreate. Marinell stands in a long line of proud and foolish virgins, and it is quite likely that Christopher Marlowe had Spenser's representations of virginity in mind when he wrote *Hero and Leander* soon before he died in 1593. Marlowe's poem casts Hero as the innocent nun of Venus who eventually realises that her role requires her to make good use of her body rather than flee all advances.[12] Marinell's defeat by the one virgin, Britomart, and his consequent deathly lethargy, is mirrored later in his near-fatal languor when he despairs of his suit for another virgin, Florimell, which sees his mother returning to Proteus for advice (4.12). Of course, it is Cymoent's advice that has helped to reduce Marinell to his perilous state, transforming him into a virgin who shuns advances, exactly how Florimell behaves and the most obvious reason why their union very nearly fails to materialize. And, pushing the point to comic absurdity, Spenser places heavy emphasis on all the other suitors who are dying for love of Marinell. In *The Faerie Queene* the poetic cliché that lovers die for lack of their beloveds is made literal, the bitter point being that the country at large would pay dearly for the queen's refusal to play the game of love.

Florimell spends Book 3 fleeing pursuers, making literal the pun that she is 'chased' rather than 'chaste'. Her adventures take a humorous turn in Canto 8 when she escapes from the lustful witch's son by jumping into the boat of an equally lecherous fisherman, an episode that is adapted from Ariosto's *Orlando Furioso*, but which has the style and manner of the less exalted genre of the fabliau.[13] Spenser indulges in one of his many smutty jokes as Florimell seeks reassurance from the fisherman that all will be well:

> But thou good man, sith farre in sea we bee,
> And the great waters gin apace to swell,
> That now no more we can the maine-land see,
> Haue care, I pray, to guide the cock-bote well,
> Least worse on sea then vs on land befell.
> Thereat th'old man did nought but fondly grin,
> And said, his boat the way could wisely tell:
> But his deceptfull eyes did neuer lin,
> To looke on her faire face, and marke her snowy skin.
>
> (3.8, 24)

The knowing response of the dirty old man illustrates that Florimell fails to understand what is going on at two inter-related levels. She cannot read obvious signs and allegories (the cockboat, the swelling of the great waters, the need for guidance and control) and so misses both the comic and the serious points of the situation. Equally, she refuses to acknowledge her unconscious desires and the drives of the body, one of the key points of the Aristotelian subject matter of the Book of Chastity, marking her as an inferior being to Britomart. When the fisherman does make his move, the narrator describes her as a 'silly virgin' (27), a description that is appropriate in Spenser's terms and which is clearly related to his perception of the behaviour of the monarch. Florimell's rescue at the hands of Proteus – another old and unattractive man – is a stark reminder of the penalties of playing the game of love when one is obviously past one's best and cannot command a decent price in the marriage market:

> Her vp betwixt his rugged hands he reard,
> And with his frory lips full soft kist,
> Whiles the cold ysickles from his rough beard,
> Dropped adowne vpon her yuorie brest:
> Yet he himselfe so busily addrest,
> That her out of astonishment he wrought,
> And out of that same fishers filthy nest
> Remouing her, into his charet brought,
> And there with many gentle termes her faire besought.

(3.8, 35)

Florimell is provided with a stark vision of what is in store for her if she fails to marry Marinell. Proteus, the god of transformation, serves to remind her of the need to transform her life and not to follow the path of England's queen, playing out ridiculous rituals of love when the meaning of the game has disappeared.[14] If not, sterility and an icy form of living death await her.

The link between virginity and death is also established in the representation of Belphoebe, another elusive virgin, who is signalled as a type of Elizabeth in the 'Letter to Raleigh' (737). Belphoebe manages to provoke lust in male characters, but is singularly unsuccessful in sorting out the resulting problems. As Judith Anderson points out, Belphoebe fails to understand the nature of 'human love. She operates in terms of absolute virtues and unearthly ideals – virginal chastity, not chaste love' (86). When Timias leads Amoret astray and earns the wrath of Belphoebe (4.7–8) – a clear allegory of the marriage of Sir Walter Raleigh and Elizabeth Throckmorton – the result is a disaster.[15] Timias, having been wounded by three foresters (3.5), was only just saved from death by Belphoebe, who nursed him back from the brink (the headnote to 3.5 informs the reader that 'Belphoebe finds him almost dead'). Now he lapses into a state of profound melancholy, retreats into the woods and cuts himself off from society, becoming a type of the 'wild man of the woods':

> His wonted warlike weapons all he broke,
> And threw away, with vow to vse no more,
> Ne thenceforth euer strike in battell stroke,
> Ne euer word to speake to woman more;
> But in that wildernesse, of men forlore,
> And of the wicked world forgotten quight,
> His hard mishap in dolor to deplore,
> And wast his wretched daies in wofull plight;
> So on him selfe to wreake his follies owne depight.

$$(4.7, 39)^{16}$$

The key word here is 'wast'. Timias, in his excessive reaction to Belphoebe's punishment, but also because of her prudish and inappropriate reaction to sexual activity, has gone from being a valued and important subject of the queen, keen and able to fight for her defence, to a useless outcast. The lines recall the common complaint against Guinevere in the last books of *Le Morte D'Arthur*, that the queen had become a 'destroyer of good knights' (382). In the Arthurian cycle the problems of the realm cannot be sorted out because of the destructive behaviour of those who are supposed to govern (revealing Lancelot's sin will only lead to a civil war, but failing to do so causes disunity which will eventually lead to the same result). Spenser is implying that Elizabeth/Belphoebe has acted just as badly as a ruler and will lead her subjects to a similar end involving the consequent death not just of large numbers of them, but also of the regime itself. Both Spenser and Raleigh favoured an aggressive foreign policy which would strongly oppose the Spanish and defend European Protestant interests and so were critical of the parsimonious instincts of Elizabeth.[17] *The Faerie Queene* makes it clear that not only has Elizabeth endangered her subjects through her own bodily politics, but she has thwarted and discarded those who can help offset her weaknesses – in the short term, at least – because of her obsessive hostility to sex.

As the story of Britomart reveals, the path of sexual awakening and maturity is painful and often very unpleasant.[18] Nevertheless, it is one that has to be followed unless one wishes to remain as an arrested adolescent. The adult love that Amoret and Scudamore, and Britomart and Artegall experience is in sharp contrast to the unsavoury encounters with aged lechers that Florimell has to endure – until she overcomes her fears and marries Marinell. The ending of the first edition of *The Faerie Queene* juxtaposed the joyful hermaphroditic form assumed by the lovers, Amoret and Scudamore, with Britomart's envious and lonely isolation:

> Had ye them seene, ye would haue surely thought,
> That they had beene that faire *Hermaphrodite*,
> Which that rich *Romance* of white marble wrought,
> And in his costly Bath caused to bee site:
> So seemd those two, as growne together quite,
> That *Britomart* halfe enuying ther blesse,
> Was much empassined in her gentle sprite,
> And to her selfe oft wisht like happinesse,
> In vaine she wisht, that fate n'ould let her yet posesse.
>
> (3.12, 46 [1590 edition])

The point to be made is that Amoret has had to suffer the trials of Busyrane in his castle (3.11–12) before she can graduate to the blissful state of mutual union. Britomart will follow suit because her union is in the future, hence the importance of the word, 'yet'. In the house of Busyrane the pains and sufferings of Petrarchan lovers are made literal and real in the Masque of Cupid, showing that love is a cruel form of war. The key, climactic image of Despight and Cruelty removing the heart of the lady and placing it in a silver basin (3.12.19–21), a sacrifice Busyrane clearly intends to repeat before he is prevented by Britomart (31–3), makes literal one of the key puns in English Renaissance literature. In order to produce life one has to die, conception depending on the female orgasm, a form of death which reduces the body's vital spirits, but without which no new life can be engendered.[19] *The Faerie Queene* is a lament for the queen's failure to die.

The poem is thus haunted by an imminent death that has not happened. The narrative drive of *The Faerie Queene* is also determined by one of the most significant deaths in Elizabeth's reign, that of Mary Queen of Scots, executed for treason on 8 February 1587, explicitly represented in Book 5, Canto 9. This event can be seen to counterbalance that of Elizabeth, and Spenser makes it clear that he reads the deaths of the two queens in symbiotic terms in his great poem. Given the question of the succession that dominated British politics throughout the 1580s and 1590s, this is hardly surprising, as Mary had the strongest claim to succeed Elizabeth should she die prematurely, and, after her death, her son, James VI, took her place as most likely heir.[20]

It is easy to see why there might have been opposition to the Stuart claim in England. Mary's biography reads like an English nightmare. She had been brought up a strict Catholic at the French court. She was the daughter-in-law of Catherine de Medici, the evil genius behind the Massacre of Saint Bartholomew's Day (1572), having married the sickly dauphin, Francis. Therefore, she had been used to unite England's two traditional foes, posing a threat alongside – at worst, in tandem with – Spain, whilst also being the heir to the throne of England. The spectre of her namesake, Mary I, who had allied herself with Spain through marriage to Philip II, signalled further undesirable associations. Mary's attempt to claim the English throne in 1558 when Mary I died, on the grounds that her half-sister, Elizabeth, was illegitimate, created further reasons for hostility. After she returned to Scotland, she was implicated in the murder of her second husband, Lord Darnley, in 1567, and married the earl of Bothwell, who was also implicated in the murder, three months later, a union which led to civil war in Scotland, Mary's enforced abdication and flight to England where she spent the last nineteen years of her life under arrest.[21] Once she had been imprisoned, Mary was the centre of a number of plots to overthrow Elizabeth and install her as monarch, actions Mary endorsed on a number of occasions despite her protestations of innocence. The three major plots were the Ridolfi plot (1571), the Throckmorton plot (1583), and the Babington plot (1586), when she allegedly dictated a letter giving her consent to a rebellion which planned to overthrow Elizabeth. Despite Elizabeth's reluctance to sign her death warrant, Mary was tried, condemned to death and executed on 8 February 1587. In short, Mary was associated with aggressive Catholicism and the murder of Protestants, an alliance between England's traditional enemies, underhand dealing and connivance, and civil war, in both Scotland and France. She was thought to be lewd, inconsistent, capricious, arrogant and deceitful.[22]

Spenser's allegory was decoded by one contemporary reader with a vested interest in the fate of the English crown. As is well known, Spenser aroused James VI's wrath through his portrait of the trial of Duessa (5.9), a transparent allegory of Mary's trial and execution. The English ambassador in Scotland, Robert Bowes, wrote to Lord Burghley on 1 November 1596 that James refused to allow the second edition of *The Faerie Queene* to be sold in Scotland, and 'further he will complain to Her Majesty of the author as you will understand at more length by himself' (cited in Maley 67–8). On 12 November, Bowes wrote again, explaining that the problem stemmed from 'som dishonourable effects (as the King deems thereof) against himself and his mother deceased.' Although Bowes claimed that he had persuaded James that the book had not been 'passed with privilege of Her Majesty's Commissioners', James 'still desire[d] that Edward [sic] Spenser for his fault be duly tried and punished' (Maley 68; *Calendar* 723). Nor was the affair over yet. On 5 March 1598, George Nicolson, a servant of Robert Bowes, wrote to Sir Robert Cecil that Walter Quinn, a poet later to enjoy a successful career at the courts of James and Charles I, was 'answering Spenser's book, whereat the king is offended' (*Calendar* 747).[23] The work, assuming it was ever completed, has not survived.[24]

James's anger is understandable, especially as he obviously thought that the poem had been published with official approval. He felt that the publication of Spenser's poem might damage his chances of succeeding Elizabeth and so uniting the English and Scottish crowns.[25] James's reading of *The Faerie Queene* – or that of his advisers – is, I would suggest, an astute one. From James's point of view, the poem was all the more scandalous for its deliberate omission of a crucial detail. *The Faerie Queene* does not actually represent the death of Mary. The canto ends with Elizabeth's counsellors, led by Zele, demanding the execution of Duessa for her numerous crimes which appear as allegorical forms before the queen: Murder, Sedition, Incontinence, Adulterie, Impietie:

> Then brought he [Zele] forth, with griesly grim aspect,
> Abhorred *Murder*, who with bloudie knyfe
> Yet dropping fresh in hand did her detect,
> And there with guiltie bloudshed charged ryfe:
> Then brought he forth *Sedition*, breeding stryfe
> In troublous wits, and mutinous vprore:
> Then brought he forth *Incontinence* of lyfe,
> Euen foule *Adulterie* her face before,
> And lewd *Impietie*, that her accursed sore.

(48)

The inclusion of incontinence as one of Mary's vices/crimes reminds the reader of such incontinent figures as Malecasta, the lustful lady who tries to seduce Britomart, in the canto that forms a bridge between the legends of Temperance and Chastity (3.1). Malecasta is described as being 'giuen all to fleshy lust' and defined by the sin of 'incontinence' (48), making a strong link between the themes of the legend of chastity and that of justice. The appearance of the figure of Adultery also seems to refer to events at the end of Book 3, when Paridell elopes with

Malbecco's wife, Hellenore (9–10), further indicating that the poem makes conscious links between allegorical episodes within its narrative. It is not such a huge step from lust to adultery to murder, one that any reader of George Buchanan's *History of Scotland* – used by Spenser as a source for *The View of the Present State of Ireland* – or his *Detection of the Actions of Mary Queen of Scots* would have observed being made.[26] The tableau might also have reminded readers of such scenes as the Masque of Cupid (3.12), suggesting that this is another rite of passage that Mercilla/Elizabeth has to read correctly and then act accordingly. In other words, the queen needs to distinguish between true and false passion in order to govern successfully.

However, if this is the case, the ending of the canto makes it clear that Mercilla is reluctant to pass the test. Despite the overwhelming case against Duessa/Mary, Mercilla/Elizabeth is overcome with pity for her plight:

> But she, whose Princely breast was touched nere
> With piteous ruth of her so wretched plight,
> Though she plaine saw by all, that she did heare,
> That she of death was guiltie found by right,
> Yet would not let iust vengeance on her light;
> But rather let in stead thereof to fall
> Few perling drops from her faire lampes of light;
> The which she couering with her purple pall
> Would haue the passion hid, and vp arose withall.

> (50)

Mercilla is undoubtedly at fault here, putting her own feelings ahead of the safety and happiness of her subjects – exactly the sort of behaviour in princes that Buchanan objected to throughout his *History of Scotland*.[27] The last lines show that she wishes to keep her feelings and tears secret, presumably aware that her subjects might well not share her pity for Mary and that she has undermined the true course of justice demanded by her most trusted inner circle of counsellors (Mercilla's errors are repeated at the end of the Book when the Faerie Queene recalls Artegall and Talus back from Ireland before they have had a chance to reform it thoroughly).[28]

Duessa, although her death is not actually described, does not appear again in *The Faerie Queene*. It is clear that she is dead, as the poem states at the start of Canto 10 that Mercilla treats the body of Duessa with excessive obsequies for a criminal: 'And yet euen then ruing her wilfull fall, / With more then needfull naturall remorse, / And yeelding the last honour to her wretched corse' (5.10, 4). The omission of the description of the execution itself seems to be deliberate, given the gory details provided elsewhere in the poem. It is also worth noting that if Spenser was attempting to preserve a sense of royal decorum in leaving Mary's head still on her shoulders, he failed to convince James. Spenser appears to be suggesting that Duessa/Mary lives on after her death, which might help to explain James's anger, as he is tarred with her brush in the poem. Book 6 shows the dangers inherent in tolerating the Catholic threat that Mary represented, principally through Spanish support for rebellion in Ireland, and its devastating effects on the rest of the British Isles.[29] Duessa's legacy, like that of Error, whose monstrous brood devour their mother when the Redcross Knight kills her (1.1.25–6), and who are actually more dangerous when dead than alive, is poisonous and destructive. More significantly, I would suggest, Duessa is transformed into the ultimate threat to order in the poem, Mutabilitie, a change in keeping with the most conspicuously Ovidian poem Spenser wrote.[30] Duessa/Mary, through her claim to the throne, does not expire when dead but lives on through her son, James, who, for Spenser, represents the same dangers as his mother.

One of the recurrent motifs of the poem is that the failure to destroy evil completely will result in its eventual return, often in mutated form. Artegall, the Knight of Justice, has to learn this lesson. He defeats Radigund, the Amazon Queen, in single combat, but throws away his sword when his senses are bewitched by her 'faire visage', enabling her to triumph and imprison him (5.5.12–20).[31] After he has been liberated by Britomart, Artegall shows no mercy to the shape-shifting Malengin, a 'wicked villain' who preys on unsuspecting travellers passing through the wilderness where he hides. Artegall has Talus execute Malengin completely with his 'yron flayle' so that

> all his bones, as small as sandy grayle
> He broke, and did his bowels disentrayle;
> Crying in vaine for helpe, when helpe was past.
> So did deceipt the selfe deceiver fayle,
> There they him left a carrion outcast;
> For beasts and foules to feede upon for their repast.
>
> (5.9.19)

Talus, on Artegall's command, destroys all remnants of Malengin, showing that he has learned the lesson of his defeat by Radigund, even if Mercilla is unaware of the dangers of false pity. His death is nothing if not spectacular, providing an even better lesson to the reader than the severed limbs and heads of traitors which adorned city walls as a means of warning against rebellion did for anyone out and about.[32] The description is self-consciously produced as a fantasy of power: Malengin's body is made to disappear, as if he had never existed, had no heirs and would signify nothing after his death. The same, as Spenser was all to well aware, was not the case with other enemies of the state, such as Mary.

Duessa's story is the most spectacular example of this repeated pattern of inversion and subversion. She first gains power once the Redcross Knight falls prey to the wiles of Archimago in Book I, Canto 2. She helps imprison the knight and inaugurate the rule of Orgoglio, appearing herself as an explicitly signalled emblematic model of the Whore of Babylon riding on a dragon (1.7.16–18). After Orgoglio's defeat, she is stripped and exposed in a cruel parody of the blazon, appearing as a half-woman, half-beast (1.8.46–50). However, just as the defeat of a monster called Error leads to the proliferation of errors and the delusive overconfidence of those whose duty it is to protect the truth, the subsequent banishment of Duessa to the wilderness only makes her more dangerous. She returns, predictably enough, to assert a previous claim to the Redcross knight at his betrothal to Una (I.12.24–36), through her messenger, Archimago. He is unceremoniously thrown into a dungeon, but the claim is not, despite Una's protestations of her prior right (33–4), laid to rest. The book ends with the knight returning to his service to the Faerie Queene for another six years, and Una 'left to mourne' (41) alone.

Duessa plays an important role in Book 4, summoning Ate from hell (4.1.19), and supporting her crimes, before she returns as the explicit allegory of Mary in 5.9.[33] As has often been pointed out, the allegory of *The Faerie Queene* is neither simple nor static and cannot be read in linear terms.[34] Figures and motifs recur and central themes are re-explored and re-thought. Duessa as Mary signals a threat to Una as Elizabeth from the start of the poem, before she returns to trouble Mercilla, another manifestation of the polyvalent Elizabeth.[35] Given this allegorical pattern it is absolutely clear that the battle between the queens is continuing in the 'Two Cantos of Mutabilitie', only published when both of them were dead.

Cynthia, who is challenged by Mutabilitie, can be read as a representation of Elizabeth, making her the same figure as Diana – Cynthia's alternative name – who is stalked by the voyeuristic Faunus, as the 'Letter to Raleigh' indicates (716). Moreover, Cynthia's steeds, one black, the other white, represent Elizabeth's colours (7.6.9), as does the black and white apparel of Una (1.1.4–5).[36] In her final words before Nature gives her judgement, Mutabilitie sets herself against Jove and his creature, Cynthia, in hostile terms which assert her right to control the universe. Despite her pretence and avoidance of the key issues, Cynthia is shown to be all too human and fallible, 'mortal borne', with her countenance endlessly changing (as cited above). These pointed lines refer to two principal issues. First, they criticize Elizabeth's vacillating and fickle style of government, in a commonplace attack on women's rule made by numerous dissillusioned, frustrated and worried men in the 1590s.[37] Second, they make the irrefutable observation that Elizabeth is reaching the end of her reign because she will die soon.[38] Her political wiles and regal bearing cannot save her body from its imminent demise.

But, more specifically, they appear to allude, albeit obliquely, to the behaviour of Mercilla in Book 5, Canto 9, when she has to be forced by her male advisers to act decisively against Duessa/Mary Queen of Scots. The main plot of 'Two Cantos of Mutabilitie' needs to be read in terms of that episode. Before she challenges Jove for the right to rule the universe, Mutabilitie challenges Cynthia's right to rule her kingdom below the moon. In defending herself, Cynthia claims her descent from Jove, but Jove, as all readers obviously would have known, was a usurper himself, just like the Tudors.[39] In fact, Elizabeth's claim to the throne was, in many ways, no better than that of Mary, who was also descended from Henry VII. For Catholics, Henry VIII's divorce from Catherine of Aragon was not recognised, so Elizabeth was illegitimate, making Mary Stuart the true heir of Mary Tudor and her cousin the real usurper. This claim, announced by Henri II of France on Mary Tudor's death, was recognised throughout Catholic Europe and formed the basis of the series of plots against Elizabeth throughout her reign.[40] This is why Mutabilitie's initial challenge is made against Cynthia. When Mercury, Jove's messenger, tries to force her to drop her claim she refuses to 'leave faire *Cynthias* siluer bower; / Sith shee his *Ioue* and him esteemed nought, / No more than *Cynthia's* selfe; but all their kingdoms sought' (7.6.18). Mutabilitie and Mary have identical aims.

'Two Cantos of Mutabilitie' dramatize the conflict between Nature and order ranged against the forces of chaos; Jove against the Titans; Elizabeth against Mary Queen of Scots; the Tudors against the Stuarts. Nature awards the victory to former on the problematic grounds that although everything changes, 'They are not changed from their first estate; / But by their change their being doe dilate: / And turning to themselves at length againe, / Doe worke their owne perfection so by fate' (7.7.58). Metaphysically this may be true, but it clearly does not square with the description of the ailing queen eight stanzas earlier, who will be prey to the ravages of death before too long. Mutabilitie, I would suggest, is a transformed version of Duessa, just as Duessa was a transformed version of Error. As such, she inherits the same allegorical mantle. The fear the poem articulates is that Mutabilitie may be evil and wrong, but that her claims – like Mary's – are impossible to resist. Mary will prove stronger after her death than Elizabeth will because she has produced life in the form of her son. The Cantos have to be read as an attack on James, who enabled his mother to live on, making the reader see that the sins of the mother were visited on the son.[41]

The narrative of *The Faerie Queene* is framed by two deaths, neither of which actually appears in the poem, but which no one writing in Britain in the 1590s could ignore. Spenser, who would only have been in his mid-forties when he was writing the second half of the poem, could expect to outlive his queen, who was by then into her sixties, and so discover what the effects of her death would be and how they would relate to Mary's death and legacy. He had good reason to fear the event, but, fortunately, his own death intervened.

## Notes

1. See Elizabeth Fowler, 'The Failure of Moral Philosophy in the Work of Edmund Spenser'. All references are to *The Faerie Queene*, ed. A. C. Hamilton (2001, rev. edn.).
2. For discussion, see Carol V. Kaske, 'Amavia, Mortdant, Ruddymane', in *The Spenser Encyclopedia*, 25–7.
3. On the relationship between *The Faerie Queene* and Italian romance, see Colin Burrow, *Epic Romance; Homer to Milton*, ch. 5. On the relationship between *The Faerie Queene* and *Le Morte D'Arthur*, see Paul R. Rovang, *Refashioning 'Knights and Ladies Gentle Deeds': The Intertextuality of Spenser's Faerie Queene and Malory's Morte D'Arthur*.
4. See Sir Thomas Malory, *Le Morte D'Arthur*, II, Books XVIII–XXI. See also Chrétien De Troyes, *the Knight of the Cart (Lancelot) in Arthurian Romances*.
5. On Spenser's apocalyptic fears see Andrew Hadfield, *Spenser's Irish Experience: Wilde Fruit and Salvage Soyl*, ch. 6.
6. See Richard C. McCoy, *The Rites of Knighthood: The Literature and Politics of Elizabethan Chivalry*.
7. See C. S. Lewis, *Spenser's Images of Life*.
8. See Kaske, 'Chastity' and J. Carscallen, 'Temperance' in *Spenser Encyclopedia*.
9. For an extended discussion see John N. King, *Spenser's Poetry and the Reformation Tradition*, ch. 4.
10. For further discussion see Anthony Low, *The Reinvention of Love: Poetry, Politics and Culture from Sidney to Milton*.

11. See Sheila T. Cavanagh, *Wanton Eyes and Chaste Desires: Female Sexuality in The Faerie Queene*, passim.

12. For comment see Patrick Cheney, *Marlowe's Counterfeit Profession: Ovid, Spenser, Counter-Nationhood*, ch. 11.

13. See Ariosto, 8.31, 47–64.

14. See John Guy, 'Tudor monarchy and its critiques', *The Tudor Monarchy*, 90. See also Arthur F. Marotti ' "Love is not Love": Elizabethan Sonnet Sequences and the Social Order'.

15. On the allegory of Raleigh and Elizabeth Throckmorton, see James P. Bednarz, 'Raleigh in Spenser's Historical Allegory'.

16. On the 'wild man of the woods', see Richard Bernheimer, *Wild Men in the Middle Ages: A Study in Art, Sentiment and Demonology*. A prototype of Timias is Yvain, in Chrétien's *The Knight with the Lion*; see *Arthurian Romances*, 330–1.

17. For discussion and analysis see John Guy, *Tudor England*, ch. 12.

18. See the overview in Judith H. Anderson, 'Britomart', in *Spenser Encyclopedia*, 113–5. See also Lauren Silberman, *Transforming Desire; Erotic Knowledge in Books III and IV of* The Faerie Queene, ch. 3.

19. See Audrey Eccles, *Obstetrics and Gynaecology in Tudor and Stuart England*, 29–31; Sara Mendelson and Patricia Crawford, *Women in Early Modern England*, 27. I owe these references to Teresa Walters.

20. See Marie Axton, *The Queen's Two Bodies: Drama and the Elizabethan Succession*, passim; Susan Doran, *Monarchy and Matrimony: The Courtships of Elizabeth I*, chs 6–7.

21. '[E]vents in Scotland in the 1560s [. . .] had been the talk of all Europe for a generation' (Alvin Kernan, *Shakespeare, the King's Playwright: Theater in the Stuart Court, 1603–1613*, 37, citing Roland Frye).

22. For details see Antonia Fraser, *Mary Queen of Scots*.

23. On Quinn, see *DNB* entry.

24. For further analysis see Richard A. McCabe, 'The Masks of Duessa: Spenser, Mary Queen of Scots, and James I'; 'Spenser and the Stuart Succession', *Literature and History* (forthcoming). On the impact of Mary's execution in England, see James Emerson Phillips, *Images of a Queen: Mary Stuart in Sixteenth-Century Literature*; Howard Erskine-Hill, *Poetry and the Realm of Politics: Shakespeare to Dryden*.

25. For the historical context see Susan Doran; D. Harris Wilson, *King James VI and I*, chs 5–9.

26. See *The History of Scotland written in Latin by George Buchanan; faithfully rendered into English* (J. Fraser) (1690), Bks 16–20; *A detection of the Actions of Mary Queen of Scots* (1721); Spenser, *A View of the State of Ireland*, 45–6, 51, 60, 63. See also Arthur Williamson, 'Patterns of British Identity: "Britain" and its Rivals in the Sixteenth and Seventeenth Centuries', 160–2.

27. For analysis see Roger A. Mason, 'George Buchanan, James VI and the Presbyterians'; J. H. Burns, *The True Law of Kingship: Concepts of Monarchy in Early Modern Scotland*, ch. 6.

28. For comment see Michael O'Connell, *Mirror and Veil: The Historical Dimension of Spenser's Faerie Queene* 154–5; Hadfield, *Spenser's Irish Experience*, 166–7.

29. Hadfield, *Spenser's Irish Experience*, ch. 5.

30. See Michael Holahan, '*Iamque opus exegi*: Ovid's Changes and Spenser's Brief Epic of Mutability'. On the cultural importance of Ovid and Spenser's rela-

tionship to Ovid as a precursor throughout his career, see Patrick Cheney, *Marlowe's Counterfeit Profession: Ovid, Spenser, Counter-Nationhood*, ch. 1; Jonathan Bate, *Shakespeare and Ovid, passim.*

31. For commentary on this episode, see Clare Carroll, 'The Construction of Gender and the Cultural and Political Order in *The Faerie Queene* 5 and *A View of the Present State of Ireland*: The Critics, the Context and the case of Radigund'.

32. See John Bellamy, *The Tudor Law of Treason: An Introduction*, ch. 5. See also the famously gory description in Michel Foucault, *Discipline and Punish: The Birth of the Prison*, ch. 1.

33. See Anthea Hume, *Spenser Encyclopedia*, 229–30.

34. See Michael O'Connell, *Mirror and Veil*, ch. 2; Isabel G. MacCaffrey, *Spenser's Allegory: The Anatomy of Imagination.*

35. On Una as Elizabeth, see Douglas Brooks-Davies, 'Una', *Spenser Encyclopedia*, 704–5.

36. See Roy Strong, *The Cult of Elizabeth: Elizabethan Portraiture and Pageant*, 71–4; Douglas Brooks-Davies, 'Una', 705.

37. See John Guy, 'The 1590s; The Second Reign of Elizabeth I?'; Helen Hackett, *Virgin Mother, Maiden Queen: Elizabeth I and the Cult of the Virgin Mary*, ch. 6.

38. See David Norbrook, *Poetry and Politics in the English Renaissance*, 152–3.

39. Hadfield, *Spenser's Irish Experience*, ch. 6.

40. See Jayne Elizabeth Lewis, *Mary Queen of Scots: Romance and Nation*, 20.

41. Why Spenser feared the rule of James is open to speculation. He may have thought that James, for all his protestations to the contrary, was really a closet Catholic; he may have associated James with the chaos of his mother's rule; he may have been strongly influenced by Raleigh's opposition to James; or he may have felt that an Anglo-Scottish union would be a disaster. For analysis see my article, 'Spenser and the Stuart Succession'.

# 3
# Psychic Deadness in Allegory: Spenser's House of Mammon and Attacks on Linking

*Theresa M. Krier*

> And in his lap a masse of coyne he told,
> And turned vpsidowne, to feede his eye
> And couetous desire with his huge threasury.
>
> And round about him lay on euery side
> Great heapes of gold, that neuer could be spent:
> Of which some were rude owre, not purifide
> Of *Mulcibers* deuouring element;
> Some others were new driuen, and distent
> Into great Ingoes, and to wedges square;
> Some in round plates withouten moniment;
> But most were stampt . . .
>
> (*The Faerie Queene* 2.7.4–5)

Mammon's piles of ore, ingots, coin, and other chunks of precious metal may stand as an emblem of one problem that allegory can pose to readers. Pursuing this problem through the House of Mammon episode in *The Faerie Queene* II, I will suggest links among the problem of thinking allegorically, greed, and death, and argue that the whole episode – the epic descent of the book's hero Guyon to an underworld – amounts to an attack on readerly thinking; Spenser represents and critiques the discourse of punitive moral-exemplum allegory (of the kind found in Dante or Boccaccio or Comes) as such an attack on the mobility of interpretive thought. This is so contrary to our usual assumptions about allegorical fictions *inviting* interpretations that I want to start by calling to mind a very different allegorical fiction about greed and a mound of gold, that in Chaucer's Pardoner's Tale.[1] Three young 'riotours,' hearing of a dangerous murderer, a 'privee theef' (675) called Death, swear to find and slay this dangerous fellow. On the way they meet an old man whose time for death has not yet come, though he is ready for it; he directs the young men to Death's place, in a grove under a tree. The Pardoner goes on:

> . . . and ther they founde
> Of floryns fyne of gold ycoyned rounde
> Wel ny an eighte busshels, as hem thoughte.
> No lenger thanne after Deeth they soughte,
> But ech of hem so glad was of that sighte,
> For that the floryns been so faire and brighte,
> That doun they sette hem by this precious hoord.

> (769–75)

Of course they have set in train the process by which they will find death after all, though they have no thought that they are pursuing it any longer; their greed and reciprocal treacheries guarantee all their deaths. All these events the Pardoner tells with economy and dispatch, so that in this part of his tale there is no ambiguity about cause-and-effect relationships among death and greed. Furthermore, there is no obstruction to the thinking of the reader about the nature of the allegory. When we hear the man who first tells the youths about Death, who has killed so many in their region, we know precisely how to take it, what sorts of resistances to death will work and what sorts will not work; we know the youths mistake the allegorical nature of the personification about whom they have been told. The Pardoner's Death has, of course, a depth and resonance that come of venerable traditions about him – Rosemond Tuve would make this kind of argument about allegorical figures of early periods, that they present us not with obscurity but with the richness of their historical lives – as well as every mortal's mysterious relationship to the limit of death – and the old man who is ready to die greatly intensifies this resonance.[2] But readers of the Pardoner's Tale and its many analogues need not twist their minds in labyrinthine ways in order to make sense of the story. The ironies of the young men's mistakings, in interpretation and ethics alike, are spare, deep, and clear at once.

Spenser's House of Mammon episode has nothing of this kind of allegory (although Tuve strongly argues for exactly this kind of force of tradition in the Mammon episode). Instead, like the heaps of disparate, unconnected metals that Mammon turns over and over, the various bits of the episode seem to invite close scrutiny, but frustrate this kind of thinking at the same time, such that readers undergo the experience of attacks on linking from the text itself. Our thought is summoned to dwell with the various persons, places, and iconographical details in Mammon's House, but how? How do we even find the gaps in the heaps of details, much less tolerate the absence of the links on which thinking thrives? The tradition of commentary on the episode is largely one of proposing a conceivable principle of coherence for all its parts, and indeed I too will be suggesting one before long. But finally it is the frustration or failure of these efforts, and the consequent relationship of text to reader, that interests me. I will emerge from my proposed principle of coherence with a suggestion about the relationships in the episode between this allegory's frustration of its readers' mental energies and the aggressive greed thematized in the episode.

In its emphasis on allegory's violence toward the reader, this proposal augments and qualifies Gordon Teskey's argument in *Allegory and Violence* about the violent relationship of allegorical plan to the characters it depicts. Speaking of Dante's *Inferno*, canto 5, which recounts Dante's meeting with Francesca da Rimini, Teskey says, 'The entire structure of the fifth canto is designed to expose allegory's primary work, which is to force meaning on beings who are reduced for that purpose to substance. [. . .] Dante is revealing in this episode the failure of allegory to accomplish [. . .] a total expulsion of life' (25).[3] I don't think this reduction *necessarily* true of every kind of allegory. But it is necessarily true of punitive, moral-exemplum allegories, and so it is not accidental that Teskey's most powerful instance of all those he treats in his allegory book is an episode in an underworld; in such a place, the fact that Francesca is dead yet maintains a sense of her continuing aliveness exacerbates her punishment (because she cannot choose extinction) and so can be said to be a cruelty on the part of the poet, but also invites us to witness the exorbitance of such punishment. Teskey's representation of allegory itself amounts to a punitive underworld, vast, hopeless, driven by 'the violent pleasure of thought' (24).

The Spenser who creates the House of Mammon in his Legend of Temperance also witnesses to the exorbitance and force, not of all allegory but certainly of punitive exemplum allegory, which he could have found not only in Dante but also in Boccaccio, Comes, and many lesser allegorical commentators. As with so many of his inherited forms in *The Faerie Queene* II, Spenser is on the way to leaving this sort of allegory behind and making clear why he will henceforth find more ease in his development of other possible relationships between thinking and poetry. He takes us on this long journey by exposing himself to his allegorical episode's violence of thought, for which I've taken as an emblem Mammon's heaps of gold and the economic, intellectual, and ethical problems it poses.

This problem of 'heaps' I would like to consider first as a phenomenon of the individual psyche trying *not* to think, then as a linguistic and ethical phenomenon, for Spenser is concerned not only with the failure of Mammon's heaps to connect internally and with the world, in a rectified commerce, but also with the excessive clutter of unwieldy, unlimited allegorical detail, and how manic excess can immobilize thinking. Any possible allegorical significance entices readers to think; a heap of promisingly but frustratingly related details thwarts and baffles the mind's movement in seeking links. Mammon's realm of death is driven implicitly by attacks on linking, a notion I borrow from Wilfred Bion (1897–1979), the psychoanalyst who developed a complex theory of thinking.

By 'attacks on linking' Bion means not chiefly overt patent attacks, for example Tantalus' sin of killing his son and reducing him to food, but attacks on *the process of thinking* that permits interpretation and, as a consequence, a sane relationship within which meaning can be created and constantly refreshed. Thinking, for Bion, is a kind of daimonic action in the sense that Diotima means when she instructs Socrates on the power of the daimonic Eros: 'A great daimon [. . .] acts as an interpreter and means of communication between gods and mortals. It takes requests and offerings to the gods, and brings back instructions and benefits in return. Occupying this middle position it plays a vital role in holding the world together.'[4]

Like D. W. Winnicott, Bion responds strongly to Freud's recurrent emphasis on the human struggle to maintain poise against an onslaught of stimuli from the enormous energies of the world; like Melanie Klein, he would also make much of the onslaught of the death drive from within. Hence the force of his notion that thinking arises under the pressure of having to *cope*:

> It is convenient to regard thinking as dependent on the successful outcome of two main mental developments. The first is the development of thoughts. They require an apparatus to cope with them. The second development therefore, is of this apparatus that I shall provisionally call thinking. I repeat – thinking has to be called into existence to cope with thoughts.     ('Theory of Thinking' 110–11)

Thinking begins not with the perception of objects but with that of relationships among objects; thinking allows the psyche to create generative, mobile, ongoing meanings from the exorbitant welter of things, stimuli, persons, internal emotions and drives. A link is the specific movement of mind in the space between objects or persons, a movement that gives rise to a verbal thought.

In his clinical practice, Bion focused on the ways that patients attacked whatever thinking occurred in the session, whether an interpretation by the analyst or an emergent perception of a link made by the analysand. (In his writing, he seems not to entertain the possibility of a legitimate attack, say against a bullying or doctrinaire interpretation by the analyst. But the question of power's effects on linking is germane to the House of Mammon, and I return to it below.) An attack on linking could be a simple resistance, but in Bion's clinical examples the attack on the link is often surprising and oblique, visceral, even murderous or suicidal. One patient, attempting to agree with the analyst's simple and positive interpretation, made an attack on this proffer of a link by beginning to stammer: 'The sounds emitted bore resemblance to a gasping for breath; gaspings were interspersed with gurgling sounds as if he were immersed in water' ('Attacks on Linking' 88). This man wanted and did not want to incorporate the analyst's idea; the stammer 'was designed to prevent [him] from using language as a bond between him and me' (91). Other examples include clients who suddenly made sharp stabbing motions or who convulsed as if attacked from within. A destructive attack on the link might be psychotic, or infantile, or sophisticated. If thinking in the form of interpretation makes possible the transformation of the client's suffering, this thinking may be hard for the client to swallow or metabolize or make use of. Still, linking and thinking, implying mental mobility and emotional resilience, are necessary if not invariably sufficient conditions for maintaining a sense of aliveness.[5]

But everyday, non-psychotic thinking itself may be used as an attack on linking; it may be rigid or opposed to 'the open growth of meaning'. Bion deduces one kind of attack from a confluence of expressions of arrogance, stupidity, and curiosity. Oedipus provides an instance of arrogant thinking masked as curiosity, used eventually to attack a mental link to the end of denying excessively painful knowledge about an historical and genealogical link ('On Arrogance' 86). He understands such attacks to issue from a death drive within the client – a development of the Kleinian death instinct, which besieges the young infant and threatens its own existence, which hates and fears all emotions as excessive, all possible links as intolerable claims from the world. For diverse reasons, it may be that 'the conduct of emotional life, in any case a severe problem, becomes intolerable. Feelings of hatred are thereupon directed against all emotions, including hate itself, and against external reality which stimulates them. It is a short step from hatred of the emotions to hatred of life itself' ('Attacks' 99; see also Eigen 40–1, 46–8). Attacks on linking/thinking are expressions of death work.

Bion develops Melanie Klein's elaborate scenarios of the very young infant in his proposals about the actions of thinking. The Kleinian infant is driven by the self-destructive energies of the death drive to fear, hate, desire, and envy the maternal breast; capable of fantasies in which it splits off feared aspects of its own violent psychic life and projects them into the mother; greedy, terrified, vulnerable, and murderous. Like Klein, Bion tries to articulate instances of an infinite, unappeasable power of death work in the individual; like Klein, he is interested in the infant's wish for knowledge; like Klein, he understands thinking *rhetorically* as an action meant to have an effect upon the person at the other side of the link. But Bion, though he takes full advantage of the richness of the Kleinian array of events in the psyche, wants to transform the impoverishing rigidity of Kleinian interpretation enforced by her attachment to the part-object:

> The conception of the part-object as analogous to an anatomical structure [. . .] is misleading because the part-object relationship is not with the anatomical structures only but with function, not with anatomy but with physiology, not with the breast but with feeding, poisoning, loving, hating. [. . .] I employ the term 'link' because I wish to discuss [. . .] relationship with a function rather than with the object that subserves a function; my concern is not only with the breast, or penis, or verbal thought, but with their function of providing the link between two objects.
>
> ('Attacks on Linking' 94–5)

Klein herself, we might say, attacks linking in her relentless, rigid focus on objects rather than on the mobile processes that link them in thought, when she unilaterally and aggressively interprets her patients for them. Kleinian part-objects nonetheless enter Bion's theorizing as bizarre objects, his name for psychotics' unrelated, incoherent fragments expelled into the world, which can never exactly enter thinking because they are not linked. Bion would say that everyone, psychotic or not, faces the economic question of how to manage heaps or surges of unrelated things. Infants and psychotics, dominated by processes of projective identification (a concept developed most elaborately by Klein and worked hard by Bion), demonstrate in extreme form how humans split off and project into another unbearable bits of the self; psychic activity is as rich in its repertoire of throwing away or disowning as it is in its repertoire of hoarding. Both are attacks on the always risky venture of linking, and both are rooted in Bion's meditations on infant greed and the infant's sufferance of the death drive. A lucky infant will have a mother who receives, tolerates, and transforms these fragments for the infant. Harold Boris says, 'The beta-elements are projected into whatever container is available, there to haunt or counterattack or to be transformed by someone else's alpha function – or "reverie," as Bion calls it. That capacity for reverie is the mother's psychic nourishing of the baby's mind. [. . .] The capacity of another to intuit and imagine one's state of mind gives life to the mind and restores life to minds gone dead' (234). Psychotics will evacuate such beta-elements, which for them have become 'bizarre objects' lacking enough links to bring them into thinking, into their environment and then find themselves tormented by them. Such a patient may have an analyst who can receive, contain, and transform the cruel fragments and help to create links, but this process itself may tend to exacerbate attacks on linking, since the patient (like an envious, angry baby) may resent and resist the analyst's ventures into thinking and linking, may envy and hate what seems to the patient like the analyst's omniscience. This paradox lends Bion's clinical accounts their pathos: the analyst suffers both for the patient and in himself, and is positioned in double-binds of thinking and linking. The analyst has the hope of creating daimonic psychic movement, linking discrete bits of the patient's life, linking with the patient, and transforming the thought processes of both of them. But humans resist the daimonic as much as they court it.

What do links made in thinking, or attacks on such links, have to do with greed or with the analysis of greed in Spenser's House of Mammon? Rather than follow Guyon sequentially through his *voie* of Mammon's realm, I turn immediately to the densest, most figurative and allusive moments in the episode, to demonstrate both the critic's urge to search for principles of allegorical wholeness, and to demonstrate the text's attacks on linking. The first moment is Spenser's representation of Tantalus, punished eternally in the River Cocytus; the second is the Garden of Proserpina. These persons and the garden itself amount to our best bet for a thematic core to the whole episode. Their tales represent manifold attacks on linking between parents and children – nurture gone awry or thwarted – in such a way that the reader experiences the episode as an attack on thinking.

Thus Tantalus embodies most starkly Spenser's links among a condition of phenomenal deadness and aliveness peculiar to punitive underworlds in epic, derangement of parental nurture, and food:

> Deepe was he drenched to the vpmost chin,
>> Yet gaped still, as coueting to drinke
>> Of the cold liquor, which he waded in,
>> And stretching forth his hand, did often thinke
>> To reach the fruit, which grew vpon the brincke:
>> But both the fruit from hand, and floud from mouth
>> Did flie abacke, and made him vainely swinke:
>> The whiles he steru'd with hunger and with drouth
> He daily dyde, yet neuer throughly dyen couth.

> (2.7.58)

Tantalus has, in one version of his myth, killed his own son, cooked him up and fed him to the gods, in order to discover whether the gods are indeed omniscient; in another version, Tantalus the rich man feasts with the gods and then betrays their secrets.[6] Spenser's allusion (Tantalus says, 'Lo *Tantalus*, I here tormented lye: / Of whom high *Ioue* wont whylome feasted be' in stanza 59) seems to speak only of the feasting/betraying tradition, yet in the context of Spenser's canto, shadowed by figures of parental nurture gone awry, Tantalus' murder and brute reduction to substance of his child cannot *not* haunt the scene. In an arrogant acting-out of curiosity that passes for thought ('Can the gods really know *everything*?'), Tantalus has attacked the link between himself and the gods, and/or the link between himself and his child, in such a way that the capacity for future creative relationship with them, and the future generation of new meaning, is aborted. He has attacked not only the child, not only his future with the child and the gods, but also their past links, his psychic representations that, in a sane situation, might have existed between them. For that matter, he has attacked food and bodily need and a maternal earth which provisions all mortals; he has attacked time and space. All of these murderous attacks are also, implicitly, disavowals of thinking, refusals to acknowledge the most primordial links and the proper direction of their movements – parents give rise to and nurture children, earth gives rise to fruits and nurtures creatures, food is by definition that which we use to sustain life.

But this powerful thematic nexus leaves key details – sometimes the absence of key details – unexplained, and the text discourages us from thinking it out, at any rate all the way through. Spenser makes Tantalus into an allegorical emblem precisely in order to elicit *and then thwart* thought, in the form of allegorical interpretation, from us. For the reader, the allegorized condition of Tantalus elicits, but then refuses, responsiveness to questions like 'What could have made him do that? What sort of man would have done that? Why did he need to know about the gods' omniscience?' or, more speculatively, 'Does the death of the son mean that Tantalus as a parent finds his child's contact with him intolerable? What would happen to a child whose parent repels recognition of him?' or, in formal vein, 'Does the poem's gap in *not* mentioning Pelops, swerving from the narrative about the murdered son, mean something?' We are left only with the blank image of the consequences of combined curiosity, arrogance, and stupidity. The peculiar deadness of a morally emblematic figure redoubles the condition of psychic deadness, or phenomenal death, which Tantalus suffers, and enrolls the reader in that deadness.

This is a kind of allegory that therefore makes for painful reading. It does so in an evident sense, of course, in that we are discomfited and perhaps sobered by witnessing the character's suffering. But it is also painful because we are asked to think, but then refused either the modal or generic features that invite further venturing on a path of thought or an open interpretive matrix that makes thinking generative and genial. Again the witty deployment of allegory in the Pardoner's Tale comes to mind as a relief from the kind of tortuous thought elicited in the House of Mammon. Closer to home, this Mammonian kind of allegory might be clarified by contrast with Spenser's Garden of Adonis, which welcomes thought from the reader and seems forever moving to generate its own links with thinking.[7] The Garden of Adonis makes thinking into something pleasurable, granting it a sense of ease and fluency. This generosity of thought is exactly opposed to the kind of thinking that the House of Mammon elicits, hard and thwarting. Guyon himself has a hard time in struggle with this relationship to thought, which is why he can respond to Tantalus only by resisting a link between himself and the other, as if he too is invited to think, then forced to the cruelty of attacking links that might arise. His itinerary confronts him on every hand with the exhausting economic problem of heaps.

Another instance of the sense of being barraged by monumental aggregates of allusive detail that invite, then frustrate, thought occurs in the description of the Garden of Proserpina. Mammon has led Guyon:

Into a gardin goodly garnished
With hearbs and fruits, whose kinds mote not be red:
Not such, as earth out of her fruitfull woomb
Throwes forth to men, sweet and well sauoured,
But direfull deadly blacke both leafe and bloom,
Fit to adorne the dead, and decke the drery toombe.

There mournfull *Cypresse* grew in greatest store,
And trees of bitter *Gall*, and *Heben* sad,
Dead sleeping *Poppy*, and blacke *Hellebore*,
Cold *Coloquintida*, and *Tetra* mad,
Mortall *Samnitis*, and *Cicuta* bad,
With which th'vniust *Atheniens* made to dy
Wise *Socrates*, who thereof quaffing glad
Pourd out his life, and last Philosophy
To the faire *Critias* his dearest Belamy.

The *Gardin of Proserpina* this hight;
And in the midst thereof a siluer seat,
With a thicke Arber goodly ouer dight,
Into which she often vsd from open heat
Her selfe to shroud, and pleasures to entreat.
Next thereunto did grow a goodly tree,
With braunches broad dispred and body great,
Clothed with leaues, that none the wood mote see
And loaden all with fruit as thicke as it might bee.

Their fruit were golden apples glistring bright,
That goodly was their glory to behold,
On earth like neuer grew, ne liuing wight
Like euer saw, but they from hence were sold;
For those, which *Hercules* with conquest bold
Got from great *Atlas* daughters, hence began,
And planted there, did bring forth fruit of gold:
And those with which th'*Eubœan* young man wan
Swift *Atalanta*, when through craft he her out ran.

(2.7.51–4)

A. Kent Hieatt, in a remarkable essay, has patiently sifted through every
allusive grain in this densely figured and allusive passage, considering
Spenser's knowledge of Proserpina, Ceres, Tantalus, Pelops, Pilate, and so
on; he works up to his proposal on the thematic import of this crux:

What, now, may we say that Tantalus and Pilate have in common, when we consider all the pressures and changes of focus in these lines concerning them, and when we remember that we are in the context of the central episode of Book II [. . .]? It seems to me that the proper answer is man's infringement upon, and arrogation of, the divine – Satanic and intemperate pride.　(35)

I would like to adapt this so as to say that Guyon and the reader encounter characters who have disavowed or deranged thinking through their spectacular attacks on linking: failure of parental nurture in Tantalus and the unarticulated thought of Proserpina's mother; Pilate's refusal to commit himself to the thought process by which he has come to the knowledge that his (divine) prisoner is innocent; members of a polis which poisons philosophers because their thinking is dangerous.

Extreme obliquity of allusive resonance thwarts the allegorical impulse to think out fully coherent links among these characters. Spenser depicts Tantalus' suffering, but makes no overt reference to his murder of Pelops. Cocytus flows around the Garden of Proserpina, the daughter whose divine mother could not save her, yet Spenser swerves from the story of Proserpina and Ceres that would make explicit a thematic core of failed parental nurture. He makes an inaccurate allusion, incorrectly linking Socrates and Critias, but both his account and the accurate versions of the two events on which he draws nicely posit a link between eros and thinking while also blocking the links that would make the allusion fully satisfying.[8] He piles up the toxic plants of the Garden faster than we can work out their interrelationships, and seeks exotic names for them as if to provoke the frustration of readerly thinking.

Hieatt notices another tantalizing, frustrating instance of such linking: there is some kind of significance in the fact that 'Tantalus's punishment should now be transferred . . . to the edge of Proserpina's garden' (where Proserpina sits under a vast tree laden with golden apples), given that it was Ceres who ate of Pelops' shoulder during the feast that Tantalus provided the gods to test them. The propinquity of these families of tales in the locus of the Garden suggests that Spenser links/thinks laterally here, as he does in so many instances. Something links together for him golden apples of classical myth, disarray of nurturant or generative relationships, food and drink that in one way or another fail to feed. The golden apples, for instance, attract to themselves classical stories of false links, deceit, tantalization. Originally a gift from Earth to Hera on the occasion of her marriage to Zeus and therefore markers of many fundamental social and familial links, the apples are in the care of the daughters of the Hesperides, from whom Hercules steals them; Hippomenes wins Atalanta by distracting her, tantalizing her, with golden apples thrown in her path as she races him; Acontius wins the reluctant Cydippe by tricking her into reading aloud an ambiguous inscription on such an apple. As James Nohrnberg points out, 'To a greater or lesser degree the various apples all suggest the use of intelligence or cunning, or lust of the eye'; he suggests that 'it is in their nature to provoke our curiosity, and this in itself is evidence for their character' (335–6).[9] In Spenser's Garden of Proserpina, they grow thick on a broad tree, but in a chthonic, death-giving matrix: all the other varieties of flora there are 'direfull deadly blacke' (2.7.51) fit to mark death, not life.[10] Comes takes the golden apples as a figure of wealth. Nohrnberg offers the wry concession that 'the apples of Mammon are provocative – this is one thing that all the mythological allusions have in common, apart from the letters *a*, *t*, *l*, or *n*' (335), leaving us with a perfect instance of a frustrating thought-teaser.

The golden apples are lodged so as to focus attention on an unex-pectedly destructive maternalized earth in Mammon's domain – as if he creates a region where the mother who repels rather than receives and transforms her child's attacks on linking has come to be represented by the child as noxious and hostile. Mammon praises the earth as the mother of precious metals, which 'in the hollow earth haue their eter-nall brood' (2.7.8), but his affection and gratitude are less convincing than his hasty pouring of his heaps of gold into a hole in that mater-nal earth when he first sees Guyon. In a fine model of aggressive evacuation of bizarre objects from the self into a maternal body, he rises in order to remove 'Those pretious hils from straungers enuious sight, / And downe them poured through an hole full wide, / Into the hollow earth, them there to hide' (2.7.6). The maternal earth, like think-ing itself in this canto, is seductive and cruel, as in its deportment toward Tantalus, when the fruit 'from hand [. . .] / Did flie abacke, and made him vainely swinke' (2.7.58). These passing references to a mater-nal earth either attacked or attacking, and the association of the mater-nal with hoarded, unlinked objects, function as swerves from, or displacements of, the ambivalent figure of Ceres: mother to Proserpina whom she cherishes and cannot preserve, yet, in unintentional attack, the one divinity who *ate* of Pelops' flesh.[11]

Most spectacularly, the Spenserian allegorizer eschews the cherishing of offspring that pervades his most important precursor text for this passage, Claudian's *De raptu proserpinae*. Children are everywhere in this remarkable fragment about the odd condition of life-and-death in the underworld. Pluto yearns poignantly for '*dulce patris* [. . .] *nomen*', the dear name of father (I.36), and envies Jove '*tibi tanta creandi copia*', so manifold a hope of offspring (I.107–8), while he himself languishes in an empty palace in the hideous realms of darkness. Ceres cherishes Proserpina because she can have no more children (I.121–5). When Pluto weds Proserpina, the shades sing them an epithalamium wishing them fair offspring (II.370–2). When Jove explains his decision to deprive men of natural abundance and make them take pains to labor for their food, Nature complains of her consequent estrangement from her human 'children'; now she is their stepmother merely (III.39–45). Ceres has haunting dreams and visions of her lost daughter (III.66–112); in one of them Proserpina cries out against her 'cruel mother' for her heedlessness and hard-heartedness (III.97–108). Proserpina's nurse, her second mother, mourns her (III.170–8). Most remarkably, in a gesture toward philosophical poetry on the nature of the universe, Proserpina's own dress bears elaborate embroidery depicting the objects and elements of the world in their birth:

> hic Hyperionio Solem de semine nasci
> feceerat eet pariter, forma sed dispare, Lunam,
> aurorae noctisque duces; cunabula Tethys
> praebet et infantes gremio solatur anhelos
> caeruleusque sinus roseis radiatur alumnis.
> Invalidum dextro portat Titana lacerto
> Nondum luce gravem nec pubescentibus alte
> Cristatum radiis: primo clementior aevo
> Fingitur et teneerum vagitu despuit ignem.
> Laeva parte soror vitrei libamina potat
> Uberis et parvo signatur tempora cornu.

(II.44–54)

In it she had worked the birth of the sun from the seed of Hyperion, the birth, too, of the moon, though diverse was her shape – of sun and moon that bring the dawning and the night. Tethys affords them a cradle and soothes in her bosom their infant sobs; the rosy light of her foster-children irradiates her dark blue plains. On her right shoulder she carried the infant Titan, too young as yet to vex with his light, and his encircling beams not grown; he is pictured as more gentle in those tender years, and from his mouth issues a soft flame that accompanies his infant cries. The moon, his sister, carried on Tethys' left shoulder, sucks the milk of that bright breast, her forehead marked with a little horn.

Passages like these invest the *De raptu* with an extraordinary tenderness, a sense of springing life, and a sense of the preciousness of children, or more accurately of the links between parents and children. This tenderness extends even to the sinners in Acheron, who enjoy an amnesty during the time of the wedding; Tantalus *'invenit undas'*, 'reaches the stream' (II.337); there is life and food and drink, not death and starvation and cannibalism; *'nullique rogum planxere parentes'*, and 'no parents wept beside the funeral pyre' (III.356).

In Claudian's underworld, limiting instances of living and dying are densely interwoven; his poem seems to aspire to the linking of narrative with philosophical poetry on the birth of things. I think Spenser is profoundly moved and influenced by Claudian's work, but suppresses its impulse toward the life-bearing of philosophical poetry, leaving implicit the pathos of sundered parent/child relationships, *in order to* demonstrate the more deadening effects of that other kind of poetic thinking found in punitive exemplum allegory. If this is true, it allows us to make sense of the gaps and swerves and near-incoherencies in Spenser's underworld; his propensity for associative linking is precisely the phenomenon of thought under attack, offered then taken away, in the realm of Mammon.

Unlinked objects in Mammon's realm mark the crossing of some interpretive threshold at which the invitation to think turns into what I have been calling the problem of heaps, aggressively aggregated objects in greedy or bizarre proliferation yet somehow without internal movement among parts. The relationship among 'the problem of heaps', attacks on linking, greed, and the actions of the death drive becomes most sobering earlier in the episode, when Mammon shows Guyon one of his rooms:

> In all that rowme was nothing to be seene,
>> But huge great yron chests and coffers strong,
>> All bard with double bends, that none could weene
>> Them to efforce by violence or wrong;
>> On euery side they placed were along.
>> But all the ground with sculs was scattered,
>> And dead mens bones, which round about were flong,
>> Whose liues, it seemed, whilome there were shed,
> And their vile carcases now left vnburied.
>
> (*FQ* 2.7.30)

These heaps of dead bodies, mere carcasses, are the logical consequence and counterpart of those heaps of coin and metals which I cited at the beginning of this essay; it becomes clear how these men could become the left-over, the remainder, to the father of greed. So it is not just that Mammon personifies Greed, though he does that; it is also that he lords it over others, he has power. His attacks on linking have murderous or death-imparting consequences for the dead men, for the demons who slave away at his furnaces, for those who unwisely try to reach the golden chain of Mammon's daughter Philotime, or Ambition (2.7.44–9), for guests like Guyon, momentarily infected with Mammon's impulse to attack linking, when he speaks in harsh, punitive terms to Tantalus: 'Nay, nay, thou greedie *Tantalus* [. . .] / Abide the fortune of thy present fate, / And vnto all that liue in high degree, / Ensample be of mind intemperate' (2.7.60).

This moment seems to me the strongest support for my argument that Spenser represents the thinking of one kind of allegory, at least, as an attack on linking, a sign of death work in the hero's way of thinking and not just in the suffering sinner. Not only is Guyon's response uncharitable, it is hostile and murderous. We know from Claudian that there is an alternative response to Tantalus and the other sinners. Tantalus speaks and wants to be understood as a suffering fellow human; Guyon speaks and wants to understand him as emphatically *not* a suffering fellow human, but as an exemplum. He refuses or distorts the kind of witness that Tantalus' condition calls for, under rubrics or language-games other than allegorical ones. One is reminded here of Lyotard's point that, in language, links among phrases of heterogeneous discourses cannot *not* happen.[12] But they can often happen as a damage or wrong to one of the engaged parties. Tantalus' articulation of his suffering, we are led to see, functions as a differend in Lyotard's sense: it takes place 'when the "regulation" of the conflict that opposes them is done in the idiom of one of the parties while the wrong suffered by the other is not signified in that idiom' (9). We are brought to this pass by the regimen of the particular kind of allegory in the House of Mammon, with its attacks on linking; allegory here serves Mammon's interests. One could say that Guyon, who faints for want of food and sleep, collapses under the combined assaults of Mammon's arguments, Mammon's inhospitality, and Mammon's mode of allegory, as Dante faints under the complex effects of witnessing to Francesca's fate. But within that allegory, Guyon cannot talk about it; the idiom of the discourse makes such talk logically impossible. The episode's traces of feeling in the gestures toward Celeno, Ceres, Pelops – these are links that Mammon or his allegorical structure has attacked. But the traces remain. As Lyotard says, 'Insofar as [what they cannot speak about] is unable to be phrased in the common idioms, it is already phrased, as feeling. The avowal has been made. The vigil for an occurrence, the anxiety and the joy of an unknown idiom, has begun' (80). Gordon Teskey might call these traces of feeling by the name of resistances to the totalizing ambition of allegory, which is a kind of greed because it wants to incorporate all or make everything over into itself.

In his hard response to Tantalus, Guyon seems to me momentarily to fail, in Lyotard's moving formulation, 'to find, if not what can legitimate judgment (the "good" linkage), then at least how to save the honor of thinking' (*Differend*, xii). Guyon as a character is not much given to expressing whatever thinking he may do. But the reader too needs to save the honor of thinking from the fix in which this allegorical episode has placed her. To recover the mobility, pleasure, and generosity of thinking, she, like Guyon, if for different reasons, needs a daimon who, as in Diotima's articulation, interprets and moves between gods and mortals (or between allegorical and non-allegorical genres of discourse). Of course I am thinking of the Angel who gorgeously comes to aid Guyon at the start of the next canto, after his collapse:

> How oft do they, their siluer bowers leaue,
> To come to succour vs, that succour want?
> How oft do they with golden pineons, cleaue
> The flitting skyes, like flying Pursuiuant . . . ?

(2.7.2)

> His snowy front curled with golden heares,
> Like *Phoebus* face adornd with sunny rayes,
> Diuinely shone, and two sharpe winged sheares,
> Decked with diuerse plumes, like painted Iayes,
> Were fixed at his backe, to cut his ayerie wayes.

(2.7.5)

In fact, Spenser compares this Angel to Cupid, who in another form is precisely the daimon Eros of whom Diotima speaks. The Angel speaks words of comfort to the Palmer, who has been separated from his charge during the whole of the Mammon episode; when the divine daimon takes his leave, Guyon is back on the pathway from death to life, and the Palmer comforts him as a parent rightly does a child. This is an affect imparted to the reader as well; the righting of parental wrongs restores to the reader the daimonic mobility of thinking out links in reading:

> At last his turning to his charge behight,
> With trembling hand his troubled pulse gan try;
> Where finding life not yet dislodged quite,
> He much reioyst, and courd [covered, protected] it tenderly,
> As chicken newly hatcht, from dreaded destiny.

$$(2.8.9)$$

The 'dreaded destiny' is punitive exemplum allegory as much as it is death. With the restoration of tenderness and cherishing between the figurative chick and its dam, Spenser releases suppressed Claudianesque affect, improves the disposition of the heretofore dour Palmer, and creates the possibility of a new kind of allegorical thinking – one allied with philosophical poetry on the birth of things, one that will emerge in the Garden of Adonis, where thinking is much more generous to the reader.

## Notes

1. All Chaucer passages come from *The Riverside Chaucer*; all Spenser quotations come from the Longman edition (1975) unless otherwise indicated.
2. See, for example, Rosemond Tuve, *Allegorical Imagery: Some Mediaeval Books and Their Posterity*: 'The images are based firmly on physical and psychological experience, often known individually, but chiefly known and made important by centuries of vicarious experience passed on to us through earlier literature; hence such images work at a deep associative level, and we are conscious of not being the first to whom they have reiterated their burden of more meant than is seen' (31).
3. Just a bit earlier Gordon Teskey has quoted Nietzsche's remark adapted in his argument, and linked Dante and Nietzsche: 'It is a mistake to suppose that the violence has nothing to do with Dante, who was [. . .] more a Nietzschean interpreter of the world than is generally supposed, and whose strength as a poet radiates from the primary work of reducing persons to substance. This work is accomplished not so much by an act of abstraction as by, in Nietzsche's words, "a tremendous *expulsion* of the principle features." The greatest allegorical poets do not simply transform life into meaning. They exacerbate the antipathy of the living to the significant by exposing the violence entailed in transforming the one into the other' (*Allegory and Violence* 24).
4. On the daimon as an intermediary see Angus Fletcher, *Allegory*, 42–8. Cleaving to this strict sense of the daimonic as free movement across an interval

leads me to an emphasis on the daimonic in allegory nearly opposite to that of Fletcher, who focuses on the daimonic agent's compulsive, automaton-like, intensively unfree behaviour. See *Allegory*, ch. 1 and *passim*.

5. As Michael Eigen puts it in a discussion of an anorexic patient, 'the indigestible must be digested, worked over, processed'. More accurately and more urgently, he speaks for the need for movement itself: 'movement between the digestible and the indigestible needs to get stimulated and sustained' (*Psychic Deadness* 18–19); otherwise the patient is frozen in death work.

6. Spenser uses the myth again in *Virgils Gnat*. On the bank of the Styx sits Tantalus 'That did the bankets of the Gods bewray, / Whose throat through thirst to nought nigh being dride, / His sense to seeke for ease turnes euery way' (386–8). See *Variorum Minor Poems*, vol. 2.

7. At a conference on Spenser in Cambridge in 2001, Kenneth Gross made the point that in the Garden of Adonis 'thoughts circulate without a clear thinker'. I have built on this observation to make an argument about how the Garden makes possible thinking our repressed and commonly unsymbolized relationship to birth, in 'Mother's Sorrow, Mother's Joy.'

8. It was Crito who was present at Socrates' death by a potion made from Cicuta, a fancy name for hemlock; Critias belongs to another event: one of Athens' Thirty Tyrants, he unjustly condemned the philosopher Theramenes to death by poison. The latter drank it with a toast 'Here's to the health of my beloved Critias.' Xenophon gives the account in *Hellenica*, but Spenser could have known the story from Cicero (*Tusculan Disputations* I.40), who draws the parallel between Socrates and Theramenes. See Upton's sorting out of the details in the *Variorum Faerie Queene*, Book II, 263.

9. See also 340–2.

10. I think it likely that Spenser's obscure allusion to the harpy Celeno, associated with defilement and food and a grotesque inversion of maternal nurture, forms for Spenser another instance of the thematic array I've been discussing; again, the precise link that would fit it to the allegory remains not only obscure but frustrating. Here are the lines, from *FQ* II.vii.23: 'Whiles sad *Celeno*, sitting on a clift, / A song of bale and bitter sorrow sings, / That hart of flint a sunder could haue rift: / Which hauing ended, after him [Guoyn] she flyeth swift.' These lines lead me to imagine that the link Spenser wishes to adumbrate throughout the episode is simply conscious acknowledgment of the feeling of bereftness.

11. At some later point in his career, in *Amoretti* 77, Spenser would again link classical golden apples, Hercules, and Atalanta, this time in contradistinction to a biblical nexus of apples, trees, maternal nurture, reliable feeding, the expansiveness of thinking. See chapters 3 and 4 of Theresa M. Krier, *Birth Passages*. Yet again, without pursuing yet another link here, I suggest that the mode of maternity in this underworld can be productively compared to the moving underworld meeting of Duessa and Night in *Faerie Queene* I.v.

12. Lyotard, *The Differend*, xii: 'A phrase "happens." How is it to be linked onto? By its rule, a genre of discourse supplies a set of possible phrases, each arising

from some phrase regiment. Another genre of discourse supplies another set of other possible phrases. There is a differend between these two sets (or between the genres that call them forth) because they are heterogeneous. And linkage must happen "now": another phrase cannot not happen. It's a necessity; time, that is. There is no non-phrase. Silence is a phrase.'

# 4
# Death in an Allegory

*Gordon Teskey*

The event of death, the moment of finality and loss, cannot be represented in an allegory, as it can be in a tragedy or a novel. The death of Antigone, of Othello or of Lear, or, for that matter, of little Nell, leaves us with the feeling that the world has changed, that our common life has become thinner, has become more pinched and mean, because something vital has left it. As Donne says in Meditation XVII, 'any man's death diminishes me, because I am involved in mankind'. Nor do we have any strong feeling, even in the context of Christian belief, that the dead person has gone anywhere in particular, to a place better or worse than the world. From where we stand the emotional focus is instead on the finality of the departure and the completeness of the loss.

In an allegory, however, the event of death is not even an event, if by 'an event' we mean a moment when the world is significantly changed. Death in an allegory is instead so rapid that it functions as a revelation of the truth of the allegorical character's being – or perhaps I should say, of the allegorical character's meaning. Death leads not to the feeling of loss but rather to a feeling of clarity gained. I mean the feeling that what an allegorical character actually is, what an allegorical character means, has at last attained its definitive form. In an oddly paradoxical way an allegorical character's death is the moment when that character is most alive as meaning, since meaning is supposed to be that character's essence. Considered as pure meaning, the allegorical character lives most in death.

There are of course scenes in which allegorical characters undergo something that resembles the death of a person, and I shall be examining one of these scenes shortly. But these characters do not undergo death as an existential event. (Such statements should not go entirely unqualified. I confess I find in the allegorical play *Everyman*, one of the most moving representations of death as an existential event. But the intensity is the result of our being made to feel with Everyman as if he were an individual.) Death itself can be, and often is, represented in an allegory, and with terrifying intensity. But this very capacity for reifying and representing Death as an individual removes the concentrated weight of seriousness and mystery which is achieved when we see a person, such as Lear, die. For we experience death existentially not as a thing but as an event.

Yet the feeling we have when we read an allegory is that death is somehow more active in it than in any other literary form. We read an ode of Keats and are seduced with the poet into feeling half in love with easeful death. But when we read an allegory, and especially when we read Spenser, we have the uneasy suspicion that death is mysteriously, imperceptibly, disturbingly present in the working of the poetry itself. The very liveliness of the allegorical figures, their frenetic, jerky, galvanic life, makes us think of dead bodies through which an electric current is passed. The figures move with something that is less than life but also with a force, with a single-mindedness, that is greater than the living can achieve.

The effect I referred to above, where what appears to be the moment of death in an allegory is actually the moment of the revelation of meaning, is programmatically developed from the beginning of the allegorical tradition, from the *Psychomachia* of Prudentius. We see this effect of revelation in every subsequent conflict allegory, from the Old French *Tourneiment Antichrist* to Bunyan's *Holy War*. (Allegories tend to fall into one of two narrative forms: conflict or quest. Spenser's quest allegory is traversed by conflicts; but it is also directed imaginatively to a second part wherein conflict would dominate – the great war between the Fairy Queen and the Pagan King.) In the *Psychomachia* each of the vices is killed by the corresponding virtue in such a way that the death becomes a revelation of what the vice essentially is. For example, the character, Worship of the Pagan Gods, is beheaded by Faith, so that her priestly fillets are laid low; her mouth, flowing with the blood of sacrificed beasts, is crammed with dust; and her eyes – since pagan rites, and the pagan gods themselves, are aesthetically pleasing – are squeezed from her head and trampled under foot. In her reading of the *Psychomachia*, Carolynn Van Dyke remarks of the even more impressive figure of Luxury, 'she is killed by her own physical nature, in revoltingly vivid detail' (53). Bunyan presents contrasting scenes of death so that we may see contrary states of the soul. But the event of death is imperceptible as anything other than a revelation of what these characters are in their spiritual essence. There is joy and there is terror when they die, but there is no sadness and no sense of loss. There is only change of place. The last thing we hear of Mr. Valiant-for-Truth is this: 'When the Day that he must go hence, was come, many accompanied him to the River side, into which, as he went, he said, *Death, where is thy Sting*? And as he went down deeper, he said, *Grave where is thy Victory*? So he passed over, and the Trumpets sounded for him on the other side' (*Pilgrim's Progress* 309).

When we turn to Spenser's *Faerie Queene*, to the rare moments when death, or something like it, is represented in that poem, we find much the same effect: the moment of death is a moment of revelation in which the allegorical character is disclosed in its essential meaning. But Spenser is considerably more subtle. Spenser is also interested, as few other allegorists are, in maintaining the sense of concreteness, of real, existential and physical being in characters who are also to function as signs. Spenser's greater emphasis on the living provokes a conflict around the rift within each character between the living and the significant. The result is an allegorical composition that is not a static arrangement of arbitrary signs, composed in accord with a simple, didactic intention mechanically applied, as romanticism would characterize allegory. Instead, we have the feeling that the allegorical characters have been instituted, like Nietzschean meaning, by force. We also have the feeling that the allegorical narrative is sustained by the continuing exertion of this force by the will. Yet this will is not simply the personal will of the poet.

Consider Arthur's fight, in the eighth canto of Book 2, with those contrastingly significant brothers, Cymocles and Pyrocles. Their significance can be read in their names, which mean water and fire, or rather 'wave' (*kuma*) and 'fire' (*pur*): the lustful and sensuous Cymocles has a character like water that flows away in waves. Whatever resolution Cymocles forms is dissipated in waves of sensual pleasure, in rising crests of excitement and descending troughs of satiety. Using Guyon's shield for his defense, the shield which bears the portrait of the Fairy Queen, Cymocles withstands Arthur's onslaught because Arthur is enchanted by the image of his love: 'His hand relented, and the stroke forbore, / And his deare hart the picture gan adore, / Which oft the Paynim sav'd from deadly stowre.' The poet then immediately forebodes Cymocles' death, and does so in language that belongs more to the spirit of heroic epic than to allegory: 'But him henceforth the same can save no more; / For now arrived is his fatall howre, / That no'te avoyded be by earthly skill or powre' (2.8.43).

So strong is this embodied, epic moment, the moment of the evil hour, that delay is required before the pagan knight can be dispatched. It is here that Cymocles, 'prickt with guilty shame, / And inward griefe,' manages to wound Arthur slightly, forcing the prince to 'reele, that never moov'd afore' (2.8.44). Arthur now returns the blow, with devastating effect:

> Whereat renfierst with wrath and sharpe regret,
> He stroke so hugely with his borrowd blade,
> That it empierst the Pagans burganet,
> And cleaving the hard steele, did deepe invade
> Into his head, and cruel passage made
> Quite through his braine.
>
> (2.8.45)

The wound is too swift and traumatic for there to be a moment in which the dying Cymocles might speak, either to curse his fatal adversary, or, like the dying Hector, to foretell the future. Nor is there, to speak more dramatically and also more improbably, time for Cymocles to repent his sins and ask to be baptized, as King Agricane does in Boiardo's *Orlando Innamorato*, in one of the most moving episodes in romance literature. From a Christian point of view there is something shocking – there is at least something dismaying – in the swiftness of this death, which leaves no opportunity for repentance and therefore no chance of saving a soul. Spenser is savagely final:

> He tombling downe on ground,
> Breathd out his ghost, which to th'infernall shade
> Fast flying, there eternall torment found,
> For all the sinnes, wherewith his lewd life did abound.
>
> (2.8.45)

Can we even say Cymocles has died? Was there a moment of death, an event of death? Or was there not instead a swift transition from a character's becoming what he is to that character's final fixity as what he is, self-tormentingly lewd? Death is a moment of departure and of loss. As what I have called an existential event, death is a moment that occurs in a pause, an interruption in the continuum which is experienced by those who witness the death as well as by the person who undergoes it. But in this scene there is no departure but a homecoming: Cymocles comes home, so to speak, to himself. And there is no sense of loss because the soul in question, Cymocles' 'ghost', is never a real soul, that is, a being at risk, on the knife-edge between one state and another. Cymocles' ghost is an allegorical soul, an essential and immutable meaning. There is no loss because this meaning flies swiftly to its home, where it is itself most truly and completely.

Nor does Cymocles' death occasion any sense of loss in his brother: it occasions only fear and rage, a chilling, immobilizing fear kindling into uncontrolled rage. One moment Pyrocles feels 'stony feare' running to his heart, leaving all his senses 'dismayd' (2.8.46); the next moment he 'strooke, and foynd, and lasht outrageously, / Withouten reason or regard' (2.8.47). Arthur weathers this storm, looking to his defense in the knowledge that his opponent will tire. Spenser summarizes this in one of his typical, iconic moments: 'So did Prince *Arthur* bear himselfe in fight, / And suffred rash *Pyrocles* wast his idle might' (2.8.48).

And now something rather interesting happens. After a series of events unnecessary to recount here, Arthur defeats Pyrocles and has him at his mercy. Instead of having Pyrocles dispatched with the brutal swiftness Cymocles was dispatched, Spenser gives us a scene in which Arthur, being 'full of Princely bounty and great mind', offers to spare Pyrocles for his 'valiaunce' if Pyrocles will renounce his evil ways, his 'miscreaunce', and swear allegiance to Arthur (2.8.51). This is easy enough to explain away as the poet's need to diversify the episode, to have one pagan die suddenly while the other dies only after contemptuously refusing offered grace. But it seems to me there is more in this than the impulse to please with variety. I would guess that Spenser himself, who was, after all, a Christian, was shocked by the death of Cymocles, by the brief impression that a real person dies here, in his sins, and that his soul flies to eternal punishment. It is true that as an artist Spenser would have sought to achieve, and enjoyed delivering, that shock, the shock of watching what seems for a moment to be a living person seized and converted into an allegorical sign. For it is the shock that makes us realize again that Cymocles is not a person like other persons, with a soul like other souls, but rather an allegorical character being violently fixed in its meaning. Yet the scene where Pyrocles is offered grace is surely meant to allay the shock to any Christian sensibility of Cymocles' sudden and unrepentant death. I said when Pyrocles is offered 'grace', but the scene is so deliberately secular that the word, 'grace', although it would have a secular meaning in this context, is avoided at first: Arthur says, '*Life* will I graunt thee for thy valiaunce' (2.8; my emphasis). Pyrocles chooses death, and does so, as he says, 'in despight of life':

> Foole (said the Pagan) I thy gift defye,
> But use thy fortune, as it doth befall,
> And say, that I not overcome do dye,
> But in despight of life, for death do call.

(2.7.52)

Spenser is answering an implied criticism of his staging of Cymocles' death by creating a scene in which other, more elevating possibilities from romance literature might come crowding in, if it were possible for them to do so. But these possibilities are open only to human agents and to human souls; and at this moment, the moment of death, Spenser, as an allegorist, must preoccupy himself with expelling the very possibilities of life which he has so assiduously built up in his allegorical characters. He must expel those possibilities of life – for life is vital, and hence always changing, always unstable, always capable of becoming other – so that the significance can come forward and declare itself as the petrific, the unchanging, the stable, the self-identical.

Note that Pyrocles does not say, as would a living person who chose defiance to the end, 'in despite of *you* I call for death.' Because he is an allegorical character who is, like most allegorical characters, formed from a symmetrical opposition – in this case of the fiery to the watery, of the wrathful to the lustful – he can only think in symmetrical terms; he therefore calls for death 'in despight of *life*' (my emphasis). In Spenser's dynamical system Pyrocles is forced back violently into the state of being of an allegorical character by speaking in opposites that can mean nothing when they are apart from each other. He calls for death in despite of life because without despite of life he couldn't call for death or even know, in the most rudimentary sense, what it is he calls for.

Only at this moment does Spenser introduce the word *grace*, as something Pyrocles refused when it was offered to him:

> Wroth was the Prince, and sory yet withall,
> That he so wilfully refused grace;
> Yet sith his fate so cruelly did fall,
> His shining Helmet he gan soone unlace,
> And left his headlesse body bleeding all the place.

(2.8.52)

Those first three lines seem to restore to Pyrocles a kind of specious humanity. Pyrocles is willful in refusing grace, a grace which means literally no more than the 'life' which was offered before (on condition of repentance and swearing an oath of allegiance). But the word 'grace' also implies theological grace, the saving of a life for the purpose of saving a soul, of preventing a man from dying unrepentant and going to Hell. Spenser gives us a little theological scene in which we are allowed to feel that Pyrocles is a real man who is offered a chance at Christian repentance, a chance that could save his soul from Hell, thus sparing us the distressing sight of another soul 'fast flying [to] eternall torment' (2.8.45). The following three verses – beginning, 'Yet sith his fate so cruelly did fall'- brutally snatch this fantasy away, reducing Pyrocles to the inhuman, to the merely significant. This reduction is so complete that Pyrocles' death, unlike his brother's, is represented in entirely, and horrifically, corporeal terms. It is also represented with Stendhalian swiftness. But is the death actually represented, or is it skipped over? We see Arthur unlacing the helmet and then we see a headless trunk befouling 'all the place' with blood: 'His shining Helmet he gan soone unlace, / And left his headlesse body bleeding all the place.' (Note that it is Cymocles who, at the beginning of the episode, in stanza 17, is unlacing Guyon's helmet when Arthur arrives.)

This is the same body that, when it had a head and was 'inflam'd with rage,' addressed the Palmer as a 'dotard vile' and warned the Palmer, in the following terms, to abandon Guyon's prostrate body: 'Abandone soone, I read, the caitive spoile / Of that same outcast carkasse' (2.8.12). The irony is that Pyrocles becomes what he describes, an outcast carcass, headless and spewing forth blood, as once he spewed forth bloody words. It is a spectacular final image of Pyroclean rage as mindless effusion. Here too, then, the allegorical character seems not so much to die – if death is the loss of what we are – as fully to become what he is.

The entire canto plays an interesting game with death, and with the language of death. The most important 'carcass' in it, although it is spoken of as dead, is not in fact dead. I refer of course to Guyon's 'fallen flesh', which, as A. C. Hamilton reminds us, is what the word *carcass* means etymologically (2.8.12; n. 5). The fallen Guyon seems dead to all present – to Archimago, to Cymocles, to Pyrocles, to Prince Arthur. (Atin arrives on the scene but is not mentioned again in it.) All except the Palmer, who has felt Guyon's pulse and seems intent on concealing from the murderous brothers that Guyon is alive, lest they kill him in his helpless state rather than merely lamenting that they cannot kill him because someone else has. Guyon revives only when the brothers are dead – in fact, he revives immediately after the image of the bleeding, headless body has been seen: 'By this Sir *Guyon* from his traunce awakt,

/ Life having maistered her sencelesse foe' (2.8.53). It is almost as if Guyon has been allowed to trade places with Pyrocles and Cymocles, to be upright again once they are laid low. The Palmer tells Guyon how Arthur defended him against 'those two Sarazins counfounded late, / Whose carcases on ground were horribly prostrate' (2.8.54).

I said that Guyon is not 'in fact' dead. But in Spenser the factual and the figurative are not easy to distinguish – or when the factual and the figurative can be distinguished they are opposed to each other wherever we find adjacent intensities of meaning. We know from the narrative that Guyon is alive, but the language keeps speaking of his death. At the conclusion of the seventh canto, when Guyon escapes Mammon's delve and reaches the upper world again, it is by breathing 'vitall aire' that he is thrown into a 'deadly fit':

> But all so soone as his enfeebled spright
> Gan sucke this vitall aire into his brest,
> As overcome with too exceeding might,
> The life did flit away out of her nest,
> And all his senses were with deadly fit opprest.

> (2.8.66 [Alpers 275])

A surfeit of vital spirits nearly kills him.

In the eighth canto, the Palmer is drawn to Guyon's side by a guardian angel who charges the Palmer with Guyon's safety, for 'evill is at hand' (2.8.8). The Palmer feels Guyon's pulse and rejoices at 'finding life not yet dislodged quight'. The Palmer then broods protectively over this frail remaining life like a chicken protecting her hatchling: 'He much rejoyst, and courd it tenderly, / As chicken newly hatcht, from dreaded destiny' (2.8.9). The evil comes, in the persons of the sons of *Acrates* (the name means 'intemperance,' more literally 'unmixed'), Pyrocles and Cymocles, accompanied by Atin and Archimago. Both Pyrocles and Cymocles assume that Guyon is dead and that his death is proof that he lived an evil life: 'Loe where he now inglorious doth lye, / To prove he lived ill, that did thus foully dye,' says Pyrocles. To this, with more seeming philosophy, Cymocles adds, 'The worth of all men by their end esteeme, / And then due praise, or due reproch them yield; / Bad therefore I him deeme, that thus lies dead on field' (2.8.12; 14).

To protect the defenseless Guyon, the Palmer speaks of him as if he were dead, knowing all the while that he is not:

> To whom the Palmer fearelesse answered;
> Certes, Sir knight, ye bene too much to blame,
> Thus for to blot the honour of the dead,
> And with foule cowardize his carkasse shame,
> Whose living hands immortalizd his name.
> Vile is the vengeance on the ashes cold,
> And envie base, to barke at sleeping fame:
> Was never wight that treason of him told;
> Your selfe his prowesse prov'd and found him fiers and bold.

(2.8.13)

The speech has no effect. Enraged that by his death Guyon has left unsatisfied his 'greedy hunger of revenging ire', Pyrocles decides to strip Guyon's armor: 'For why should a dead dog be deckt in armour bright?' (2.8.15).

At this the Palmer delivers the second of the two speeches to Pyrocles in which he speaks of Guyon as dead. The Palmer exhorts Pyrocles not to disgrace himself by seeking revenge on a dead body, and he implores Pyrocles not to commit the sacrilege of taking the clothes of the dead. Finally, the Palmer asks that Pyrocles leave Guyon the accoutrements of knighthood so these can be displayed on Guyon's hearse and steed at his funeral – a remarkable image of Guyon as dead. In reply, Pyrocles offers another image of the destiny of the body before them: to be eaten by (entombed in) birds:

> Faire Sir, said then the Palmer suppliaunt,
> For knighthoods love, do not so foule a deed,
> Ne blame your honour with so shamefull vaunt
> Of vile revenge. To spoil the dead of weed
> Is sacrilege, and doth all sinnes exceed;
> But leave these relicks of his living might,
> To decke his herce, and trap his tomb-black steed.
> What herce or steed (said he) should he have dight,
> But be entombed in the raven or the kight?

(2.8.16)

As Pyrocles and Cymocles begin to despoil Guyon, Arthur arrives and greets Pyrocles and Cymocles, who receive the greeting churlishly. Only then, as he turns to the Palmer, does Arthur see Guyon:

>Then turning to the Palmer, he gan spy
>Where at his feete, with sorrowfull demaine
>And deadly hew, an armed corse did lye,
>In whose dead face he red great magnanimity.

>(2.8.23)

Of course, by 'dead face' we are to understand the poet to mean that the face of Guyon seemed dead to Arthur, as it does to the others, excepting the Palmer. But with this knowledge the sight is for us too a grim, heroic image of death.

Arthur asks the Palmer how the man before him died and learns that the man is not dead, yet 'cloudes of deadly night / A while his heavie eylids cover'd have' (2.8.24). When informed of Pyrocles and Cymocles' intentions, Arthur takes his turn at dissuading them, entreating pardon for 'this dead seeming knight' without, as he says, debating the issue of their presumed right to despoil him. Would not they like to show mercy on a 'carcasse' that is already in the lowest state of fortune – 'Whom fortune hath alreadie laid in lowest seat'? (2.8.27)? They would not. Cymocles' reply is violently morbid, speaking of Guyon as a 'vile bodie', 'outcast dong', and 'dead carrion' on which, nevertheless, he is determined to wreak his vengeance: 'The trespasse still doth live, albe the person die' (2.8.28). To this Arthur replies – again, with remarkable mildness – that Cymocles is of course right on that point, 'So steitly God doth judge.' The entire ethical calculus of revenge, including the proposition that it is noble to take revenge on a living man but ignoble to take revenge on a dead one, is undone by this phrase. Still, there is reason to appeal to Cymocles' self-interest: he should consider how his honor will be stained 'with rancour and despight' by raising his hand against the dead (2.8.29). At this, Pyrocles calls Arthur a felon and 'partaker of his crime' and strikes at Arthur with his, Arthur's, own sword, *Morddure*. The fight ensues and Cymocles and Pyrocles are killed, as we have seen. Cymocles soul flies swiftly to Hell and the headless trunk of Pyrocles is left on the ground.

What are we to make in this canto of the ferocious, death-fixated language and imagery, directed to a person who is not in fact dead? I mentioned that the narrative point of this misdirection onto the living of language for the dead is the Palmer's intention of concealing from the despoilers that Guyon is alive, lest they kill him. But by the time Arthur arrives and attempts to dissuade them there is no further tactical reason for this subterfuge. Instead of debating the knightliness of raising one's hand against the dead Arthur might more reasonably say that Guyon is alive, though helpless, and now under his, Arthur's, protection. But Spenser is interested in the question of taking revenge on a dead body. He is also interested in how the psychological energies of rage and concupiscence have deep somatic consequences, how they fasten on the body and will not leave it easily even at death. We realize now that the point of putting Guyon on the brink of death, keeping him unconscious throughout, is to isolate and emphasize these somatic consequences – the unconscious power of rage and concupiscence as habits – which take hold on the body at a level deeper than the senses themselves: 'By this Sir *Guyon* from his traunce awakt, / Life having maistered her sencelesse foe' (2.8.53). The 'sencelesse foe' is death, which is beaten back when Guyon returns to his senses; but it is also, as Hamilton remarks, the morbid effects represented by Cymocles and Pyrocles. While manifesting themselves in the senses, rage and concupiscence fasten on the body addictively, on a level deeper than the senses themselves. Mammon's delve, in the preceding canto, was about greed, the desire that fixes on a goal outside itself, moving the body toward it. This canto is about vices that become fixed deep within body, establishing needs that regularly announce themselves in the senses, crying to be appeased. But they are anchored much deeper than the senses, which is why rage and concupiscence do not diminish when the external objects by which they are excited are removed.

There is, however, a further point to Guyon's being in this canto both alive and dead. This point is concerned not with Spenser's specific intention in moral theorizing but with the character of Spenser's art, with the status of death in an allegory. As I said at the outset, death cannot be represented in an allegory as an existential event, as a rupture in the continuum and a moment of absolute loss. If Guyon *were* dead the entire mood of the poem would change from the theoretical and the moral to the tragic. We see in the Mordant and Amavia episode with which the second book of *The Faerie Queene* opens the risk that actual death poses to the stability of the allegorical narrative – though it is a risk Spenser brilliantly takes, and wins. Spenser obviously cannot take such a risk with Guyon, for that would not be a risk at all but a certainty of failure. Spenser has instead taken a different and perhaps more challenging risk in having the hero of this book in a divided or even paradoxical state: death is in Guyon but Guyon is not in death.

It is just this state of the body – as having death at work within it but not being dead – which characterizes the allegorical sign, and especially the allegorical personification. I have spoken elsewhere of the violence of allegorical idealism, whereby abstractions abduct, seize, and tear open physical bodies in which to represent themselves as embodied, and therefore as real. (A model of this can be found in the idealistic but obsessively mediated language of Neoplatonism, in which the material world is an emanation of the ideal. But this emanation which is the material world becomes resistant to its origin and has to be violently 'seized' by the ideal in a moment of *raptus*. Only then may be it be turned back to its source, converted – the term is *conversio* – into a meaningful realm in which every physical thing is a sign of something higher.)

In each allegorical body, as in the allegorical text itself, there is a rift between the material and the ideal and a struggle occurring around it. The rift is seen in the very word *allegory* (*allo* + *agoreuo* 'other + speaking'), the precise meaning of which oscillates continually to either side of the rift. For the *other* can denote either the ideal meaning, which is 'other' with respect to the physical sign, or the physical sign in itself, which is 'other' with respect to the meaning. An allegory says something other than it means and means something other than it says.[1] This then is the significance of Guyon's paradoxical state, of his being at once dead and alive. The boundary within him between the living and the dead is not so much a boundary as a rift between his meaning as a pure allegorical sign and his vitality as a narrative figure in quest of the wisdom that comes from struggling with meanings and striving for truth.

In Cymocles and Pyrocles we see the destiny of pure allegorical signs, which become fixed emblematically. This emblematic fixing is at once the fulfillment of what Cymocles and Pyrocles are, as signs, and the expulsion of everything in them that is vital: 'those two Sarazins confounded late, / Whose carcases on ground were horribly prostrate' (2.8.54). But once an allegorical sign becomes fixed in this way it can no longer function in the narrative. It can only be observed for a moment before the observer – the 'Dante,' for example, who travels through the *Commedia*, or the Guyon who travels through Mammon's delve – passes on.

In the eighth canto of the Legend of Temperance something like death seizes upon Guyon and holds him in a state that brings him as near as he can come to being himself an allegorical sign. The allegorical poet is always in danger of allowing whatever it is in the poem that keeps the poem alive, that keeps the poem's narrative moving, and that keeps us caring about the characters who move in that narrative, to fall into the shadow of absolute, determinate meaning. Recall the verses in which the Palmer finds that Guyon has a pulse:

> At last him turning to his charge behight,
> With trembling hand his troubled pulse gan try;
> Where finding life not yet dislodged quight,
> He much rejoyst, and courd it tenderly,
> As chicken newly hatcht, from dreaded destiny.

> (2.8.9)

I see in this moment an image of what I suppose to have often been Spenser's state of mind as he contemplated where to turn next in the evolving project of *The Faerie Queene*. I imagine him wondering for a moment, after each lucid formulation of meaning, if there is any life left in the game. He finds that there is, rejoices at its presence, and fosters it protectively as he goes on. But the life in this game needs this protection just because it works in such intimate proximity to death.

## Note

1. See Teskey, *Allegory and Violence*, 6.

# 5

# 'After the First Death, There is No Other': Spenser, Milton, and (Our) Death

*Roger Kuin and Anne Lake Prescott*

Death has no entry in *The Spenser Encyclopedia*.

That sentence can be read in several ways, and should: the present essay is in some ways a meditation upon it.[1] It is true that Death has a literal 'entry' in *The Faerie Queene*: summoned by Order, he and 'Life' conclude the Mutabilitie Cantos' great procession of Time's circling component parts (7.7.46). His 'grim and griesly visage' seems to give the parade a dark final period, a breaking of its self-renewing circles, but the narrator hastens to add that 'Yet is he nought but parting of the breath.' He is also hard to discern, a mere 'shade': 'Unbodied, unsoul'd, unheard, unseene.' If so, it is hardly surprising that despite his many effects he makes so little appearance as himself among *The Faerie Queene*'s multitude of characters and visible figures. 'Parting of the breath' is hard to personify, as is 'nought'. There is, however, much to say on Spenser and Death – or at least on Spenser and death. Here we concentrate on Book 1 of the *Faerie Queene* because the Legend of Holiness contains two episodes which may prove enlightening; and our focus is upon readers and reading rather than readings.

As this book's title mentions Milton, we may perhaps begin with him. He was an absorbed reader of Spenser, so much so that we might see him as having *become* one of the earlier poet's 'afterlives'. We are not here concerned with Dryden's claim that Spenser was Milton's Original, nor that he was Spenser's Poetical Son, nor (at least directly) with Spenser as his inspiration in writing works 'exemplary to a Nation'.[2] What we want to attend to is Milton's rapt listening to his predecessor's 'sage and solemn tunes',[3] the seriousness of his ear, the concentration and focus of his inward I. In his poetical filiation Milton was a fine and most individual apprentice; in the depth of his attention he was an

78

exemplary reader. Such a reader Spenser himself seems to have hoped for: of his 'rimes' he says:

> Yet if their deeper sence be inly wayd,
> And the dim vele, with which from comune vew
> Their fairer parts are hid, aside be layd[,]
> Perhaps not vaine they may appeare to you.
>
> (Dedicatory Sonnets)

Thus the poet to stern Burghley, who was no poet as Milton was but who would have approved at least the Latin Secretary's commitment to his God and to his country's good. And Milton listened both with a poet's ear and with a pupil's rapt attention to the sage and serious poet's voice. It is hard for us to think of Milton's world as basking in summer sunshine, yet such a reading as he gave Spenser we may perhaps recognize in this passage from novelist Danièle Sallenave's *Le Don des morts* ('Gift From the Dead'):

> Literature – novels, poetry, literary fiction – completes, accomplishes this movement of soaring, of leaving the world behind; when the movement is there, literature is in tune with it; when it's not there, literature demands it. A child reading is like a child when it's sick: it is stretched full-length, it doesn't move, it doesn't hear, outside, the glorious call of July. 'What's wrong with you?' its mother asks, 'Are you ill? You're so quiet.' 'No,' says the child, 'I'm reading.' (98)

And if this summer child should grow up to be John Milton, there will quite naturally come a time when the 'dim vele' of England's very best stories will aside be laid (though not discarded), his eyes lift from the page, and his mind attend to Holiness, to Justice, and to Courtesy. Poetry, not instead of but under God, will have been found to interpret life for him, to console him – it did so to the end – and to sustain him. The study of poetry made him a poet; the absorbed reading, the rapt marking, the profound learning and the inwardly digesting of poetry – of Spenser's poetry, which concerns us here – made him a sage and serious man.

In that sense, a *provocateur* might say that Milton was the last reader of Spenser. The last, he might be brought to explain, for whom the veil was not the text's only or its chief reality. For Dryden, the special grace of Spenser's moral fiction was already fading; for Pope it was alive, but obscurely so and indefinable: 'I don't know how it is, but there's something in Spenser that pleases one as strongly in one's old age as it did in one's youth' (qtd in Spence i 182). A lifelong affection is shown to be unaccompanied by clear understanding of its moral or aesthetic causes. And by 1819, Keats's Madeline elopes to the accompaniment of a feast of images superficially 'Spenserian' but from which the intellectual and moral content has been leached by the passing years. Even the most Spenserian of nineteenth century poets, Tennyson, cannot read in his great master the moral of the metaphor or the metaphor of the moral. Since Tennyson, the readers of Spenser may have included poets, but they have more typically been professors; and professors whose profession has, in the last hundred years, become steadily more professional, indeed professionalized. John Milton, the *provocateur* still whispers, insistently, may have been Spenser's last reader of undissociated sensibility.

Within this sensibility, Holiness still matters. Accordingly, it is with Holiness in mind that we will attend to Spenser and to Death, and examine two episodes in Book 1 of the *Faerie Queene*. Death has no entry in *The Spenser Encyclopedia* – and rightly so: the deaths that occur in the epic are mostly the simple, brutal and well-deserved ends of the allegorically wicked.[4] Malengin has all his bones broken 'as small as sandy graile' (5.9.19); Pyrochles, who refuses grace, is left a 'headlesse body bleeding all the place' (2.9.52); Duessa's death is tactfully elided between the 'strong constraint' that overrides Mercilla's mercy and the last honour the Queen yields to her 'wretched corse' (5.9.4). Throughout the poem Death, when it comes, is unproblematic as befits a continuous allegory: as the evildoers are (mostly) not human beings but representations of the ideal reader's infected will and its vices, their end is brisk and unlamented.

Much more gripping, much more telling, and much more important are the moments when Death comes near, the hair's-breadth escapes and rescues. For these happen not to our vices but to us, or to those who represent us; and we are summoned by them to take notice even as our knuckles whiten. Of such episodes in Book 1, two especially engage our attention.

After the first death, there is no other. The first death is a might-have-been death: the Castle of Orgoglio. The first death, likewise, is a very-nearly-death: the 'hollow cave' of Despair (1.9.33). After those two, there is no other at all. There is sainthood, and eternity. (The dragon-fight is waged by Saint George, which contributes to its air of unreality, for the knight has crossed over into Holiness and is no longer Everyman, or Everyreader, and the risk is thus finally minimal.)

Orgoglio is a mystery, Despair an enchantment. Why is Pride a mystery? Because he comes after Lucifera, whose House is Pride also. That house is decoded for readers even before their arrival at the gate: 'To sinfull House of Pride, Duessa / guides the faithfull knight' says the quatrain announcing Canto 4. Within, her identity is made unmistakable by her coach, which is drawn by the six *other* Deadly Sins, and her pre-eminence and hellishness by the fact that Satan himself condescends to be her coachman (1.4.16–36). Within her Cantos are met Duessa, paynim knights, and the full panoply of the Underworld, described as 'hell' in the title-quatrain to Canto 5. It is with commensurate relief, then, that we accompany Everyman through the privy postern, through a lay-stall of unburied corpses fallen through 'that great Princesse *pride*', and along a dunghill of carcasses which forms his, and our, last 'dreadfull spectacle of that sad house of *Pride*' (1.5.52–3). We, with him, conscious of our allegorical journey, breathe half-amazed the clean air of deliverance at having left Pride, the greatest sin, behind. Indeed, we want to insist here, for a moment, on the seriality of the reading experience, too often lost in scholarly and critical discussion: sometimes it is important to forget the 'work's architecture' to re-encounter the sequentiality and suspense proper to an art that takes place *in time*. After all, Book 1 descends in part from medieval pilgrimage allegory. On this particular sequence of pride's challenge to a wayfaring knight, moreover, one could do worse than consult Erasmus' much-read *Enchiridion* [1503] and its rueful comments on the human tendency to escape from worldly pride only to fall into moral smugness.[5]

When, then, the knight – Everyman, Everyreader still – rests, relieved but still exhausted, by a spring in a clearing, we feel with him the cooling shade, our sweat also is dried by the '*breathing* wind' (a *pneuma*, an *anima*, a *ruach*: why should it not be blessed?), our mind too is delighted by the cheerful birds' 'sweet music': Phlegeton's shade still hangs heavy on our memory, and this *locus amoenus* is a balm to our corpse-haunted soul. The knight, we should remember, is (with us) represented in the proem, which announces Deceit, as 'the guiltlesse man' (1.7.1): and when Fidessa meets him here, we should read the text's words with care and without prejudice. We know, of course, what he does not: that she is not what she seems. But it is the guiltless man she entertains with guile; and the entertainment is perhaps not as erotically licentious as today's hardened critics regularly imagine.[6]

After some pretty reproaches on her part, tempered with honie sweet, they 'gan of solace treat'. They bathe in the pleasaunce of the joyous shade, and the knight drinks of the bubbling spring.

> Yet goodly court he made still to his Dame,
> Pour'd out in loosnesse on the grassie ground,
> Both carelesse of his health, and of his fame:
> Till at the last . . .

(1.8.7)

How we read this entertainment depends in part on the antecedent of the participle and the adjective, which is left indeterminate. Some would argue that it is probably the Dame who is poured out; and it may well be she also who is careless of his well-being and his reputation. 'Making goodlie court' does not necessarily denote, nor even connote, a fully completed sexual activity which would fit neither Redcrosse's nature as we know it nor the status of guiltless unknowing victim of deceit here presented by the text.

Reinforcing this is, of course, the matter of the spring. Its sacred Nymph happens at this time ('as it then befel', 1.7.4) to be out of favor with Diana for taking a break while hunting: its waters are doomed to weaken a drinker. But the gentle knight 'hereof [. . .] unweeting was', and indeed the text suggests no way he could have known. Although he continues to make goodly court to his Dame, the water has already assailed his courage with curdled cold, chilled his cheerful blood, and made him feel feverish: hardly a fit condition for enjoyable fornication, and moreover not brought about by whatever the degree of dalliance in which he is engaging. It is therefore with a shock no less great than Redcrosse's own that we hear the bellowing and feel the trembling of the trees. A twenty-foot giant is bad enough: one who is son of Earth and Æolus is worse. A monstrous mass of earthly slime puffed up with empty wind he may be, but he is filled also with sinful crime; and when, after several stanzas of mounting terror and imminent defeat, we hear Duessa cry his name, we are filled with bafflement as with debilitating spring water. We had left Pride behind: how can this be Orgoglio?

Our decoding is here brought up short by an aporia: a blocked path nevertheless unavoidable. And the task is made no easier by the episode's ending. Not under his own power and Dwarf-advised does Everyman make his way out of this castle: instead, all his flesh shrunk up like withered flowers (1.8.41), he must be rescued by a Personage of whom we have no understanding. For what do we, truly, know of Magnificence? The mystery, as the French say, for us remains entire. The episode of which the centrality proclaims its urgency is one which baffles our moral and our intellectual powers – ours, late readers, especially.

Why, we asked, is Despair an enchantment? No mystery he. Depression is surprisingly seductive.[7] His name, unusually for a major character, is unambiguously English and allegorical; his nature is immediately apparent. There is no doubt about his horror: he is a wicked wight, his cave is dark, doleful, dreary like a greedy grave, and the landscape is littered with the self-slain and thus damned dead. There is seemingly nothing attractive about its inhabitant either: he is melancholy and sullen, his eyes deadly dull, his cheeks rawbone, his clothing a congeries of rags, as though to indicate the sordid fragments of biography and self-accusation with which he taunts Redcrosse, or perhaps the uncontextualized quotations and gap-filled logic of his enticingly repellent arguments.

And yet this horror, this death-in-life, entices even the rescued Everyman, and brings him so far under his spell that his hand actually lifts the dagger to make an end to his life, his soul, his story, and his text. How does this come about? Why is Despair an enchantment? Unlike Duessa and Orgoglio, this very-nearly-death does not circumvent or short-circuit Everyknight's, and Everyreader's, intelligence. Indeed, it makes goodly court to our erected wit. Despair is given the most perceptive reasoning of any creature on the side of Evil. Beside his hollow, quiet, knowing voice Pyrochles is a blusterer, Duessa a gold-rush tart, Archimago a smarmy wizard, and even Mammon (no slouch at advertising) an unconvincing huckster. Despair does not try to overwhelm. He speaks slowly, and pauses to let his interlocutor reply. Not once does he pretend to be a holy hermit or a fair dame. Not once does he offer goods or wealth or power. And not once does he talk down to us, or treat us like fools.[8]

On the contrary, he appeals to the highest knowledge in us: the *architektonikè*, which stands (said Sidney) in the knowledge of a man's self (82–3). Such knowledge, like the Reason that produces it, is in Spenser's age not value-free. It is a *moral* knowledge, and it is to this moral knowledge, this moral intelligence and clear-eyed understanding, that the cursèd man appeals. His arguments, patiently expounded, chill the knight's blood more effectively than any forest spring. And they have the added quality of effacing the distance between Redcrosse and ourselves. For Despair, in clear and cogent words, says what we all, in our Vietnam-scarred culture, learnt to say. After Auschwitz and My Lai there is no more room for comforting fictions, for plume and pennant. Knights are murderers, and their profession is that of more-or-less-hired killers:

> It is a God-damned lie to say that these
> Saved, or knew, anything worth any man's pride.
> They were professional murderers and they took
> Their blood money and impious risks and died.
> In spite of all their kind some elements of worth
> With difficulty persist here and there on earth.[9]

They live by what the Gospel condemns:

> All those great battels, which thou boasts to win,
> Through strife, and bloudshed, and avengement,
> Now praisd, hereafter deare thou shalt repent . . .

> (1.9.43)

And the sooner their horrible lives are put an end to, the less defini-
tively they will have exiled themselves from Heaven: 'hee, that once
hath missed the right way, / The further he doth goe, the further he
doth stray' (ibid.).

He is hollow-eyed, Despair, but he is appallingly clear-sighted, whatever the lapses in his (theo)logic that Una so crisply identifies. Not for
him the comforting half-truths of propaganda. He has seen right to the
bottom of Redcrosse, not only as a knight but as a man: he knows every
detail of Orgoglio's dungeon; he knows every moment of the betrayal of
Una; he knows that his knowledge will be to Redcrosse a sword. More
than a sword, it is an enchanter's staff: as Moses struck water from the
rock, Despair strikes from Redcrosse a flood of new self-knowledge,
an ocean of new *self*-consciousness. As the spell takes hold, none of
Redcrosse's (and our) previous knowledge – that this is a horrible
allegorical figure, that despair is a Bad Thing, that he is surrounded
with suicides – matters: it is all drowned in this new and merciless clarity.

> The only hope, *or else Despair*
> Lies in the choice of pyre or pyre—
> To be redeemed from fire by fire.[10]

These words of a later poet are nevertheless precisely applicable to
Spenser's faith: this miserable Carle is the only alternative, not only to
Hope, but to Faith itself. Like Pogo's Enemy, he is Us, and more than
ever. Despair – then as now – is an enchantment.

So much for the exposition: let us venture on a brief development.
There is something particular about Orgoglio which is both a difficulty

and a clue. His name makes him Pride, as his nature makes him both unstoppable and a windbag. Why can he be vanquished by Magnificence (which, as a value, we so often now hesitate to understand or allow)? Because he works evil *to knighthood*: 'through presumption of his matchlesse might, / All other powers *and knighthood* he did scorne' (1.7.10). Magnificence is not knighthood: it is Royalty, the virtue of Princes.

Despair, if we will read again his most convincing arguments, attacks the knight *as knight*: 'never *knight* that dared warlike deed, / More luckless disadventures did amate.'[11] Spenser makes this clear in the stanzas that lead up to Redcrosse's encounter with the seducer when we see a pale Sir Trevisan bareheaded, fleeing in terror, with a shameful rope around his neck 'In fowle reproch of knighthoods faire degree' (1.9.22; honourable knights facing violent death merit steel, not hemp). Dishonoured, he is in better shape than his friend Sir Terwin, self-murdered with a rusty knife, an implement hardly more honourable than Trevisan's rope. Despair's honeyed voice can lead the unwary, or perhaps especially the all too wary and introspective, into both death and degradation.

The Legend of Holinesse's most dangerous deaths threaten, then, the Everyman *knight*: in Spenser's intended reader (and in us), that which knighthood represents. In *The Faerie Queene*'s original readers – whether courtier, lady-in-waiting, knight of the shire, lady of the manor or younger son – these deaths assail the knighthood that was their (or their husbands', fathers', lovers' or sons') profession and pride, their *raison d'être*. We should not be misled by the anachronism of tilting in exquisitely-engraved armor in an age of gunpowder. It was the sense of knighthood that gave Lord Willoughby (who called courtiers 'reptilia') and Sir Philip Sidney their readiness to risk their lives for a cause. Nor should we be misled by even such knighthood's pastness. There is that in us also which these deaths attack, and which we might call our age's equivalent to knighthood – the *miles christianus* (or *agnosticus*), the armed innocent abroad, the seriousness at which our sophistication has almost learnt to smile.[12]

Orgoglio is the death of distancing, the death by distancing. He is humankind 'grown great though arrogant delight / Of th'high descent, whereof he was yborne' (1.7.10). Such a race, having been placed above all Creation, knowing itself but a little lower than the angels, becomes in truth a *Herrenvolk*, full of an elemental pride, masters under God (Who often seems comfortably absent) of all they survey – Giants indeed. To such a humanity, to such a metaphysically-exalted race, what is knighthood? Filled with complicated rules, irksome denials, and unconvincing ceremony (an Order of a *garter*?), it is flummery, a foolishness. Its elaborate armor is as hot, heavy and cumbersome as T. H. White describes it in *The Once and Future King's* unforgettable fight between King Pellinore and Sir Grummore Grummursum.[13] It is much better removed when reading books (as Federigo da Montefeltro, Urbino's Good Duke, did not know or heed[14]) or when resting from a hair-raising escape in charming company under a cooling breeze. Cuisses, at least, can be left off, even when riding into battle at Zutphen. . . . Such a master race, its erected wit reaching even unto the stars, has no need for codes and plumes: it can make and unmake Kings.[15]

Despair is the death, not of the erected wit but of the infected will. It also attacks knighthood, but from the other side. Whereas Orgoglio's pride separates the knight from the man and exalts the latter at the former's expense, the ghastly reasoner under the cliff conflates the two and – much more dangerously – attacks *the knight as man*. Time and again he stresses this in the progression of the appellations: 'foolish man', 'most envious man', 'ô man of sin', ending with 'die soone, ô Faeries sonne'. It is *as man* that a knight's will is infected – such an infection, he hints, is as incurable as it is inescapable. And yet Despair reserves a particular torment of perverted rationality for knighthood. For knighthood, so far from improving the condition of fallen man, merely (in every sense) makes it worse: it is *as a knight* that Redcrosse has not only taken part in, but actively sought out, all those 'great battels' in which his very victories make the greater sin, with blood to be repaid. It is *as a knight* that his falsing with perjury his faith to his Lady mild (1.9.46) makes him doubly a man of sin. It is *as a knight* that he has been amated with luckless disadventures; it is *as a knight* that he is revealed as far more repulsive a sinner than if had he been a simple miller or a plowman.

Despair is a death that saps knighthood by undermining its codedness through morals, not metaphysics. It paints the institution and all it represents as a whited sepulchre hiding elemental wickedness and unbridled sin – as, indeed, a kind of multiplier of normal human fallenness, making the latter more reprehensible by lending it pretension. And its specious but oh-so-convincing rationality also crosses gaping gulfs of time to reach our offices and studies: behind every earnest English poet writing in a small Irish castle, it persuades us to see as the only *real* reality a Smerwick massacre. Despair expounds only truths (even if also omitting some major ones), and this is his awful strength: he tells Redcrosse nothing he cannot, miserably, acknowledge. Despair is more than death: it is what someone once characterized as the essence of Hell – to have one's secret shames and fears about oneself authoritatively and implacably confirmed, without appeal. After such deaths, such might-have-been deaths and such very-nearly-deaths, Cælia's house is a pleasant pain.

It will have been noticed that in this discussion of death and knighthood, pride and knighthood, despair and knighthood, we have from time to time hinted at a crossing of the gulf of ages. It is to this crossing that we now address ourselves – led by the serious shade of Milton, by the sage and solemn tunes of Spenser, and by the absent presence of Death itself.

To confront the next part of the argument we will bring in more recent voices.

> Death, in the human horizon, is not that which is given, it is that which is to be done: a task, that which we seize actively, that which becomes the source of our activity and our mastery.
>
> (Blanchot 'L'œuvre' 115)

> That which I describe here in order to define, in the banality of its features, meaning as temporizing deferral is the classically determined structure of the sign.        (Derrida 'La différance' 9)

It is, say the semiologists since Saussure, in the deferring of closure that meaning is created and that language has its space of activity. They apply the principle to language; but Blanchot, whom we have just seen writing, characteristically, of Death, seems to move this concept into a wider context relevant to our concerns. If Death, as closure, becomes the source of our activity, that activity is something we create as meaning, as meaning*ful*, as significant, in the deferral of Death. Nevertheless, what we thus create is (Derrida reminds us) the sign as 'classically structured': as standing for a reality; as in fact symbolic.

Yet symbol (which is emphatically not allegory, still less Spenserian allegory) is suspect. Blanchot again:

> Symbolic reading is probably the worst way to read a literary text. Each time we are embarrassed by too strong an utterance, we say, 'It's a symbol.' The wall that is the Bible has thus become a gentle transparency where melancholy colors the little fatigues of the soul.
>
> (Blanchot, 'Le livre' 126)

Symbol itself, in other words, becomes an act of deferral, the putting-off of embarrassing forces, *a fortiori* of the authenticity that is Death. And symbol, dependent as it is upon what Derrida would call a meta-physic, always implies a reality.

At the same time symbol, sign, significance, meaning, interpretation are, if not currently our favourite words, nevertheless and still the stuff of our métier, the warp and woof of our professional activity, our professional mastery. Let us, in the face of Milton and Death, consider Spenser, *our* appropriated Spenser, in the light of this. We have seen, above, that the first death of Orgoglio, the first death of Despair, touched Redcrosse and knighthood; that Redcrosse is Everyman and Everyreader; that we too share in a knighthood, however altered; and that Orgoglio and Despair are not only menaces *to* us, but in some lights and under some angles, *are* (portraits of) us. Their might-have-been Death might have been ours (mastery): with their very-nearly-Death we are very nearly associated (Smerwick). Potentially, then, *The Faerie Queene*, like Blanchot's Bible, is a Wall, an avalanche waiting to start sliding. It is an uncomfortable text, a text that 'dé-range', which untidies us, which dis-orders us, or would if we let it, with truths too close to home. Do we, like Spenser, like Milton, really want to think about holiness, about temperance, about chastity?

What, then, do we do with such a text – we, the professionals, we the professionalized, we the specialists? What can we do to keep at bay its embarrassing force, to stop or escape the avalanche, to make the wall transparent? The answer is all around is. For three or four generations now, we have created a vast and complex structure, a *knowing-machine*[16] of scholarship and a second, parasitical, *interpreting-machine* of criticism that like the goodly frame of Temperance, 'gins . . . fairely to rise'. It is a structure of many mansions and complex elements, still growing. Like the House of Alma, it is built up of three chief elements: the solid quadrate of the base is made up of articles; the triangle consists of conferences and sessions; and the circle's perfection is filled with books, both editions and monographs. Like the vessel Argo, it constantly replaces its parts without ever losing its identity. Like Xanadu, the Internet daily extends its domes in dimensions of virtuality. And it has one added and remarkable feature: while constantly interpreting, while everywhere seeing and decoding signs, it must never interpret and decode itself.

If, though, for a moment we permit ourselves this forbidden activity, we perceive that this busy structure, this knowing and interpreting machine, exists for the creation of meaning. Ceaselessly interpreting the

(Spenserian) Text, it creates (indeed, becomes) another text: a complex text with the perspective, the prospect, of covering the Text entirely with a structure of interpretation. And, as a text, it creates its meaning by deferral.[17]

This needs some explanation. How, we might ask, can a structure, a text, of interpretation be a structure of deferral? After all, its *raison d'être* is the Text, Spenser's text: it exists for the highest and most selfless reasons – to make the Text accessible, to help new readers and intrigue long-time adepts, to interpret and to debate. How can this be deferral? If the French thinkers of the twentieth century's second third have taught us anything, it is the value of a *different regard*. Barthesian semiology, for instance, always teaches us to ask, of a phenomenon or an utterance, What (*else*) does it *mean*? And here, faced with Spenser in the conjunction with Milton and with Death, it occurs to us to direct this semiotic regard upon the complex structure, the text, which we might call Spenserism. In order to do this more comprehensibly and more systematically, we will borrow some methodical basics from the Riffaterrean semiotics of poetry. Riffaterre's method teaches us to see the text as existing on two levels: the heuristic level, of straightforward meaning, and the semiotic level, of significance. The reader's activity, the praxis of passing from the first to the second level, he calls *semiosis*.

The first step is to look, in the first (or heuristic) reading of the text, for anomalies, for what Riffaterre calls 'ungrammaticalities'. If we look for these in the text that is our profession, in Spenserism, a major ungrammatically at once meets the eye. The structure (the text), we have said, is one of knowledge and, especially, of interpretation. It exists to decode and to interpret the Spenserian Text. But – and here we arrive at the ungrammaticality – *for whom* does the structure, the text of interpretation, exist? This vast and increasingly elaborate text, this exponentially growing structure, interprets the Spenserian Text to whom? Our swift defensive answer is: to students. For the structure is an *educational* structure, and has grown up in universities. In this fact there lies already the germ of an ungrammaticality, and there is a defensible thesis that the Text's preservation in universities has risked killing it elsewhere; but let us give this educational interpreting-machine the benefit of the doubt and accept it, for the moment, without insistent question. In no way does this remove the ungrammaticality. For within the university – the North American university especially, which largely created the structure in the first place – the structure's public, the text's supposed audience, is dwindling and in many places courses are disappearing. With some heartening exceptions, outside the academy readers of the kind that Milton might have recognized and Spenser sought are becoming extinct.[18] The ungrammaticality of a growing structure of interpretation serving a shrinking public seems undeniable.

A second ungrammaticality is the increased professionalization of the structure. It is not now thought possible or proper to interpret *The Faerie Queene* without eight to ten years of formal post-secondary study; and no graduate student or assistant professor can afford to ignore the pro-liferating structure of information and interpretation.

A third is that while the original Text recedes farther and farther from the knowledge, interests and concerns of the contemporary reader, the structure of interpretation insistently (and sometimes hectoringly) connects it with what it perceives as urgent contemporary issues. It does not do so directly, as Spenser might have done, by asking what Holiness, Temperance and Courtesy could contribute to, say, a newly multicultural society (or, indeed, vice versa); instead, it projects its concerns upon the Text and forms its interpretative structure in current discourses and assumptions.

In Riffaterrean semiotics, once the ungrammaticalities are discerned, we proceed to look for an *interpretant*: 'a sign that translates the text's surface signs and explains what else the text suggests' (Riffaterre 81). Such an interpretant, in this case, has been provided by the structure's creation of the present volume. Like all interpretants, it first of all belongs fully to the surface level of the text. A volume of academic, scholarly and interpretative articles on 'Spenser, Milton, and Death', appearing in America in the early years of the twenty-first century, to be sold to university libraries and a few scholars, and to be read by the authors' acquaintances and a few graduate students, may be said fully to participate in the text, the professional structure, the goodly frame of Spenserism, here under review. But in it there is one sign which is itself anomalous and makes it into an interpretant. For here we are con-cerned not, as recent conference round-tables have it, with 'Spenser and Sex' or 'Spenser and Science'; here we are not examining 'Milton and Republicanism'; here we are looking at Death. And it is Death which will be, in *this* text, the Riffaterrean interpretant.

For Death, as Blanchot says, is the source of our activity, of our mastery: it is the universal, the most basic object of deferral. And so Death, providentially appearing in the surface or literal level of our text, unites the ungrammaticalities and sets in motion the semiosis, the movement in our observing minds from meaning to significance. The structure of this significance now shows itself to be a *structure of defer-*

*ral.* The massive collective text of interpretation, the constantly changing, exponentially growing, ever more rigorously professional knowing-machine of 'Spenserism' is united by this significance.

What, then, does it defer? What is the Death that creates its activity? Our semiotics will not be complete without an answer to this question. Language, we know, takes place in the deferral of closure; our activity as thinking humans takes place in the deferral of Death. What does our hive-like house, with its quadrate of articles, its triangle of conferences, and its circle of books, defer?

We may now, perhaps, go back to the beginning of this essay, and to knighthood. There we saw that Orgoglio and Despair, the mystery and the enchantment, the might-have-been death and the very-nearly-death involving, respectively, the erected wit and the infected will, did not speak only to Elizabethan courtiers but, most uncomfortably, to us. What this suggests is that our structure of knowledge, our ceaseless and insistent text of interpretation, exists as a *deferral of the Text – of Spenser's Text.* We have, in Blanchot's words, made the Text into a symbol: we are, indeed, still making it, our labors are aimed at making the wall transparent. We are convinced that this symbol stands for a reality – that somehow this structure of ours, this knowing and interpreting machine, *is* the reality. Yet if we listen, we will find Blanchot's words directly challenging: to adapt his phrasing, do we not color with relevance the little avoidances of the soul? What do we do with the uncomfortable text that is *The Faerie Queene?* We spin it into theory, we castigate it or co-opt it with ideology, we castrate (or spay) it with scholarship, we threaten its life with a railway share, we pursue it with forks and hope.[19] We create an Encyclopedia about it – about it and about. We treat it, in fact, like Death itself.

Death has no entry in *The Spenser Encyclopedia.*

Yet Death we may defer, but Death we cannot ignore. So let us perhaps end by leaving semiotics and asking, What might we do with such a Death? What might we do with the Spenserian text? Easy answers are denied us. We cannot unlearn what has been learnt, undo what has been done. All our learning cannot restore Milton's reading of *The Faerie Queene.* But Death, and Derrida, and Blanchot, and Bataille, may give us a clue.

We may, for instance, refuse the metaphysical implications of our deferral, of our symbolic insistence on a reality underlying our activity. Doing so would exchange deferral for *differral* (if we may so translate

Derrida's *différance*), and create for our activity a space of hitherto unimagined freedom. Interestingly, even within an older structure of knowledge there is a pointer to such an exchange, in the difference between symbol and allegory, and especially Spenserian allegory: if we attend to Spenser's allegory, as A.C. Hamilton has for many years reminded us, we see that unlike symbol it cannot be paraphrased, only *read*; that its moral teaching is coextensive with its text; and that its skilful reader needs to be equipped with the Arnoldian quality of tact (116). Differral would allow us to exercise all the extraordinary ingenuity of our collective mind in the dimensions of pluralism, discontinuity and uncertainty so characteristic of the modern world.[20] And it would allow us to do so while reading Spenser with a seriousness which, though it can never be Milton's, would nevertheless be an equivalent in its scrupulous and affectionate attention to the text's moral aesthetic, in its rapt absorption of Spenser's serious and allegorical game.

Valuably, we might try to extricate ourselves from the Procrustean and entrapping structure we have created, by the complex exercise of *undistancing*. Again, the answers cannot be easy: but such an exercise might produce a reading of Spenser which would not only employ all the cumulative experience of scholarship, but reintegrate these into what one might call a new simplicity. Such a reading would recognize that, as Blanchot put it, Death is not that which is given, but that which is to be done: that Death is for each of us to be accomplished, and that likewise, as Barthes said, the Text is to be accomplished. Such a reading, then (and the writing it would not fail to produce) would engage Death (which, we should remember, for Spenser had little sting and no victory), and Holiness, and Temperance, and Chastity, and Friendship, and Justice, and Courtesy, and even Magnificence, in a dimension both public and private: with the panoply of our learning but with the courage of our Death.

> And the end of all our exploring
> Will be to arrive where we started
> And know the place for the first time.[21]

## Notes

1. The *index* to the *Spenser Encyclopedia* includes several references under 'death'. As an *entry*, 'Death' appears subsumed under 'Life'. Although doubtless as haunted by death as most sentient human beings, and despite many references to it (see a concordance of his works for an impressive list), Spenser wrote nothing like Ronsard's 'Hymn to Death': *memento mori* and *contemp-*

*tus mundi* are found less, or less explicitly and less often, in his verse than in that of many other writers of the time. A MLA database search on Spenser and death turns up very little (one of the few articles is Patricia Vicari's). Dying plays a role in the allegory, of course, although many have noticed the high survival rate of Spenser's villains: such figures have important jobs to do in a fallen world. It might be valuable to examine why and under what circumstances Spenser's characters do *not* die – from poor Malbecco in Book 3, now one of the undead and a mere noun ('Jealousie'), to the giant Disdain in Book 6 who must live at least a little in the hearts of pretty women lest they become pushovers. The deaths of other allegorical figures are more likely to signify the demise or control of forces within the protagonist (or ideal reader) than the disappearance of those forces in the world we inhabit.

2. See *Reason of Church Government*, Preface to Book II, in *Milton's Prose*, 111, citing classical drama.

3. 'Il Penseroso', l. 117.

4. Kathrine Koller notes Spenser's characters die or kill physically 'with very little display of emotion'. There are of course exceptions, Mordant and Amavia being among the most interesting.

5. See, for example, in *The Enchiridion of Erasmus* the remark that when 'all the rest of the passions have been subjugated, only the infirmity of empty glory lies in ambush, even in the midst of virtues' (76). Many other passages seem relevant, not least the reminder that 'the foe emerges from the depths of our own nature, just like the earth-born brothers of poetic fiction' (63; this must mean Jason's dragon-teeth soldiers, but 'earth-born' also suggests giants).

6. The authors do not wholly agree here, Prescott being willing to think Redcrosse engaged in at least quasi-fornication with Duessa, the great Whore herself. (On Orgoglio as a giant phallus, see J. W. Schroeder's ingenious 'Spenser's Erotic Drama: the Orgoglio Episode'.) More skeptical, Kuin points out that whatever the Elizabethan use of the word 'pride' to mean sexual arousal or prowess, the sin itself would be Lussuria, not Orgoglio. We agree that even if the giant figures overwhelming desire, among other energies, in this context 'looseness' on the 'grass' of the flesh allegorizes (and perhaps helps explain) religious infidelity.

7. On Despair see Harold Skulsky, 'Spenser's Despair Episode and the Theology of Doubt', and his essay in the *Spenser Encyclopedia*. In 'The Left Hand of God: Despair in Renaissance Tradition', Susan Snyder, who quotes Spenser *passim*, notes despair's connection with Prodigal Son dramas and to varieties of *tristia*. She cites theologians who call Despair's logic – the longer a life the more sin and the more damnation – 'the devil's syllogism' (a fairly benign version that Spenser would have read is 'The lenger lyfe, the more offence' [see *Tottel's Miscellany*]; it concludes that since Death is the end of strife, 'Wherefore come death, and let me die'). As Snyder says, Una's reply is not an 'answer at all but a transcendence'. Other authorities called Despair the child of Luxuria and cited the dangers of idleness. One common theory was that although religious melancholy might promote suicidal thoughts it could also be the first step to redemption. Thomas P. Roche, in 'The Menace of Despair and Arthur's Vision, *Faerie Queene* I.9', comments on Amor's role in the episode's context, reading Una's rescue of her knight as signifying that 'only Love can kill Despair'.

8. His closest modern parallel may be the urbanely nihilistic dragon in John Gardner's *Grendel*.

9. Hugh MacDiarmid, 'Another Epitaph on an Army of Mercenaries', replying to A. E. Housman's original 'Epitaph'. It is interesting that MacDiarmid either did not notice, or chose to ignore, the irony of Housman's title, which quotes the Kaiser's contemptuous assessment of the British Army in World War I.

10. T. S. Eliot, *The Four Quartets*, 'Little Gidding', 4, 5–7. Our italics.

11. Skulsky, 'Spenser's Despair' (227), rightly says that the episode is not an 'ordinary chivalric encounter', but here, as with Mammon's disturbing reminder to Guyon that being a knight takes riches, knighthood is put in question.

12. After the attacks on 11 September 2001, for a time, at least, 'New York's finest' and 'New York's bravest' played a chivalric role in the public's imagination.

13. See pages 61–7 of T. H. White's *The Once and Future King*, for example: 'When they had got their weight properly distributed in front of them, so that they were just off balance, each broke into a trot to keep up with himself. They hurtled together as it had been two boars. They met in the middle, breast to breast, with a noise of shipwreck and great bells tolling, and both, bouncing off, fell breathless on their backs' (64).

14. See Pedro Berruguete (attrib.), *Federico da Montefeltro and his son Guidobaldo* (1476–7), Urbino, Ducal Palace.

15. It should, in this context, be remembered that William of Orange's *Apologia* and the Dutch Estates' Placard of Desertion were, even by their authors, written with considerable self-consciousness if not trepidation, and were seen by legitimists as not only treasonable but sinful.

16. We create this term by analogy with Gilles Deleuze and Félix Guattari's 'desiring-machine' in their challenging article 'Bilan-programme pour machines désirantes': 'Man constitutes a *machine* as soon as this nature is communicated by recurrence to the ensemble of which he forms a part under given specific conditions'.

17. Hence the brilliance of David Lodge's finale in *Small World* when the naïve protagonist asks an audience of professors at the MLA conference what would happen if they could persuade everyone. The flowers in Central Park start to bloom now that the grail hero has asked his question, but in fact consensus would kill the profession. English studies is endless romance, not epic – and not yet elegy.

18. For Spenserians there are important exceptions, although some poet-admirers (John Hollander, notably) are also academics. Other exceptions are at least amusing, as witness an episode of *Star Trek Voyager* in which the captain of the Enterprise is seen catching up on her *Faerie Queene* (a slim volume, we see as the camera sweeps over it, and in prose).

19. Faithful to the machine's ethos, we here append an endnote directing the reader to Lewis Carroll's 'The Hunting of the Snark', a possibly allegorical (or possibly symbolic) text.

20. Roger Kuin, *Chamber Music: Elizabethan Sonnet Sequences and the Pleasure of Criticism, passim*. As one Spenser scholar said after a talk at Kalamazoo, 'If I thought Spenser was just illustrating moral truths I wouldn't be interested'.

21. T. S. Eliot, *The Four Quartets*, 'Little Gidding', 4.27–9.

# 6
## Anatomizing Death

*Linda Gregerson*

## Eating death

> Out of every corner of the woods and glynnes they came creeping
> forth upon their hands, for their legges could not beare them; they
> looked like anatomies of death, they spake like ghosts crying out of
> their graves; they did eate the dead carrions, happy where they could
> find them, yea, and one another soone after, insomuch as the very
> carcasses they spared not to scrape out of their graves...
>
> (Spenser *A View of the State of Ireland 101–2*)

Death is not merely a pervasive thematic presence in the writings of
Edmund Spenser; it is a foundational political, moral, and psychological premise. It is also, I shall wish to argue later, the ground rhythm of
cognitive method and aesthetic apprehension. The passage cited above,
from Irenius' eyewitness description of the Munster famine, is arguably
one of the most haunting portrayals of human extremity in early
modern literature. Irenius does not produce this piece of eloquence in
order to arouse pity and commiseration in the heart of his interlocutor,
however. Or rather, the pity and commiseration his words arouse (and
Eudoxus professes to experience both emotions) are not intended to
produce intervention on behalf of the sufferers. Pity – sorrow for the
other – and commiseration – sorrow for the other self – are collateral
effects in the present instance and, more to the point, they are tactical
problems. For the business of the moment is a policy recommendation:
the Munster famine is adduced as evidence that the decisive subjuga-
tion of Ireland is a realistic and desirable goal, can be brought about by
means of so many English footmen, so many horsemen, so many gar-
risons, so many months of victualling, so many pounds of her Majesty's

treasure, provided the power of her Majesty's sword is augmented by the instrumental power of starvation. Pity must not be allowed to blunt the sword. The Irish have been reduced to carrion before; to carrion they can and must be reduced again. Which prompts us to ask what it is that can inspire the embrace of death on such a scale.

Or this other embrace, which Irenius also professes to have witnessed at first hand: '[A]t the execution of a notable traytor at Limericke, called Murrogh O'Brien, I saw an old woman, which was his foster mother, take up his head, whilst he was quartered, and sucked up all the blood that runne thereout, saying, that the earth was not worthy to drinke it [. . .]' (*View* 66). The raw power of Irenius' account appears to be grounded as much in admiration as revulsion, and in something else as well: the sheer spectacle of an affiliation the English imposition cannot touch. At the very moment when the colonizing imperium chooses to exercise its power over life and death, the colonizing construction of law and lineage encounters a wholly alien, wholly resistant configuration of fosterage, blood, and earth. Yet Irenius insists the scene is legible. He adduces the bloody imbibing at Murrough O'Brien's execution as part of his survey of Irish custom, which survey in turn entails a genealogical survey of the nations and cultures – Scythian, Spanish, Gaulish, British – from which the Irish are said to derive. The action of Murrogh O'Brien's foster mother is adduced as a kind of genetic trace, a Gaulish survival in 16th century Irish culture, though with one significant permutation: the Gauls were said to have drunk the blood of their enemies in battle, while the Irish drink the blood of their 'friends'.

What unites these two verbal portraits, that of the Munster famine and that of Murrogh O'Brien's execution and its aftermath, is not merely the figure of consumption – the Irish eat their dead – but also the figure of anatomy. Anatomy: (1) the artificial separation of the different parts of a human or animal body in order to discover its structure and economy, (2) a corpse shrunken to skin and bone, (3) a living being reduced to 'skin and bone', a withered or emaciated creature, (4) the dissection or dividing of anything material or immaterial for the purpose of examining its parts, analysis. The English quarter the body of Murrogh O'Brien. His stepmother reincorporates his blood. The English survey and anatomize Irish culture. 'This ripping of auncestors, is very pleasing unto me', says Eudoxus. The 'old customes, and . . . coniecturall circumstances' from which Ireneus infers 'the descents of nations' afford 'great pleasure and delight' (53, 61). One might argue that Eudoxus' phraseology, his 'ripping', betrays the shadowy predation that links even the most disinterested colonial ethnography to more explicit deployments of force, and surely this link is real. The consolidated resonance of a foster mother's grieving is for Irenius just one more piece of evidence that Irish culture is not amenable to reform but requires instead a ruthless extirpation. But the reader ought also to linger over the announced categories of pleasure and delight, discomfiting as those categories may be in the context of so much bloodthirstiness. At the conclusion of their dialogue, Eudoxus extracts from Irenius the promise of a further conversation, a conversation devoted to the 'observations, which you have gathered of the antiquities of Ireland' (161). That is, the absorbing textures and delightful prospects of the delineated colonial field – its rich antiquity, its complex adaptations, its implicit testimony to the coherence of the surveying mind – repeatedly waylay the expedient 'remedy' it is the ostensible business of the *View* to promote. To anatomize Ireland is to constitute that country as a field of knowledge, a field for the production and advancement of English epistemology.

Finally, there is a deep and troubling etymological substrate to Irenius' plans for reducing the Irish to submission by means of starvation. Conquest in Ireland has ever been close cousin to dearth, in the full double sense of sixteenth-century usage. In the Oxford English Dictionary, 'dearth' marks an etymological trail from 'glory', 'splendor', and 'dearness or costliness' to 'scarcity'. On some level, this testifies to a durable economic verity: the price of corn is savagely high when crops most disastrously fail. But dearth in Spenser's *View* marks another economy as well: the high price and high valuation of a cultural order that is said to warrant the *production* of famine, the explicit use of famine as an instrument of cultural propagation. The Englishman who anatomizes death in the colonial field insists that even the disintegrative process is an articulation of structure. To anatomize the body, or the body of a subjected nation, is to divide it into parts in order that it may be read. Death in its eloquence may escape or loosen the binding strictures of political and religious doctrine – it does so repeatedly in Spenser's poetry as in his *View* – but the recurrent imperative in Spenser's writings is to insist that death *has* a body, that it is legible.

In *Paradise Lost*, by contrast, Death has no proper body. Milton insists again and again upon its derivative status, its belated and contingent appearance on earth, its founding and perdurable absence of form:

> . . . The other shape,
> If shape it might be call'd that shape had none
> Distinguishable in member, joint, or limb,
> Or substance might be call'd that shadow seem'd,

> For each seem'd either; black it stood as Night,
> Fierce as ten Furies, terrible as Hell,
> And shook a dreadful Dart; what seem'd his head
> The likeness of a Kingly Crown had on.

> (*PL* 2 666–73)[1]

Loosed upon creation, Death stuffs his 'Maw, [his] vast unhide-bound Corpse' (*PL* 10 601). In Milton's unfallen Paradise, eating is a measured ceremony, both a corporal and a social form of sustenance. In the fallen world, Death's feasting exceeds all measure, quite literally knows no bounds. Death's appetite is never satisfied: it is tautological (the body Death feeds is already a corpse); it is dispersive or entropic rather than consolidating (the body Death feeds has no binding integument). Death's force may gather to a point (the dart can 'sting'), but that force is a radical loosening. The power of the dart, like the power of the maw, is dissolution.

Since death has no distinguishable form, but assumes the form of that which it inhabits, Eve may eat of the fruit and, for the space of her sinning, deceive herself about its nature: 'Greedily she ingorg'd without restraint, / And knew not eating Death' (9 791–2). Death having begun its disintegrative work in her, Eve may then estrange herself from her own motives and become a vector for death's continuing infection. In the soliloquy that immediately follows her eating of the fruit, she contemplates the relative odds of self-promotion (the competitive advantage of keeping new knowledge to herself) and spousal murder (the fallback precaution of sharing deadly fruit with Adam). Her resolution taken, she casts the sharing of the fruit as an act of love, but she speaks more truly than she intends: 'On my experience, *Adam*, freely taste, / And fear of Death deliver to the Winds' (9 988–9). Delivered to the winds, propagated by the winds, that fear, and death itself, will reach the furthest corners of creation.

In Book 10 of *Paradise Lost*, the narrator surveys the consequences of the Fall for the beasts of the land, the birds of the air, the fish of the sea, the stars in the firmament. And he explains the disastrous climatic change, from perpetual temperateness to 'pinching cold and scorching heat' in the following terms.

> At that tasted Fruit
> The Sun, as from *Thyéstean* Banquet, turn'd
> His course intended.

> (*PL* 10 687–9)

We are told in classical sources that the Sun averted his face when Atreus served his brother Thyestes the flesh of his own sons. How is it that eating the flesh of an apple can be equated with the horrors of cannibalism and the murder of offspring? Adam, as ever, is a fast learner. Observing the animals as they fall to devouring one another, Adam knows at once that this turning of kind against kind, this radical deformation of nature, proceeds from him:

> All that I eat or drink, or shall beget,
> Is propagated curse. O voice once heard
> Delightfully, *Increase and Multiply*,
> Now death to hear! for what can I increase
> Or multiply, but curses on my head?

> (*PL* 10 728–32)

If Spenser proposes a colonial expansion based on dearth, it is because he imagines that the consequences of death will be self-limiting, focused upon an intractable native population. Once the victims of hunger have consumed themselves and one another, the ground will be cleared for biological and cultural propagation of another, better, English kind. In *Paradise Lost*, Death is the true colonialist; his expansion universal. Eating itself becomes a species of violence once Adam and Eve have fallen. This is part of the closed logic of providence: those who disobey will die, and with them all their heirs. Adam and Eve and all the as-yet-unborn now dine at death's table.

## Loving death

In Canto 9 of the Book of Holinesse, Redcrosse Knight discovers the body of a 'wofull louer' who has who has plunged a rustie knife into his own breast. The knight is outraged and threatens to avenge this spectacle upon its 'author' (*The Faerie Queene* 1.9.37).[2] But the author explicates the spectacle thus: 'He there', he says, this 'he' being the dead Sir Terwin:

> He there does now enioy eternall rest
> And happie ease, which thou doest want and craue,
> And further from it daily wanderest:
> What if some litle paine the passage haue,
> That makes fraile flesh to feare the bitter waue?
> Is not short paine well borne, that brings long ease,
> And layes the soule to sleepe in quiet graue?

> Sleepe after toyle, port after stormie seas,
> Ease after warre, death after life does greatly please.

(1.9.40)

These lines are spoken by Despair. In other words, the author of *The Faerie Queene* ascribes to the author of self-murder lines that are arguably the most ravishing in all his poem. It is almost impossible to detect, or rather to master, the flaw in logic here, so powerful is the pull of syntactical and sonic reiteration in the final couplet: the parallel phrasing, the parallel caesurae, the insinuating rhyme, even the extra foot in the alexandrine seem to bind the series of analogies with the force of near-tautology. This is no mere forward march: when the perfect iambs of the first seven lines give way to the far more seductive rhythms of a doubled metrical inversion (*sleep* after *toil*, *port* after *storm*, and so on), intellection succumbs to the senses.

Or nearly so. Redcrosse manages a reply, and his reply is doctrinally correct – it is God, not His creatures, who must set the terminating limit on life – but his rhetoric is so saturated with that of Despair (he speaks in an extended metaphor, he construes death as the soldier's reprieve from a nightwatch) that it is difficult to be certain about subsequent shifts in speaker attribution. A notable feature of Spenser's ten-stanza excursis on the subject of self-murder is that lengthy portions of it might be spoken by either Redcrosse or Despair: not only is the latter's eloquence infectious, but it also mimics the vocabularies of Christian conscience ('The lenger life, I wote the greater sin' 1.9.43) and Christian argument ('Is not [God's] deed, what euer thing is donne, / In heauen and earth? did not he all create / To die againe?' 1.9.42). Redcrosse has himself recurrently called upon death, and has come to look like death, a 'pined corse' (1.8.40), during his long captivity in Orgoglio's castle: the encounter with Despair is narrated redundantly, and allegorized recursively. As are the erotic encounters that give despair and death their foothold: the sleeping and waking visions of a licentious Una, dalliance with Una's licentious surrogate Duessa, even the ostensible 'rescue' that spares Redcrosse's life and establishes Duessa as Orgoglio's consort. These wanton couplings are spiritually barren but institutionally fecund: judging from the contents of Orgoglio's castle, they have generated nothing less than the thousand-year imperium of Roman Catholicism.

It is only Una's intervention, penitential progress through the House of Holinesse, and the visionary revelations of a figure named Contemplation that restore Redcrosse to the covenant of grace. Contemplation is himself an emaciated figure very like the deathly anatomy to which

Redcrosse had declined in the Castle of Orgoglio: 'Each bone might through his body well be red' (1.10.48). And the vision Contemplation shares with Redcrosse, the vision Redcrosse longs to enter, is that of death. This is death with a difference of course; its lofty towers are the towers of New Jerusalem. But if it is a motivating vision, it is also a problematic vision from the standpoint of earthly quest: 'O let me [. . .] streight way on that last long voyage fare' (1.10.63), begs Redcrosse. And his request is a reasonable one. He has moved from one death-longing to another, from bad to good, from soul-sickness to a vision of rebirth. But death remains the gateway. To which orthodoxy can only answer: Not yet.

Adam eats death for company's sake. He knows the nature of the fruit, or knows at least what it entails, and eats it anyway: 'to Death devote [. . .] / And mee with thee' (*PL* 9 901, 906). Adam eats because the story requires it and because Milton could not untie the conundrum of the double fall, no more than theologians before or since have been able to untie it, and Adam dies therefore of misguided love, or uxoriousness. And when he awakens to what he has done, he loves the thought of death:

> . . . How gladly would I meet
> Mortality my sentence, and be Earth
> Insensible, how glad would lay me down
> As in my Mother's lap!

> (*PL* 10 775–8)

When Eve awakens to what she has done, she too is drawn to the preemptive embrace of death. But her proposal is the more remarkable because it is not mere impulsive outburst but the result of careful and considered calculation: 'If care of our descent perplex us most', she says, 'Which must be born to certain woe, devour'd / By Death at last', it yet lies in our power 'Conception to prevent' (*PL* 10 979–81, 987). She proposes to replace the nuptial embrace of Adam with a preemptive embrace of Death, either by abstaining altogether from the act of generation, which will limit Death's ravening to Adam and Eve alone, or if prolonged abstention proves more than they can manage, to 'supply / With our own hands [Death's] office' (10 1001–2), committing active suicide. The prospect takes one's breath away. For Eve's proposed self-murder is quite consciously an act of genocide as well: the suicide she is drawn to is not single, nor merely double, but racial. Eve's view is more sweeping than that of Irenius.

## Death and poetic form

The two poets we habitually construe as bracketing the thinkable limits of the English Renaissance – Spenser the Tudor colonialist, Milton the revolutionary – work with inherently opposed figurative fields when they take death for their explicit subject: Spenser habitually renders death by means of fixed anatomy and sharpness of outline; Milton renders death by means of formlessness. Moving from figuration to the realm of poetic form, we contemplate a kind of double chiasmus or crossover. The poet gravitates toward antidote, each his own, and, according to the logic of inversion, each adopts prosodic formulas conspicuously at odds with those of the other. The poet writes against death not in general but in particular, against death as he instinctively apprehends it. And because Milton's formal propositions are the easier to describe, I shall ignore chronology and begin with them.

Milton's prosodic command is the firmest in the language. It is mindful, it is unwaveringly deliberate, it treasures the rigor and the suppleness, the orchestrated expectation of the line as one might treasure life itself. Phrase by phrase and syllable by syllable, Milton generates the conscious 'sense' of his verse by means of a variable opposition between syntax and poetic line, 'the sense variously drawn out from one Verse into another' (Milton 210). The clarity of this prosodic method, the key to its simultaneous freedom and its control, depends in the longer poems upon the suppression of competing compositional units, the suppression, that is, of stanza and rhyme.

Even within the distilled expectations of a shorter form – the sonnet – we can see this formal imperative at work. Take, for example, sonnet 19:

> When I consider how my light is spent,
>> Ere half my days, in this dark world and wide,
>> And that one Talent which is death to hide,
>> Lodg'd with me useless, though my Soul more bent
> To serve therewith my Maker, and present
>> My true account, lest he returning chide;
>> 'Doth God exact day-labor, light denied',
>> I fondly ask; But patience to prevent
> That murmur, soon replies, 'God doth not need
>> Either man's work or his own gifts; who best
>> Bear his mild yoke, they serve him best; his State
> Is Kingly. Thousands at his bidding speed

> And post o'er Land and Ocean without rest:
> They also serve who only stand and wait'.

In the Italianate sestet, the separation of end rhymes is compounded by an aggravated enjambment until the stabilizing symmetry of rhyme words (need, best, state, speed, rest, wait) is almost entirely withdrawn from immediate auditory apprehension. This by a poet for whom visual rhymes – eye rhymes – had withdrawn to the realm of shades. The injunction Patience delivers to the man of faith is that of unrelenting vigilance: no soothing, sonorous reiterations will pass for action in the harsh light cast by eternity; you must stand (at attention) and wait.

For a structure fully as rigorous as that of the sonnet, but as far from the traditional sonnet in pacing and proportion as verse may be, we may consult the slightly more than sonnet-length passage that constitutes the first sentence of *Paradise Lost*:

> Of Man's First Disobedience, and the Fruit
> Of that Forbidden Tree, whose mortal taste
> Brought Death into the World, and all our woe,
> With loss of *Eden*, till one greater Man
> Restore us, and regain the blissful Seat,
> Sing Heav'nly Muse, that on the secret top
> Of *Oreb*, or of *Sinai*, didst inspire
> That Shepherd, who first taught the chosen Seed,
> In the Beginning how the Heav'ns and Earth
> Rose out of *Chaos*: Or if *Sion* Hill
> Delight thee more, and *Siloa*'s Brook that flow'd
> Fast by the Oracle of God; I thence
> Invoke thy aid to my advent'rous Song,
> That with no middle flight intends to soar
> Above th'*Aonian* Mount, while it pursues
> Things unattempted yet in Prose or Rhyme.

We call this syntax Latinate, by which we mean to refer to the firm architecture of sub- and super-ordination of which Latin and other highly inflected languages are capable. And, indeed, the architectural solidity of this sentence is all but palpable, as an old-fashioned school-room device makes wonderfully clear (see Figure 6.1)[3]. 'Blueprint' is too weak an analogy for the structural revelation a diagram of this sentence affords: its power is more like that of a CAT scan.

The poet builds an elaborate edifice of interlocking modifiers cantilevered (brooding) over the abyss, secured at one point only, by the

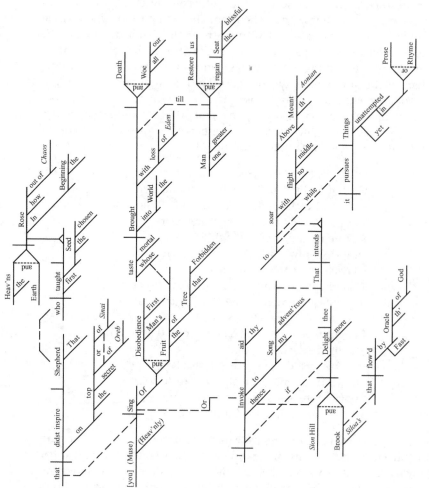

*Figure 6.1  Paradise Lost 1 1–16.*

narrowest possible main clause, by *sing*, a single monosyllabic word in the imperative mood. *Muse* is not the grammatical subject; *muse* is an appositive. The grammatical subject, as is all but universally the case in the imperative mood, is 'understood', which understanding is both the premise and the project of the poem. 'Something understood', writes Herbert in the ravishing breakthrough that constitutes the soul in prayer.[4] Milton's speaker summons the divine second person (or His attendant emanation, which is all to the same effect; the god is required to exist) by an act of will, the sheer coercive act of grammatical address, and simultaneously by an act of complete submission, by conceding power to a second person who must always be construed as first, the single underwriter of the universe. And under the (unspoken) name of this single underwriter the poet claims to stand.

The imperative mood has no tense and therefore is not bound by the ordinary divisions of time. The heavenly intercessor the poet summons is eternal, as is the vision this intercessor is summoned to provide. Yet Milton's sentence unfolds in time and, in its temporal contours, enacts a compressed version of the epic poem it launches, a cognitive progress in which prolepsis and retrospection are inseparably entwined. The story the poet proposes to tell is that which made the present what it is and what, except for this story, it need not have been: a time inflected by mortality. Death enters the world and the sentence as a contingency, as the grammatical object of *brought*, which action is governed by the grammatical subject *taste*, which is itself the property of *fruit* and, conceptually if not grammatically, of *disobedience*. So Death, which to those of imperfect apprehension seems to impugn the perfect goodness of a perfectly powerful and perfectly knowing God, is unveiled in the context of its proper subordination: as the mere by-product of sin.

The invocatory sentence unfolds in a meantime, the time between first disobedience and final redemption: 'till one greater Man / Restore us'. Much is elided here, not least the whole of history. Redemption is problematically lodged in a deferred time all its own. The Incarnation, which Christians have been taught to construe as their redemption, has retreated into an ever more distant past, while the promised defeat of death this Incarnation was supposed to entail has retreated to an ever more difficult-to-imagine futurity. Is it futurity at all? The clauses that posit a limit to death and 'all our woe' may be imagined to contain a suppressed auxiliary verb: 'till one greater Man / [shall] Restore us, and regain the blissful Seat'. But they may as plausibly belong to the realm of the subjunctive, the grammatical mood that governs wish, hypothesis, and conditions contrary-to-fact.

This much of the traditional sonnet the sixteen lines of the anti-sonnet retain: the vocational foundation, the production of poetic voice as an attempt to conjure the beloved into being. The beloved, in this case the Creator, is addressed not by name nor attribute nor local habitation but by 'meaning'. You: you know who you are; you spoke to Moses as now I ask you to speak to me. Do you prefer Siloa's brook to Sinai? Do you prefer to be imagined as a muse? an angel? the third part of Trinity? May I call you Light, or Urania, and not be misunderstood? 'The meaning, not the Name I call' (*PL* 7 5), lest you refuse me on a technicality.

The first sentence of the first book of the story that comprehends all others pivots at its center on a double beginning: 'who first taught [. . .] / In the Beginning'. In the beginning the heavens and earth rose out of Chaos. In the beginning of their life as a nation of faith, the chosen were taught the story of creation, which story has been gathered in a book. In the beginning, when death was still unknown and, more, was not inevitable, there was a Word where now are only words, which obsessively reiterate the breach in meaning even as they attempt to heal it. First causes are beyond our immediate apprehension; on the other side of the division made by sin, beginnings can only be inferred retroactively. What can be apprehended immediately, what is in fact reiterated in every present moment, is the cause of first division, so 'disobedience', or rather, the 'Of', the preposition that makes disobedience the grounding condition of all that is to follow, launches the poem. Grammatical agency belongs to the one who 'sings', but who is that? The poet who commands but is himself the child of sin and thus requires enlightenment? Or the muse who is commanded? Both are agents in the secondary sense, servants to something prior. It is the business of the sentence to launch the song, and this it does. Before the sentence can end, it must vest the song itself with grammatical agency; it is the song that 'intends to soar'. Intention is the bedrock of Milton's prosody. Denying death all morphological distinction and all original presence, conceding to death only the borrowed and perpetually deteriorating shape of that in which it takes up residence, the poet crafts a song that, line by line and sentence by sentence, defies dissolution. Spenser's is a very different project.

I have written elsewhere about the overdetermined and competing formal contracts – to pentameter and alexandrine, to a nine-line pattern of reiterated rhyme, to the divergent representational planes of epic persona and allegorical personification, to the triple and septenary formulas of fairy tale and biblical narrative, to the inherited figures of erotic praise and the evolving figures of Protestant politics, to the forward momentums of narrative and the lingering of exegesis – that make *The Faerie Queene* exceed all usual methods of authorial control.[5] Five parts adrenaline and five parts inertia, the poem is chronically ahead of itself and chronically in arrears on its promises. It is fraught with redundancy, hiatus, and aggravated, crossbred, layered oppositions. Ungainliness is the soul of its poetic method; unfinished, it seems to us now, is what it was always destined to be. If Milton's syntax defies dissolution, Spenser's seems to woo it. These attributes are commonly observed and plausibly attributed to the distinctive generic affiliations of Milton's and Spenser's major poems: the relative dominance of Virgilian epic on the one hand and Ariostan romance on the other. I am arguing at present that something else – some opposition between poetic method and the perceived anatomy of death – is also at stake. And I would like in this context to consider two of Spenser's shorter poems.

## Death and generation

The undersongs in Spenser's wedding poems are those of a river and a wood. The river is a tidal river, obedient to the cycles of the moon and shadowed by temporality; it passes through a city whose 'bricky towres' are obedient to the cycles of worldly pride and shadowed by pride's decay. The river may flood or may dry up altogether, but the poet of the *Prothalamion* bids 'not yet': 'Against the Brydale day, which is not long: / Sweete *Themmes* runne softly, till I end my Song' (*Prothalamion* 17–18).[6] The woods are the woods of a rich estate, the source of wealth and title, obliging to merchants' daughters (*Epithalamion* 167) and to young men of the town (*E* 261), willing to second and sustain their public celebrations: 'The whiles doe ye this song unto her sing, / The woods shall to you answer and your Eccho ring' (*E* 54–5). But the posts and walls that are sprinkled with wine in honor of a colonial wedding will in three short years be overthrown and the colonist forced to flee. The woods are the same woods that Irenius knows to be sheltering the remnants of an earlier and hostile population. The uneasiness that assumes melodic contours in the *Epithalamion*, as in its Thames-side sister, is in part a species of social and political foreboding. But the singer's darker intimations also go beyond the temporal: bride and bridegroom turn to the act of generation under night's 'broad wing' (*E* 319).

The *Prothalamion* opposes a troubled mind to beneficent natural elements and derives from the social and political realm a crisis of soul. Like Redcrosse Knight in the sway of Despair, the speaker who makes his way toward the banks of the Thames at the beginning of the poem suffers more from failures of spirit, and from recognizing his failures of spirit, than from circumstance, distressing as circumstance may be. The blessings of a bountiful creation have been all but lost on him:

> Calme was the day, and through the trembling ayre,
> Sweete breathing *Zephyrus* did softly play
> A gentle spirit, that lightly did delay
> Hot *Titans* beames, which then did glyster fayre:
> When I whom sullein care,
> Through discontent of my long fruitlesse stay
> In Princes Court, and expectation vayne
> Of idle hopes, which still doe fly away,
> Like empty shaddowes, did afflict my brayne,
> Walkt forth to ease my payne . . .

(Prothalamion 1–10)

The very syntax bespeaks a mind in pursuit of shadows. 'Calme was the day [. . .] When I [. . .] Walkt forth': well enough. The interruptive clauses in which Zephyr plays, a spirit delays, and beams glister admittedly digress, but 'lightly', gratefully, in the manner of the breeze itself: this portion of the sentence can be parsed. But how shall we parse the clause (clauses?) that purport to explicate the 'I'? 'I whom sullein care [. . .] did afflict?' This much would be plausible, but what then of 'my brayne', which awkwardly competes with 'whom' (meaning 'I') for the position of direct object of the verb? The preposition that introduces 'idle hopes' appears to promise some tighter delineation of 'expectation vayne', but the second phrase seems to reiterate rather than properly to modify the first. Sullen care appears to have derailed the sentence. While passing through the byways of idle hopes and empty shadows, the grammatical subject ('I') forgets the extent to which he has promised, by means of syntactical contract, to secure the dependent clause: 'When I whom sullein care [. . .]'. The force of grammatical agency passes willy nilly to the idle hopes and empty shadows; they afflict 'my brayne'; the subjective binding force of 'whom' is abandoned.

The speaker does in some sense rescue the sentence when he 'walks forth', recovering the thread of action and, not so incidentally, the force of the containing clause. And he will, in the course of the poem, regain the shores of human kinship and studied hopefulness, but despair will retain its undertow. The poem's reiterated movement is 'against': 'Against the Brydale day, which is not long'. *Against* bears a temporal imprint of course: it may signify anticipation or temporal approach, as in 'ever gainst that season comes / Wherein our Saviour's birth is cele-brated, / This bird of dawning singeth all night long' (*Hamlet* 1.1. 158–60). Spenser's wedding song is sung before (*pro*) the bridal chamber (*thalamos*), in anticipation of (against) the bridal ceremony, which will not be long in coming (it is almost here).

*Against* may also signal a sort of exchange, a scale of reciprocity or return: 'Against his great love, we have only obedience to offer' ('Against,' *OED*, entry 14). In honor of the ceremony that binds the bride to bridegroom, and both to the larger community, the poet offers his song as a form of tribute and anticipatory payment for benefits received. The bridal day marks the public claim in private contract and private affection. The principals and their attendants are surrogates for a larger interest. The merest passerby is understood to have a stake in orderly alliance and sanctioned propagation. His song constitutes a formal gift or offering and in this guise it is recuperative. Like the more specific praise accorded to a patron of the wedding in Stanza 9 ('Great *Englands* glory and the Worlds wide wonder'), the bridal tribute restores a system of reciprocal obligation whose disruption has occasioned the poet's discontent. His song is offered *on account*, as antidote to disappointment and social unravelling.

But *against* is also and always oppositional. The song that celebrates the pleasures and the fruitful issue of a chaste bed imagine those bless-ings as 'confounding' foes (*P* 105). 'Fairness' is chronically partnered with foulness, as though beauty could not be known except as the product of contradistinction: even the silver river, the lifeline of the poem, seems 'foule' next to the swans it bears (*P* 48). And swans them-selves are 'fowles': the fair/fowl pun bespeaks an endemic apprehension, as do the remarkable yokings of 'Loves dislike' and 'friendships faultie guile' (*P* 99). Milton will later insist this mode of knowing is acquired: to know one thing by means of another, to know good by means of evil, is the epistemological fruit of the Fall. Spenser paints in more inef-fable gradations, but the over-againstness so chronic in this poem bears witness to a similar divide between the mortal and the transcendent. Wishing to attribute to the sister brides and their pair of bridegrooms a more-than-earthly brightness, he likens them to the double set of twins engendered on fair Leda by Jove. But those twins are the children of rape; only by an act of violence can godhead be thought to enter the human directly.

Which may be why both temporal and topographical point of view are so elusive in the *Prothalamion*. The speaker describes himself in Stanza 1 as walking along the banks of the Thames, yet in Stanzas 3 and

7, and therefore in the stanzas that fall between them, he appears to be observing a bridal progression from the banks of the tributary Lee. He is both inside (Stanzas 8–10) and outside (the stanzas preceding) the city of London. The particularity with which he binds perspective at the beginning of the poem, in the confession of sullen care, as later in the recital of birthplace and family ('London, my most kyndly Nurse', 'a house of auncient fame' *P* 128, 131) and in the lament for his patron Leicester (*P* 138–42), this grounding in personal history and aspiration gives way, albeit inconsistently, to overview.

The refrain is at once a bridge and a divide. The bridal day now 'is', now 'was', and its temporal oscillation is far more complex than the mere alternation of present and past. The 'Brydale day' in Stanza 1 is not, not yet, the day on which Katherine and Elizabeth Somerset will celebrate their betrothal to Henry Guildford and William Petre. Not yet tethered to individuated circumstance and expectation, the bridal day enters the poem obliquely, by way of an extended ornament: the riverbank and meads are adorned with flowers 'fit' for the decking of 'maydens bowres', which bowers bring the verses by way of association to 'Brydale day'. So too in Stanza 9, where the refrain is grounded in a direct address to the Earl of Essex:

> Faire branch of Honor, flower of Chevalrie,
> That fillest *England* with thy triumphes fame,
> Joy have thou of thy noble victorie,
> And endlesse happinesse of thine owne name
> That promiseth the same:
> That through thy prowesse and victorious armes,
> Thy country may be freed from forraine harmes:
> And great *Elisaes* glorious name may ring
> Through al the world, fil'd with thy wide Alarmes,
> Which some brave muse may sing
> To ages following,
> Upon the Brydale day, which is not long:
>   Sweet *Themmes* runne softly till I end my Song.

(*P* 150–62)

The governing verb is 'is', but it no longer signals the present tense, nor does this 'Brydale day' primarily anticipate the one on which three prominent English families will seal an advantageous alliance. The bridal day imagined here bespeaks a much more sweeping futurity, a consummation not of young men and women but of the Elizabethan state.

How is it that 'was' can enter the refrain at all? The *Prothalamion* is all before the fact (*pro*), all anticipatory. In the simplest sense, 'was' signals the transition to historical narration. In Stanza 2, the poet begins his turn to the particular, the topical, wedding: the nymphs gather flowers 'against' the bridal day which 'was' not long, that is, would not be long in coming; within the historical narration, this 'was' is a species of futurity. And 'was' obtains as well in Stanzas 3, 4, 5, and 7, all the stanzas that concern themselves with the actual, the bound-by-place-and-person wedding. The modulated refrain in Stanza 6 ('Upon your Brydale day, which is not long: / Sweet *Themmes* run softlie, till I end my Song') can accommodate the present tense again not because it digresses from the Somerset marriage to something more abstract but because it is more specific yet, beginning inside an interpolated 'lay':

> Ye gentle Birdes, the worlds faire ornament,
>
> . . .
>
> Joy may you have and gentle hearts content
> Of your loves couplement:
>
> . . .
>
> Let endlesse Peace your steadfast hearts accord,
> And blessed Plentie wait upon your bord,
> And let your bed with pleasures chast abound,
> That fruitfull issue may to you afford,
> Which may your foes confound,
> And make your joyes redound,
> Upon your Brydale day, which is not long:
> Sweet *Themmes* run softlie, till I end my Song.
>
> (*P* 91–108)

In the present stanza, it is only the second line of the couplet that is sung by the poet; the first line is sung directly to the bird-brides by an attendant nymph.

I have been writing as though that other temporal marker, 'not long', were unambiguous, but of course its ambiguity is the most resonant in the poem. Even in those syntactical configurations that bind 'not long' most clearly to the realm of expectation – when the bridal day is most explicitly said to be, or to have been, nearly upon us – the phrase has a way of escaping its bonds, overshadowing imminence with brevity. Thus the justness of Eliot's adaptation in 'The Fire Sermon':

> Sweet Thames, run softly till I end my song,
> Sweet Thames, run softly, for I speak not loud or long.
>
> (T. S. Eliot, *The Waste Land* 183–4)

If ever an inversion decisively fulfilled an earlier poetic incarnation (and in eloquent illustration of the author's own theories about poetic tradition), this is it. Spenser's bridal day is fleeting. Even in the visionary ninth stanza of the *Prothalamion*, when national and political culmination are imagined as sung to 'ages following', the culmination is 'not long'. That culmination is most unambiguously brief which is most sweepingly, least topically, invoked: in the first and final stanzas of Spenser's poem. Brevity is the one eternal verity. Like the river and the song, the bridal day is mortal: mortality is what it celebrates.

## Death again

> Ye learned sisters which have oftentimes
> beene to me ayding, others to adorne:
> Whom ye thought worthy of your gracefull rymes,
> That even the greatest did not greatly scorne
> To heare theyr names sung in your simple layes,
> But joyed in theyr prayse:
> And when ye list your owne mishaps to mourne,
> Which death, or love, or fortunes wreck did rayse,
> Your string could soone to sadder tenor turne,
> And teach the woods and waters to lament
> Your dolefull dreriment:
> Now lay those sorrowfull complaints aside,
> And having all your heads with girland crownd,
> Helpe me mine owne loves prayses to resound,
> Ne let the same of any be envide,
> So Orpheus did for his owne bride,
> So I unto my selfe alone will sing,
> The woods shall to me answer and my Eccho ring.

*(Epithalamion* 1–18)

When, in the *Epithalamion*, the wedding song is sung by the bridegroom himself, the living terms of its refrain are 'answer' and 'echo'. Its musical poles are song (including songs of 'dolefull dreriment' and 'th'unpleasant Quyre of Frogs' E 11, 349) and silence; its rhetorical poles are prohibition and solicitation; its temporal poles are futurity and something yet more tenuous. This echoing refrain inhabits a temporality even more complex than that of the refrain in the *Prothalamion*. In some iterations, the song appears to be sanguine: 'The woods shall to me answer and my Eccho ring' (*E* 17–18). In others, more tentative and petitionary: 'Be also present heere, / To helpe to decke her and to help to sing, / That all the woods may answer and your eccho ring' (*E* 71–3). And in others poised upon a paradox of presence and omission:

> Why stand ye still ye virgins in amaze,
> Upon her so to gaze,
> Whiles ye forget your former lay to sing,
> To which the woods did answer and your eccho ring.

> (*E* 181–4)

'Answer' is partnered more often than not in these verses by a modal auxiliary ('shall', 'will', 'may', or 'should') conveying obligation or intent, hoped-for or probable futurity. Sometimes 'answer' enters the verses by way of 'that' ('That all the woods may answer'), which governs the subjunctive. Three times 'answer' is prefaced by the hortatory 'let'. In one very problematic case, in Stanza 23, the final line of the stanza seems to escape the bonds of syntax altogether. The one condition in which the woods are never made to answer nor their echo ring, not once in the course of twenty-four stanzas, is the present indicative.

For two thirds the length of his poem, in sixteen stanzas out of twenty-four, the bridegroom promises or prompts an echoing 'answer' as a positive good. The groom 'will' sing. The muses, the nymphs of Mulla, the handmaids of Venus, the minstrels and choristers, the young men of the town, the very angels are enjoined to sing. The answering woods and ringing echo are construed as a sustaining endorsement of the bride's beauty and her bridegroom's happiness. But with the bedding of the bride in Stanza 17, and for the duration of the poem, the force of the refrain is largely inverted:

> Now it is night, ye damsels may be gon,
> And leave my love alone,
> And leave likewise your former lay to sing:
> The woods no more shal answere, nor your echo ring.

> (*E* 311–14)

Not only has the singer turned to silence and prohibition. He has also turned from an imagined sympathy with the social and the natural worlds to a place of oppositional and precarious 'safety' (*E* 325). In the language of a formal spell or blessing, very like Puck's formal blessing of the bedchambers in that other midsummer wedding poem, *A Midsummer Night's Dream*, the singer now enjoins the woods to suppress the fearful sounds of screech owl, stork, and raven. He peoples the world outside the bridal chamber with 'false treason' and 'sad afray' (*E* 323, 327). He fears 'housefyres' and 'lightnings' (*E* 340), 'false whispers' and 'lamenting cryes' (*E* 336, 334). If the bedding of the bride betokens pleasure and fecundity, it also betokens danger: the groom from his wedding chamber calls upon Juno to protect his love in childbed.

The *Epithalamion* is not a poem of despair. The getting of children is a virtuous delight and a continuing re-enactment of creation, the bestowing of beneficent form: a 'chast wombe informe[d] with timely seed' (*E* 386). Children breed comfort. Posterity is an enlargement of spirit. But children are not an escape from mortality, quite the contrary. Children increase mortality's count, and for the parent, they increase mortality's consequence. Spenser's auto-epithalamion celebrates the work of generation and the union of flesh and celebrates perforce the flesh's strict entailment, which is death. The one is corollary to the other. It is Wallace Stevens rather than Eliot who has best glossed the essential act of praise:

> Beauty is momentary in the mind –
> The fitful tracing of a portal;
> But in the flesh it is immortal.

> ('Peter Quince at the Clavier')

And for short time an endlesse moniment.

## Notes

1. Here and elsewhere, citations from Milton's poetry will be based on the *Complete Poems and Major Prose*, ed. Merritt Y. Hughes (Upper Saddle River, NJ: Prentice Hall, 1957).
2. See *The Faerie Queene*. Ed. A. C. Hamilton (London and New York: Longman, 1977).
3. My thanks to James Winn for the original template and to Anthony Cece for technical assistance.
4. Herbert's sonnet is itself a remarkable exercise in syntactical abridgement, enacting the cognitive drama of prayer, the effort to reach the divine by means of submission, in a series of exclusively nominative phrases:

Prayer (I)

Prayer the Churches banquet, Angels age,
  Gods breath in man returning to his birth,
  The soul in paraphrase, heart in pilgrimage,
The Christian plummet sounding heav'n and earth;

Engine against th'Almightie, sinners tower,
  Reversed thunder, Christ-side-piercing spear,
  The six-daies world-transposing in an houre,
A kind of tune, which all things heare and fear;

Softnesse, and peace, and joy, and love, and blisse,
  Exalted Manna, gladnesse of the best,
  Heaven in ordinarie, man well drest,
The milkie way, the bird of Paradise,

    Church-bels beyond the starres heard, the souls bloud,
    The land of spices; something understood.

  *The English Poems of George Herbert*

5. See *The Reformation of the Subject: Spenser, Milton and the English Protestant Epic* (1995).
6. Here and elsewhere, citations from Spenser's shorter poems will be based on *The Yale Edition of the Shorter Poems of Edmund Spenser*, eds William A. Oram, Einar Bjorvand, Ronald Bond, Thomas H. Cain, Alexander Dunlop, and Richard Schell (New Haven; London: Yale University Press, 1989).

# 7

# Reading, Death and the Ethics of Enjoyment in Spenser and Milton

*Marshall Grossman*

Whatever else it might entail, thinking about Spenser, Milton, and death is a literary historical exercise: Literary because these thoughts will deal with verbal forms – genres, tropes, schemes. Historical because changes in literary forms disclose traces of history embedded in the context of the work, and because literary innovation – the disposition of old and new facts into new configurations, both figural and narrative – is itself a historical event. *The Faerie Queene* and *Paradise Lost* are implicitly joined by commonality of sources and models – most notably *The Aeneid*, the *Gerusulemme Liberata* and Tasso's accompanying discussion of allegory – and by their bardic ambitions. They are explicitly joined by Milton's explicit refusal 'to dissect / With long and tedious havoc fabled knights / In battles feigned [. . .]' (9, 29–31).[1] One literary historical event that transpires between them is a troping of narrative form from allegory in Spenser to what might be called a narrative of historical causation in Milton, and a consequent shift from exemplary to dialectical presentations of character – that is, from characters whose history grows out of what they are, to characters whose history accounts for what they have become.[2] In even broader terms, I think this shift in narration signals or incorporates a shift from mimetic verisimilitude to expressive authenticity as the governing criterion of poetic truth.

Admittedly, these generalizations are broad enough to require a book or two. I raise these big questions now only as context for a more modest meditation on the differences in the narration of death in *The Faerie Queene* and *Paradise Lost* and what those differences might begin to tell us about the joys of reading these two poems. The broader literary history of a transition from mimesis to expression is only suggested as a process, part of which may be possibly exemplified by these two specimen texts.

# 1

Thinking seriously about Spenser and death is hard. It is possible to suspect that, at least in *The Faerie Queene,* Spenser did not take death very seriously – not the way, for example, that Augustine, or Milton or Lacan did: as incorporating stages and degrees, transitions and trans-figurations, requiring a plot and theory of its own. Spenser's creatures just seem to die and be done with it, perhaps secure in the knowledge that whatever thing they have represented in their textual lives will quickly reappear, reinvested elsewhere in the fecund landscape of Faeryland: as when Priamond is cleft through 'His weasand pipe' by Cambell: 'Thence streames of purple bloud issuing rife, / Let forth his wearie ghost and made an end of strife.' But,

> His wearie ghost assoyld from fleshly band,
> Did not as others wont, directly fly
> Vnto her rest in Plutoes grisly land,
> Ne into ayre did vanish presently,
> Ne chaunged was into a starre in sky:
> But through traduction was eftsoones deriued,
> Like as his mother preyd the Destinie,
> Into his other brethren, that suruiued,
> In whom he liu'd a new, of former life depriued.

> (4.3.12–13)[3]

Death here is not the final act conferring meaning on a life history, but rather the divagation of a textual motif, disappearing beneath the warp only to reemerge elsewhere in the design.

A qualitative difference between the representations of death in *The Faerie Queene* and in *Paradise Lost* is integral to the different pleasures afforded by these texts. I will characterize them, respectively, as plea-sures of anticipation and deferral, in the former, and of the terrible fascination of retrospection in the latter. In short, Spenserian death is always something to come, so that 'the readiness is all', while Miltonic death has always already arrived. It comes in the epic's first lines 'with the 'fruit / Of that forbidden tree, whose mortal taste / Brought death into our world and all our woe' (*Paradise Lost* 1, 1–3), and we learn in Book 2 that even before it entered Eden, Death was already lustily chasing its mother about the gates of hell, having been conceived on her by Satan in heaven, at the start of the angelic rebellion. Thus Death both begins and antedates Milton's narrative.

The differently deadly pleasures of Spenserian and Miltonic death are, in turn, consequent to the different procedures of reading elicited by *The Faerie Queene* and *Paradise Lost*. One gets *Paradise Lost* into one's head and when it is all there, wonderful things happen – connections are made, echoes heard, expectations revised and meditated on. But, as David Miller has remarked, one cannot get *The Faerie Queene* into one's head. At least, I've never been able to get it into mine. It won't fit. In fact, every time I read it, it wiggles and creeps around the pages, as though it might be writing itself all over again; in Faeryland what seems furniture one moment or one reading comes alive the next. Nothing holds still, except perhaps the Bower of Bliss, in which stillness itself figures death, or, at least, the life-in-death of the supine Sir Verdant in Acrasia's curiously maternal pieta. Even more distressing than the mysterious antics of the wayward words on the page I am reading, is the conviction that the words on the page I have just turned have already rearranged themselves, doubled or tripled in number, sent perhaps a false, perhaps a snowy Florimell, down one previously undiscovered forest path, Una, or a dream spright, or Duessa down another.

In contrast, as a text in which death has always already occurred, *Paradise Lost* is never read but always re-read, as it is itself a re-reading of Genesis 1–4, and of Augustine's re-reading of Genesis 1–4 at the end of *The Confessions*, and of countless other hexameral writings. The title and the opening lines tell us what will have happened at the end so that each narrated episode we encounter is (re)read according to its anticipated consequence, even as it unfolds.

Take, for example, the complex triangulation of the reader's position with respect to a crucial moment in Book 4 of *Paradise Lost*. At this point Satan has entered Eden and observes Adam and Eve, who are also introduced to the reader as Satan observes them. While Satan watches, disguised in the form of various edenic animals, Adam speaks to Eve, praising God for the bounty of the garden:

> . . . he who requires
> From us no other service than to keep
> This one, this easy charge, of all the trees
> In Paradise that bear delicious fruit
> So various, not to taste that only Tree
> Of Knowledge, planted by the Tree of Life,
> So near grows death to life, whate'er death is,
> Some dreadful thing no doubt . . .

> (4.419–26)

To read these lines is to experience the dissonance between Adam's innocence of the meaning of *death* and one's postlapsarian self. Not only does the reader recognize that his or her perspective on the scene is the consequence of the choice Adam will make, but also that Satan too hears Adam's words and will use his superior knowledge of *death* and Adam's ignorance to bring 'death into our world, and all our woe'. The reader has met *Death* in the allegorical character of Satan's son in Book 2, and presumably knows also yet another revision, which Adam will learn only in Book 12, 'that suffering for truth's sake / Is fortitude to highest victory, / And to the faithful death the gate of life' (569–71). The scene must therefore be read as a moment unfolding in time that is always already transformed by its most temporally remote consequences. For Adam, *death* is perceived as a formless 'dreadful thing' that lies in consequence of transgression, while the presence of evil is unseen; for the reader, Adam's innocence is the anamorphic stain that can only be glimpsed when Satan's presence is momentarily forgotten.[4] The principle of reading at work is that every view is a partial view of some unseen totality and meaning can only be stabilized by bringing the story to an end. As Hegel's owl of Minerva flies at dusk, Milton's narrative voice becomes clear only in the moment that it falls silent.

While *Paradise Lost* can only be re-read, *The Faerie Queene* can only be read, because it exceeds and evades memory as effectively as *Paradise Lost* captures and contains it. To read it over is less to read it again than to extend indefinitely an always incomplete first reading. In fact, we cannot even try to read *The Faerie Queene* to find out what happens in the end, because its end is a phantom evoked in the impossibly grand design of twenty-four books suggested in the 'Letter to Ralegh', which renders incompletion a part of the poem's formal design, nor do we reread it to understand each episode as contributing to the end we have discovered. Between the end promised in the 'Letter' and the end effected after six books, and the possible second end of the fragment of 'Mutabilitie', which would be at best the middle of an end, gaps not bridged by any narrative are circumscribed, insisted upon and left blank. These silences, so carefully surrounded by noise, exemplify the weakness of death in *The Faerie Queene*. The poem is interrupted but not decisively. Were another book or two discovered somewhere in the vicinity of Kilcommen, we would happily restart it even now. As Jonathan Goldberg pointed out, the endlessness of *The Faerie Queene* is not a contingent but a formal feature of Spenser's narration.

While the reader of each Spenserian stanza dies for the suspended moment of the alexandrine's sixth foot, only to draw breath and begin again with the pentameter of the next new stanza, the propulsive para-graphs of *Paradise Lost* press us forward to the silence at the end.[5] No one ever mistakes Milton's own sequel, *Paradise Regained,* for a contin-uation. Stylistically, as well as thematically, the 'brief epic' is a different book.

It makes historical sense that Spenser's mercurial text should serve the hermetic intention of the allegorist, while Milton's text, especially in its last two books, works toward but does not reach the self-consciously Protestant plainness its author will achieve in *Paradise Regained.*[6] But a literary historical understanding of the difference between Spenserian and Miltonic representations of death ought also to account for the dis-tinctness of each performance as a matter of form, and then specify the mediations by which the difference in form responds to and transfigures history. Some of this work has been done by Gordon Teskey, for whom *The Faerie Queene* and *Paradise Lost* exemplify two formally different prin-ciples of narration, which he labels allegorical and dialectical respec-tively. 'In Spenser,' Teskey writes 'error is represented *diegetically,* in all the various forms offered by narrative romance. In Milton, error is rep-resented *dialectically,* as the negation of all that is good' ('From Allegory' 9). As Milton's God, the father, sardonically explains:

> O sons, like one of us man is become
> To know both good and evil, since his taste
> Of that defended fruit; but let him boast
> His knowledge of good lost, and evil got.
>
> (11, 84–6)

These two narrative modes establish and partly mediate the semantic gap between the spatial and the ethical aspects of the word *error,* which retains the *errancy* of wandering in Spenser's poem, but comes to mean *that which will turn out to have been a morally* wrong choice in Milton's. Indeed, Milton famously marks the transition between the two senses of *error* in his descriptions of a prelapsarian river, 'Rolling on orient pearl and sands of gold, / With mazy *error* under pendant shades' and Eve's 'unadorned golden tresses' worn 'Dishevelled, but in *wanton* ringlets waved, / As the vine curls her tendrils . . .' (4.238–6; 305–7), which force us to read the innocence of Edenic *error* and *wanton* against the moral judgments they will have become for us.[7]

But perhaps the most dramatic witness of the distinction between these two narrative modes may be seen in Milton's grafting of Spenser's dragon of error onto Hesiod's account of the birth of Athena to gener-ate the meta-allegorical characters, *Sin* and *Death.* Milton's Sin:

> seemed woman to the waist, and fair,
> But ended foul in many a scaly fold
> Voluminous and vast, a serpent armed
> With mortal sting: about her middle round
> A cry of Hell-hounds never ceasing barked
> With wide Cerberean mouths full loud, and rung
> A hideous peal; yet when they list, would creep,
> If ought disturbed their noise, into her womb,
> And kennel there, yet still barked and howled
> Within unseen.

(*PL* 2, 650–9)

This description of Sin retains a good part of the language Spenser used to describe the dragon of error and her whelps:

> Her huge long taile her den all ouerspred,
> Yet was in knots and many boughtes vpwound,
> Pointed with mortall sting. Of her there bred
> A thousand yong ones, which she dayly fed,
> Sucking vpon her poisonous dugs, eachone
> Of sundry shapes, yet all ill fauored:
> Soon as that vncouth light vpone them shone,
> Into her mouth they crept, and suddain all were gone.

(*FQ* I, 1, 15.1–5)

Two details of Milton's imitation of Spenser are particularly illustrative. The first is the way that the contents of Error's stomach, revealed in her 'vomit full of bookes and papers' (I.1.20.6), are retained in Milton's version but condensed into the single word, *voluminous* (that is, full of volume[s]), used to describe Sin's 'scaly folds'. The second is Milton's condensation in the scene of Sin and Death at the gates of hell of the Dragon of Error from the first canto and the more formidable dragon of Sin from the eleventh canto of *The Faerie Queene* I. There is something platonic about Spenser's dragons and the dragonlets they spawn. The mother dragons are corporate representations that function as the source and sustenance of error and sin in the multiple substantive forms in which they are encountered in the sensible realm. They are, one might say, accumulative – each new despicable thing issues from and returns to the dragons' dark wombs, but each also retains its particular character. Like the interpretations of a parable, the spawn of error are offspring but not repetitions of the mother text. Milton's conflation of Spenser's dragons of error and of sin, however, posits an identity of cause and effect that collapses all wandering in time and space into an originating mistake or 'first disobedience', that must be retroactively reconstructed. Sin is the mother of error and every error is a sin, spawned and residing beneath 'many a scaly fold / voluminous and vast'.

In *The Faerie Queene* and, interestingly, *Areopagitica* – in which *The Faerie Queene* is curiously misquoted – the result of error is generally, more error, a wrong turn, a prolonged quest with Truth at the ever receding vanishing point.[8] In short, error is story-telling itself, an 'endlesse werke' of self-generation. It is negatively figured in the dragons, but it is also figured positively as spontaneous and fecund transmutation, as in the description of Adonis, hidden within the mount of Venus and productively engaged in and by Spenser's marvelous middle voice of *jouissance*: 'Ioying his Goddess and of her enioyd' (III,6, 48.2):

> All be he subiect to mortalitie,
> Yet is eterne in mutability,
> And by succession made perpetuall,
> Transformed oft and changed diuerslie:
> For him the Father of all formes they call;
> Therefore needs mote he liue, that liuing giues to all.

> (III, 6, 47.4–9)

If mutability accommodated by narrative form evades death in *The Faerie Queene*, narrative captured by repetition manifests it – as in the diurnal repetition of Cupid's mask in III.12 – until it is disrupted by Britomart after she perspicaciously decides that the way to be 'bold enough' but 'not too bold' is to 'stand and wait':

> Where force might not auaile, there sleights and art
> She cast to vse, both fit for hard emprize;
> For thy from that same roome not to depart
> Till morrow next, she did her selfe auize,
> When that same Maske againe should forth arize.

> (III, 12, 28.1–5).

Nothing in the text explains how Britomart knows the mask will be replayed the next day. Rather, her correct assumption rests upon her (and our) intuitive grasp of Spenserian narration. One might say that when a Miltonic character is faced with a choice and goes through the wrong door, he or she drops immediately into an abyss without end: 'to bottomless perdition, there to dwell' (1.47), but the Spenserian knight finds only the wrong – or least optimal – path on the other side of the door and keeps on walking. The path may be infested with dragons, evil hermits, lustful and duplicitous ladies and sexually perverse magicians, but encountering and overcoming these obstacles increases the traveller's perspicacity, until he or she intuitively wanders back onto the right road. Britomart makes the right choice in Busyrane's Castle because she trusts in an idea of copia through cyclic repetition that is embedded in the natural landscape of Faerieland:

> The morrow next appeard with ioyous cheare,
> Calling men to their daily exercize,
> Then she, as morrow fresh, herselfe did reare
> Out of her secret stand, that day for to out weare.

> (III, 12, 28.6–9)

Only the textual silence constitutes a threat to allegory's death-defying errancy, but Spenser, with seeming purpose, cancels silence, as the closure threatened by the embrace of Amoret and Scudamour at the end of the 1590 text is literally crossed out in 1596, and Colin's breaking of his pipe in Book 6 does not seem seriously to impede the narrative force of Calidore's pursuit of Pastorela.

In *Paradise Lost*, self-generation is presumptuous and erroneous, though it may begin as innocent as the wandering of unfallen Eve's wanton tresses; error is never just a turn, but always a wrong turn, and always, in fact, the same wrong turn. Error and death issue from the 'voluminous' folds of Sin, to throw their shadow over our fallen view even of the unfallen world, even though it will not be until Book 10, that Sin and Death build their interstate highway from hell to earth to ease what will have become a daily commute. Miltonic narration captures the energy of Spenser's textual dissonance and condemns it to the death of always returning to the same, perpetually reenacting man's first disobedience and precipitate drop into the 'darkness visible' of the morally obtuse. If Arthur moves through *The Faerie Queene* as presumptive end-product of the unification of all virtues, Sin haunts *Paradise Lost* as his uncanny negation: the compulsive ground of solipsistic pride that inevitably subverts Arthurian magnanimity and its components. For this reason, I would say that, in *Areopagitica*, when Milton sends Guyon down to the cave of Mammon *with his Palmer*, while Spenser did not, the error is a canny one. What solace is the poor Palmer against the centripetal power of spiritual pride envisaged as an obsessive-compulsive repetition latent in every instance of self-assertion?

Reading Milton's narration of death yields its pleasures: the promise of meaning that resides in the imagination that past and present will always prove to have been determined by their anticipated end. As Roland Barthes has noted, this sort of narrative offers the continual conversion of sequence to consequence. Such relief from the energetic exigency of temporal life is easily experienced as pleasure. For Milton, the alternative appears to be uncreation and chaos.

Spenser pre-emptively defers his encounter with death as he pre-emptively defers the end of his 'endlesse werke', while Milton writes from the much more organized perspective of the already dead, threading every detail of each narrative episode through the closure that Spenser, perhaps hysterically, denies. The distinction thus obtained is that between the ever-unfolding destiny of an energy that lives through death by exceeding all of its possible forms and the architectural brilliance of an energy bound and preserved within a vast structure of causation, the capture of sequence by consequence that ingests and engulfs death as climax – like Eve, who, tasting an apple, 'engorged without restraint / And knew not eating death' (*PL* 9, 791–2), or the psalmist, who 'walks in the shadow of death' but fears no evil – or, more recently, the Heideggerian, thrown into being and 'living toward death'.

The great, bloody opening of Robert Bresson's film, *Lancelot du lac*, with its rapid sequence of vignettes of knights clanking their way through a dark wood and hacking each other to death in a series of seemingly random encounters discloses the dark exhaustion that lurks at the end of the Arthurian Quest. In *The Faerie Queene*, however, this profoundly moving image is also gratefully haunted by the battle in *Monty Python and the Search for the Holy Grail*, in which a stubborn knight continues issuing verbal challenges as he loses first one arm, then the other, then a leg, and another, blood spouting in torrents from the torso, as the Knight continues to deprecate his adversary.

Against this defeat of death through the comedy of excess, place the vision of Cain and Abel through which Adam first encounters death in *Paradise Lost*:

> His Off'ring soon propitious Fire from Heav'n
> Consum'd with nimble glance, and grateful steam;
> The other's not, for his was not sincere;
> Whereat he inly rag'd, and as they talke'd,
> Smote him into the Midriff with a stone

That beat out life; he fell, and deadly pale
Groan'd out his Soul with gushing blood effus'd.

(11.441–7)

I suppose that the 'streames of purple bloud issuing rife,' which 'Let
forth' Priamond's 'wearie ghost and made an end of strife', and Abel's
'Soul' 'Groan'd out . . . with gushing blood effus'd' as well as the theme
of 'inly rage' in both texts, share a common source in Vergil's report of
the life of Turnus passing indignantly from his body at the conclusion
of the *Aeneid*:

> '. . . *Pallas te hoc volnere, Pallas*
> *immolat et poenam scelerato ex sanguine sumit,'*
> *hoc dicens ferrum adverso sub pertore condit*
> *fervidus ast illi solvuntur frigore membra*
> *vitaque cum gemitu fugit indignata sub umbras.*[9]

To navigate the Spenserian and the Miltonic tributaries of this Vergilian
stream is to explore differing constructions of the border crossed by
these 'souls' as the characters they animate pass from life to death; the
two tributary streams trace also the border between a mimetic inscription as porous with respect to death as its allegory is to history and the
evocation of inwardness that purports to transubstantiate historical
experience into truth at once revealed and possessed – digested and
assimilated to its own substance: between the forward motion of errors
issuing from the dragon's womb and the history of an error, mobile yet
trapped in Sin's scaly folds, 'voluminous and vast'.

## 2

[C]ould we but forgoe this Prelaticall tradition of crowding free consciences and Christian liberties into canons and precepts of men . . .
I would not despair the greatest design that could be attempted to
make a Church or Kingdom happy. Yet these are the men cry'd out
against for schismaticks and sectaries; as if, while the Temple of the
Lord was building, some cutting, some squaring the marble, others
hewing the cedars, there should be a sort of irrationall men who
could not consider there must be many schisms and many dissec-
tions made in the quarry and in the timber, ere the house of God
can be built. And when every stone is laid artfully together, it cannot
be united into a continuity, it can but be contiguous in this world;

neither can every peece of the building be of one form; nay rather the perfection consists in this, that out of many moderat varieties and brotherly dissimilitudes that are not vastly disporportionall arises the godly and the gracefull symmetry that commends the whole pile and structure.          (*Areopagitica* 2.554–5)

*Areopagitica* is a written simularcrum of an oral address about composing and reading printed pages, and its evocation of the building of the temple is a self-contained allegory of the rhetoric of historical contingency. The above passage also supplies a protocol for reading a dialectical (as opposed to a diegetic) narrative. History itself is envisioned as a story in which the interconnection of various episodes, each with its own motives and causes, will become legible only through the perspective of the end. Somehow, when the 'godly and gracefull symmetry' of the structure emerges from the 'brotherly dissimilitudes' of independent workers toiling in contiguity, it will be seen that their contiguous works will have been, in fact, continuous – in ways the workers themselves could not have anticipated. Since the temple of which Milton writes is a written, indeed, a edifice built of printed books – the reconstruction of lost truth through the unifying sublation of the sum of an unimpeded human discourse – it is clear that the emerging continuity may be thought of as the rationalization of a series of metonymies by a controlling metaphor: resemblance emerges from the ground of adjacency. It is also clear that Milton's figure gives intellectual history a narrative shape, in which each book is an episode in a single action that will not be understood except from the perspective of its ending.

In a political reading of this passage, William Kolbrener remarks, 'out of the contiguity and particularity intrinsic to the fallen world, Milton perceives at least the possibility of "continuity," a "perfection" organizing and ordering difference' (11). For Kolbrener, the trope of contiguity within continuity serves to preserve the integrity of the concrete particular – of the individual and his or her acts – even as it reveals the collective totality in which it is destined to be subsumed. Kolbrener sees in this an implicit mediation of a public sphere: 'Milton's own self-constitution as one who wishes to "promote" his "Countries liberty" (2.487) occurs only within the context of the public realm (which he helped to define), where the individual is at once independent *and* mediated' (12). I would add to this reading an emphatic recognition of the force of the future anterior tense. The contiguity of the individual effort is experienced, but the continuity will be seen only after the

Temple is completed. The myriad stories of human endeavour will have become history only in the perpetually deferred synchrony achieved at the end of individual endeavour, when the unfolding of time as contiguous event is abolished by the continuity of providence. As I said earlier, this moment may be understood in rhetorical terms as the moment when metonymy is arrested by metaphor and association gives way to meaning.[10] The human action and choices unfolding in time are always already mediated by an anticipatory prolepsis of this ever deferred unification – much as the efforts of the carpenters and brick layers at a construction site anticipate the shape of the competed building that will subsumes their individual and specialized endeavours, except that the architectural plan is revealed only partially and at temporal intervals.[11] From the viewpoint of the individual worker, however, the completion of the project also raises the specter of unemployment. Such moments constitute death; no character survives the mythos of which his or her ethos is the effect.[12]

To this, we may contrast again Spenser's tale of Priamond, Diamond and Triamond. The brothers' lives are extended past death by an extension of the plot in which they arise. This extension is in fact a repetition. Priamond fights Cambell and 'dies', but only to transmigrate to Diamond, who continues the fight; Diamond similarly 'dies' and then reappears in Triamond. The fight is then fought again. Life renews itself and persists, on the same level. Spenser's allegory renders time as geographical space, as in the common 'life is a journey' motif. Death on this model is arrival, but the prefatory fantasy in the 'Letter to Ralegh', of a 24-book poem, presenting 12 private and 12 public virtues, ensures that no one ever arrives in *The Faerie Queene*. Moreover, we are told in the 'Letter' that were the poem to reach its middle (or its first end) the non-existent twelfth book would bring us to its beginning with the assignment of quests at the court of Gloriana. As with the diurnal return of the Masque of Cupid, the proposed structure of *The Faerie Queene* itself exemplifies a path whose 'ending' leaves one at the gate and ready to begin the journey once again. Spenser proposes that his edifice, if completed, would bring the 12 (or 24) virtues into a unity in the 'magnanimity' of Arthur. This unity is no more narratable than is that of Milton's anticipation of an end of time, when 'God shall be All in All' (*PL* 3.341). But Spenser's text very significantly substitutes its own interminable analysis of magnanimity for the post-apocalyptic silence proposed by Milton's.

Arthur moves through *The Faerie Queene* as the form of perfected virtue, of which each metonymic knight-virtue is but a part. As such, magnanimity cannot be narrated. Each of the knights undertakes an action that exemplifies and develops his ethos as distinct mode of action. But, as magnanimity is the common ground of all the distinguished virtues, to narrate it would require Spenser to tell all his stories at once; Arthur moves through the text as the image of this metaphoric unification of virtues to suggest that ethos is the author of mythos, that virtue inheres in the person and not the act, but this quest to unify character and action is structured as infinitely deferred – and as internalized by Artegal, whose also deferred marriage to Britomart will have given rise to the future that is the present of Elizabethan England. Similarly Gloriana, Mercilla, Bellephoebe and and Britomart may be figured as anticipatory types of Elizabeth I, but each remains the ethos of her mythos and cannot be sublated into a proper representation of the Queen.

> In that Faery Queene I mean glory in my generall intention, but in my particular I perceiue the most excellent and glorious person of our soueraine the Queene, and her kingdome in Faery Land. And yet in som places els, I doe otherwise shadow her. For considering she beareth two persons, the one a of most royall Queene and Empresse, the other of a most virtuous and beatifull Lady, this latter part in some places I doe expresse in Belphoebe.                                                                    (*Letter to Raleigh* 16)

In *Areopagitica*, however, space is subsumed in time. The image of the building of the temple is used to suggest an analogous collaborative intellectual construction undertaken by 'the sad friends of truth'.[13]

> Truth indeed came once into the world with her divine Master, and was a perfect shape most glorious to look on: but when he ascended, and his Apostles after him were laid asleep, then strait arose a wicked race of deceivers, who as that story goes of the *Ægptian Typhon* with his conspirators, how they dealt with the good *Osiris*, took the virgin Truth, hewd her lovely form into a thousand peeces, and scatter'd them to the four winds. From that time ever since, the sad friends of Truth, such as durst appear, imitating the carefull search that *Isis* made for the mangl'd body of *Osiris*, went up and down gathering up limb by limb still as they could find them. We have not yet found them all, Lords and Commons, nor ever shall doe, till her Masters second coming; he shall bring together every joynt and member, and shall mould them into an immortall feature of loveliness and perfection.                                                      (*Areopagitica*, 2, 549)

Where *The Faerie Queene* figures time as a journey through space, during which the knights discover their virtues in and through their geographical disbursal, *Areopagitica* again figures time as the medium of a centripetal (re)collection. Personifying an originally unified Truth that has been – literally – dismembered, rendered into fragments, Milton assigns to 'the sad friends of Truth' the task of collecting and reconstructing the body. But this reconstruction cannot be achieved in time, because only the second coming will re-assign each written word its *proper* meaning. True to his Aristotelian inspiration, Spenser's construction of magnanimity is largely a matter of acquiring habits. His aim of fashioning a gentleman is not in itself transcendental, but rather a set of worldly situation in which different virtues are called upon and expressed. To acquire a virtue is to be habituated to doing the right thing in varied and unexpected circumstances. Also true to Aristotle, the knights of *The Faerie Queene* claim no existence beyond their actions, no ethos beyond mythos. Milton's dialectical narration, however, tends to leave the mimetic for the sublime so that 'the race of time / Till time stand fixt' is but the antechamber of death: 'beyond is all abyss, / Eternity, whose end no eye can reach' (12.554–6).

The ethics of enjoyment lie in the alternative pleasures offered by these two texts and the modes of narrative they represent, for each fosters a different relation toward death, silence and closure. Doubtless there are historical determinants at work in the appearance of one or the other mode of narration in a given time and place. However, my interest here has been the implications of reading in the present. It strikes me that a reader's choice of the infinite unfolding of contiguity offered by Spenser or the dialectics of metaphoric totalization offered by Milton can profoundly affect the way he or she lives in the world. The ethics of reading inheres in its ability to put the choice before us.

## Notes

1. John Milton, *The Complete Poems*, ed. John Leonard (London: Penguin, 1998). On the formal implications of Milton's rejection of an Arthurian subject, see Teskey, 'Milton's Choice of Subject in the Context of Renaissance Critical Theory'.
2. For a more detailed discussion of literary historical events in general and the transition from allegory to narrative in particular, see my *The Story of All Things: Writing the Self in Renaissance English Narrative Poetry*. See also, Gordon Teskey, 'From Allegory to Dialectic: Imagining Error in Spenser and Milton'.

3. Edmund Spenser, *The Faerie Queene*, ed. Thomas P. Roche, Jr, with the assistance of C. Patrick O'Donnell, Jr, (Harmondsworth, Middlesex: Penguin, 1978).
4. I refer, of course, to Lacan's description of the subject split between the act of seeing and the imagination of being seen. The pleasure of reading Miltonic narrative is entry into a closed symbolic system in which one can almost see oneself seeing, see oneself in the present instance as seeing Adam and as Adam seen by Satan, see Lacan, *The Four Fundamental Concepts of Psycho-Analysis (Seminar Book XI)*, 79–90. See also: *The Seminar of Jacques Lacan Book VII The Ethics of Psychoanalysis 1959–1960*, 272–3.
5. See Kenneth Gross, '"Each Heav'nly Close": Mythologies and Metrics in Spenser and the Early Poetry of Milton'.
6. On Milton's relegation of properly historical action to the final two books of *Paradise Lost*, see Teskey, 'Milton's Choice of a Subject' 57.
7. See Christopher Ricks, *Milton's Grand Style*, 109–17.
8. Alluding to *Faerie Queene* 2.7, Milton has Guyon in the Cave of Mammon incorrectly accompanied by his Palmer. In his gloss on the passage Ernest Sirluck observes that Spenser separates Guyon from the Palmer before the knight's meeting with Mammon 'partly to show that the mere habit of temperance is sufficient to withstand the solicitations of that God' and suggests that 'Milton is in this matter less Aristotelian than Spenser; he is less disposed to rely on the security of habit; in all significant situations, choosing [. . .] is, for him, active reasoning' (*Complete Prose Works of John Milton*, 2, 516n. 109). Sirluck does not dwell, as a Spenserian might, on the high price Guyon pays for his reliance on habit, but in the context of my argument, his observation is acute. Following the *Nicomachean Ethics*, Spenser represents character through habituated choice, whereas Milton's dialectical narration represents choice as determinative of character.
9. *Aeneid* 12.948–52: ' "Tis Pallas, Pallas who with this stroke sacrifices thee, and takes atonement of thy guilty blood." So saying, full in his breast he buries the sword with fiery zeal. But the other's limbs grew slack and chill, and with a moan life passed indignant to the Shades below.'
10. For a more detailed explanation of this rhetorical procedure see *The Story of All Things: The Writing of the Self in English Renaissance Narrative Poetry*, 45–51.
11. For an extended discussion of the dialectical structure of *Paradise Lost*, see my, '*Authors to themselves*': Milton and the Revelation of History', 177–96.
12. On the homologies of repetition, narrative closure and death, see Peter Brooks, 'Freud's Masterplot', *Yale French Studies* 55/56 (1977) 280–300. See also Jonathan Culler, 'Fabula and Sjuzhet in the Analysis of Narrative: Some American Discussions'.
13. On the importance of collaboration in *Paradise Lost*, see Amy Dunham Stackhouse, 'Disseminating the Author: Milton and the Trope of Collaboration', unpublished dissertation, University of Maryland, 1998, 98.

# 8
## Sublime/Pauline: Denying Death in *Paradise Lost*

*Rachel Trubowitz*

Writing in 1936, in the historically resonant moment between the two Wars, Walter Benjamin detailed the disappearance of death from the public stage of modernity, recounting the ways in which death had vanished from common sight, was pushed to the social and intellectual periphery, sublimated and forgotten. 'Dying,' writes Benjamin, 'was once a public process in the life of the individual and a most exemplary one; think of medieval pictures in which the deathbed has turned into a throne toward which the people press through the wide open doors of the death house. In the course of modern times, dying has been pushed further and further out of the perceptual world of the living' (93–4).

This essay turns to *Paradise Lost* as an important early site of modernity's reformation of death, its displacement from 'the perceptual world of the living'. While death is very much 'alive' in many of Milton's texts, his vivid depictions of death are counterpointed by his symptomatic response or, more precisely, non-response to the Crucifixion – Christianity's monument to death and its most potent and widely circulated image. It is telling that Milton attempted only once to address the Crucifixion directly, in his early poem, 'The Passion', and that this attempt short-circuits. The poem's eight stanzas, all introductory, break off before rendering the climactic scene of Christ's dying agony. Never again would Milton write directly on the Passion, preferring only to hint, suggest, or foreshadow Christ's exemplary death. In *Paradise Regained*, for example, he writes not of the Passion, as his title would suggest, but of the Temptation, which he treats as a type of Passion, highlighting the figure rather than the fulfilment. In *Samson Agonistes*, we learn only second-hand of Samson's inscrutable death, since Milton chooses to leave the seeming climax of his drama undramatized, only hinting at its possible role as typological anticipation. Even in early poems, such as 'Upon the Circumcision' and 'The Nativity Ode', Milton never directly represents the Crucifixion's centrality to Christian history.

What are we to make of Milton's sustained detours around the Crucifixion? The most ready answer of course is that Milton as an iconoclastic Puritan conscientiously refuses to celebrate the Christian death-icon. But, it is also possible to read Milton's decentring of the Crucifixion as a 'logical' working out of his culture's disavowal of death as a 'public process', which, as Benjamin observes, can be seen as a defining mark of modernity. As recent studies detail, customary perceptions of death, the afterlife, and funereal rites and rituals underwent radical revision during the sixteenth and seventeenth centuries.[1] When the consolatory devices of the old religion (the doctrine of Purgatory, prayers for the dead, among others), which helped to make death a meaningful communal experience, were dismantled by the dramatic cultural, social, and religious transformations that the period was to witness, death was cut free from the past and the public stage, and remade into a private and 'modern' experience. But, if no longer meaningful or valuable in customary terms, reformed or 'modern' death was also difficult for the newly individualized psyche to comprehend and represent. When Mass, for example, was condemned by the English Church as an outmoded and 'primitive' communal ritual, even Christ's exemplary death became less palpable, public, and hence conventionally significant – thus, Milton's afore-mentioned reluctance to put the Crucifixion on the page, despite its customary centrality to Christian history and doctrine.

This essay argues that, rather than the Crucifixion, Milton comes to focus in his late verse on inward articulations of mortal terrors, on, more specifically, the melancholia afflicting the newly privatized post-lapsarian subject in the face of 'modern' death – a melancholia that cannot be redressed or 'worked through' by any received public modes of consolation. In *Paradise Lost*, it is Adam who, after the Fall, models the fraught subjective forms of Reformed grief, who is the first 'modern' melancholic – a role that coheres with his historical obsolescence, as we shall soon see. Adam's deadlocked but, paradoxically, also open-ended lamentations (for example, his self-entrapment in the ever-widening psychic abyss he opens up by his melancholic soliloquizing) can tell us much about how death, grief, despair, and mourning were transformed not only by Reformation challenges to the doctrine of Purgatory, customary funereal rites and ritual, and so forth, but also by republican and regicidal antipathies to kingship, theatre, genealogy, and historical memory.[2] Especially when read in relation to Book 12, Adam's lament highlights the intimate interrelations between Milton's postdynastic vision of the national future and his 'modern' disavowal of death.

## 1

Before turning to Adam's lamentations, it is necessary, however briefly, to account historically for the melancholic impasse that death presents to Adam. Broadly put, death, like almost everything else in Reformation culture, was 'disenchanted' as were the shrines, relics, statuary, chantries, and liturgy that had hitherto made death not only a meaningful, and, in the case of the Metaphysicals, even an erotic, experience, but a communal one as well. By abstracting and internalizing death, reformers from Tyndale to Milton aimed to dispel the old religion's 'vulgar errors' concerning the afterlife, especially the doctrine of Purgatory, as Stephen Greenblatt has recently argued, thereby releasing believers from a state of servile fear that could be exploited for financial gain through the buying and selling of indulgences.[3] Protestant efforts to de-ritualize death were, as such, undertaken quite deliberately to put an end to 'papist' corruption. But, this reforming movement became a victim of its own successes, undone by its own internal logic. The same disdain for ritual that helped to demystify the Catholic 'cult of death' inadvertently also helped to generate a Protestant 'mortality crisis' by sparking the unthinkable and publicly unspeakable heresy that death was not the gateway to spiritual rebirth but that it was instead an empty state of negation, 'signifying nothing' (Watson 1–15).

Ironically perhaps, this heretical perception of death as negation proved to be a fruitful source of cultural, artistic, and political inspiration in the Jacobean period, compelling new aesthetic and cultural strategies for restoring death's lost communal and ritual dimensions – new means for unthinking the unthinkable thought that death, and hence life, was meaningless. Of these new vibrant Jacobean forms of returning death to the public stage, two stand out as most successful: the Jacobean drama (and *Hamlet* in particular) and the cult of monarchy. The Jacobean stage served an important public consolatory function in the absence of traditional religious rituals, ceremonies, and prayers: 'If the English Church no longer permitted Christ to play so explicit a physical–sacrificial role in the tragic ritual known as Mass, then some new form of tragic hero would have to become our advance scout into the unknown country of death. If prayers for the dead were discouraged in churches, then revenge on behalf of a ghost would be performed in theaters.' Like the new tragic hero, the sacralized body of the monarch became a displaced communal outlet for mortal terrors. Under Elizabeth I and James I, the figure of the monarch functioned as an 'immortality-surrogate', with an eternal body and body politic; the monarch was granted 'the power to impose death partly because that function implies an obverse power to preserve life (as in the curative force of the royal touch)' (Watson 9, 16). Stage and crown, themselves intersecting cultural and political arenas (as when Edward the Confessor touches for the King's Evil in *Macbeth* and James I styles himself as 'the royal actor' in *Basilikon Doron*), helped to restore communal meaning and moral purpose to death, thereby offering partial resolution to the period's 'mortality-crisis'.

But what happens to death and to the crisis of mortality when even these reformed means of communally living with and triumphing over death are dismantled? How is death imagined after the closing of the theaters in 1642, the execution of Charles I in 1649, and the restoration of monarchy in 1660? Put another way, what special challenges did mid-century regicides and republicans like Milton face in trying to rewrite (and un-write) death in internal, post-dynastic, and anti-theatrical terms? It is, after all, the throne and the theatre-like 'death house' that, as Benjamin observes, place death on the public stage and into the 'perceptual world of the living'. Milton, we recall, mocks the life-sustaining powers imputed to kingship by having Death, that shapeless 'shape', wear a crown: 'what seem'd his head / The likeness of a Kingly Crown had on' (2.672–3).[4] The conjoint anti-monarchical and anti-theatrical implications of these lines, with their emphasis on Death as 'seem'-ing and 'likeness' and on his 'Kingly Crown', are unmistakable. For Edmund Burke, however, Milton's allegory of Death epitomizes the 'sublime' (Burke, 61). As David Norbrook observes, Burke considers 'the menacing obscurity of "what seemed his head" [. . .] a quintessentially sublime line; and its sublimity has regicidal overtones' (Norbrook *Writing* 460). The 'sublime' implications of Milton's regicidal allegory of Death deserve our attention, since, as we shall see, poetic sublimity represents one of Milton's most compelling responses to the special representational challenges that death presents after 1649. The 'sublime', I contend, offers Milton a politically accented, aesthetic mechanism for resolving the 'mortality crisis' in the absence of the stage and crown after the foundation of the Commonwealth, a point to which we shall soon return.[5]

*Paradise Lost* reminds us, in short, that the Civil War period forms a discrete, but surprisingly under-examined chapter in the 'modern' history of death. The studies noted above offer fascinating observations about 'death', especially in the Jacobean period, but each makes only occasional references to Milton and to English republican culture more generally. This may be because for Watson, for instance, *Paradise Lost* rehearses the same 'mortality crisis' that informs the Jacobean texts upon which he centrally focuses (Watson 41–2). By contrast, Greenblatt suggests that, by the time Milton comes to write *Paradise Lost*, the 'mortality crisis', at least insofar as the doctrine of Purgatory and the 'cult of death' are concerned, had been resolved and had little urgency (Greenblatt 38). Pointing both Watson's and Greenblatt's intriguing observations in a slightly different direction, I suggest that if Milton's easy dismissal of the once-formidable idea of Purgatory closes off a distinct period in the history of 'death', it also opens up a new one, which must be understood in its own terms. And if Milton, in writing of death in *Paradise Lost*, faces the same crisis of meaning and representation that enriches the Jacobean drama, he resolves that crisis through different but equally compelling literary and aesthetic strategies than do the Jacobeans.

Much was very specifically at stake during the tumultuous period between 1640–60 in controlling 'death', since mastering 'death' also promised mastery of 'life', a concept that radical Puritanism, regicide, civil war, and republicanism had dramatically altered over the course of this rapidly changing temporal interval. As noted, by the time Milton comes to write *Paradise Lost*, Protestant believers were freed from such palpable mortal terrors and fears as the pain and suffering to be endured in Purgatory; but they also became newly vulnerable to amorphous, 'inward', and potentially atheistic afflictions, i.e. disaffection, despair, and melancholia, which the civil wars' radical devaluation of both traditional and reformed Jacobean consolatory devices, especially the cult of monarchy (culminating in the execution of Charles I), helped to encourage. Rather than the gateway to immortal life, 'modern' death, or death experienced without the customary machinery of church, stage, or crown, was perceived as the *summa* of all misery. As John Wollebius writes in his chapter on misery in his 1650 tract, *The Abridgement of Christian Divinitie*: 'God comprehended all mans misery under the name of death. Gen. 2.17' (86). In light of the comprehensive misery that the thought of death appears to provoke at this uncertain cultural moment, it is telling that Parliament put forward a Blasphemy Bill

(1648–50), which made atheism into a capital crime. The civil wars, in short, forced England to face widespread bloodshed and destruction at the precise moment in which the nation was least equipped to make customary collective sense of these horrific experiences. To be sure, English republicanism was fuelled by the exhilarating millenarian promise of a liberatory 'apocalypse now'. But, after the formation of the Protectorate in 1653, this imminent salvific future seemed to anti-Cromwellian sectarians such as Fifth Monarchist prophet Anna Trapnel, among many others, to be a false promise. Indeed, the period's vulner-ability to heightened psychic malaise threatened to strike a death-blow to the very idea of the republic itself, since the new state as imagined by Milton and other republicans, as Sharon Achinstein importantly argues, demanded an activist and engaged citizenry[6] – a citizenry, I would add, that could not be allowed to be become disaffected, derailed, and demobilized by mortal terrors.

It is in relation to these historically specific implications of death in the Civil War period that this essay places *Paradise Lost* and, more specif-ically, Adam's lament. Milton's epic, I argue, can tell us much about why and how English republicanism necessitated not only new religious and political forms of death-denial but also new aesthetic forms as well – a poetics of forgetting the terrifying and socially unproductive states of despair and denegation, which death, in its 'purest' or most skepti-cal form, threatened to unleash with heightened intensity. In its most ambitious scope, then, this essay reads Milton's epic as an attempt to formulate a postdynastic poetics and politics of death, shaped in two main ways: first, by the Paulinism that increasingly informs especially the later writings; and, secondly, as already intimated, by Milton's renovation of the Longinian sublime as republicanism's central aes-thetic category.

Milton's radically Pauline theology has been an ongoing critical concern, but, as newly reassessed by Jason P. Rosenblatt in relation to Milton's Hebraism, it has special relevance here, since Milton's Pauline understanding of 'carnal Israel', as we shall see, is intimately tied to the ways in which death is re-imagined in Milton's writings.[7] Milton's poetic sublimity plays an important role in Norbrook's important recent study of English republican culture. As Norbrook points out, enhanced civil war interest in 'the sublime' and in Longinus's treatise, *Peri Hypsous, On the Sublime*, 'was found in royalist as well as Parliamentarian circles, but Milton and his followers gave the sublime a distinctively republican accent'. Milton 'had placed Longinus on his ideal syllabus in *Of Educa-tion*, and praised poetry as "that sublime art"; it was appropriate that the first English translation of Longinus should have been composed by [Milton's] young disciple, John Hall'. (Hall's translation was published in 1652.)[8] Most important for my purposes is that for Milton, Wither, and other anticustomary poets, Longinian sublimity allowed for a 'soaring fancifully above due limits' (Norbrook 137); the prospect of death as the ultimate limit, I would suggest, helps to inspire Milton's use of the sublime.

But while Milton's Paulinism and his sublime republican poetics have each served separately as the focus of recent scholarly reappraisal, surprisingly scant critical attention has been paid to the ways in which the two inform each other. Despite their apparent disparities, however, Milton's anti-corporeal Pauline theology and his iconoclastic poetic sublimity conjointly shape his 'modern', postdynastic vision of death. Paul's devaluation of the body was to allow Milton to devalue nature, and, more specifically, the 'natural' promise of endless progeny that dynastic government allows kingship to make. At the same time, in devaluing nature and kingship, Milton also prepares the ground for his 'sublime' post-apocalyptic ideal of antidynastic community, which negates, or 'purifies', all 'natural' justifications for kingship and the received social conventions, religious rituals, and set forms that helped to support dynastic government, clearing space for the 'entirely artificial' relations that Raymond Williams suggests characterize the modern nation-state.[9] Upon this 'entirely artificial', *tabula rasa* site, Milton inscribes his 'post-natural' vision of collective social harmony – a vision indebted to the spiritual unity and community celebrated in Galatians 3:24: 'There is no longer Jew or Greek, there is no longer slave or free, there is no longer male and female; for you are all one in Christ Jesus.'[10] Unlike the natural body, the sublime, post-natural body of Milton's Pauline, antimonarchical polity is subject neither to decay, corruption, and death, nor to any of the 'carnal' particularities of nation ('Jew or Greek'), class ('bound or free'), or gender ('male or female') that limit and hence impair the exercise of free will.

In *Areopagitica*, Milton represents his ideal of free, departicularized but decidedly 'post-natural' community in his resonant depiction of the newborn English republic as the arisen Samson. In a sublime flight of prose-poetry, Milton pushes the organic analogy between the healthy 'natural' body and the English body politic 'to breaking-point' (Norbrook *Writing* 137). It is precisely this 'breaking-point' moment, in which the organic model of dynastic government is emptied of meaning and value, and hence, for Milton, of divinity as well, that I am interested in exploring in *Paradise Lost*, and, more specifically, in Adam's lament. For Milton, this moment of rupture between God and Nature, and between the godly, universal republic of the reformed future and the temporal, particularized kingdoms of the outmoded past – kingdoms for which, as Books 11 and 12 make clear, the 'carnal Israel' of Hebrew scripture forms the prototype – makes it possible to rewrite 'death' in salvific, postdynastic, Protestant terms. In marking the irreparable break between the 'old' corrupt dispensation and the birth of the 'new' salvific future moment, or, in other words, the negative/positive, 'there is no longer', moment of Galatians 3:28, the reformed 'body' (once natural and particular/insular, but now sublime and universal) of the godly English nation remakes 'death' into a thing of the unredeemable past, for which Milton and the republic he imagined no longer had any use.

Death, for Milton, emerges, in other words, as a generalized sign of 'the primitive'. While beyond the scope of this essay, I would never-theless like to note that Milton maps death not only onto the Israel of Hebrew scripture, reducing it into a nether world of shadowy types and cryptic figures, but also onto other 'archaic', usually Catholic, and, more often than not, Oriental times and places – onto, in other words, all spatiotemporal zones beyond the pale. Consider, for example, the passage in Book 3, in which Satan is compared to 'a Vulture on *Imaus* bred' (431), which crosses various Asian wastelands (first, the 'snowy ridge' of the Himalayas, where 'the roving *Tartar* bounds', and then 'the barren Plains / Of *Sericana*' [432, 437]). In prelapsarian geography, the future Gobi desert is but 'barren Plains', but as a postlapsarian, site, this Chinese wasteland becomes the seat of 'all things transitory and vain' (446), of, more precisely, Limbo, or 'the Paradise of Fools' (496) or, in other words, of Purgatory, itself reduced, as Greenblatt points out, to an empty superstition, a 'dead' concept.

## 2

Milton's anti-dynastic vision of Reformation thus crucially depends upon his wresting authorial and political control over the discourse of death. Undoubtedly, the boldest attempt that Milton and other regi-cides made to steal 'death' from the Stuarts and to rewrite it in repub-lican terms was performed by the trial and execution of Charles I, a subject of excellent recent scholarship.[11] This was an intervention, however, that ultimately failed, since Charles's death reactivated the barely repressed 'cult of monarchy', which helped to turn the king back into an 'immortality-surrogate', as the many elegies to Charles that poured forth after the execution testify. Briefly put, in executing

Charles, the regicides (temporarily) won the battle over political sovereignty, but they lost the war over 'death'. Milton's framing of Charles's death in *The Tenure of Kings and Magistrates, Eikonoklastes*, and other prose tracts remains an intriguing topic, but what I would like to isolate here are some of the specifically poetic means through which Milton attempts, time and again, to master 'death' as both a political and a literary subject. Having failed to steal 'death' from the Stuarts, Milton returned again and again to death in less topical political contexts as a way not only to redress and rewrite the topical scene of Charles's death, but also, more generally, to rescue the English people from despair and melancholia, among other socially unproductive emotions, which, as noted above, threatened to deal an affective death-blow to the new intellectually and emotionally engaged liberal subject, which Milton's writings helped not only to create but to preserve (as a literary construct) after the defeat of the Cromwellian state.

For this reason, I am especially interested in the period from the late 1650s and into the Restoration, when death increasingly 'animates' Milton's writings as he, and other failed republicans and religious radicals, tried to work through 'the experience of defeat', to borrow Christopher Hill's term.[12] This is of course also the same period that sees the emergence of Milton's late great poems, from which I would like to isolate Adam's long, tortured soliloquy about loss, misery, and death. This soliloquy is among Milton's most fully realized articulations of mortal fear and dejection. It also offers especially clear insight into the ways in which English republicanism's radically anticustomary and antitheatrical prospect of death newly inflects the period's 'mortality crisis', especially after the official 'death' of the republic in 1660. More specifically, Adam's lament subjectively rehearses Milton's efforts both to rupture Restored dynasty's claim to divinely sanctioned 'natural' supremacy and to posit the republican 'sublime' as the domain of a decidedly 'post-natural' and hence truly 'godly' nation, in which liberty of conscience, and moral feeling could be freely exercised – a domain to which Milton's epic more generally provides access. On the one hand, Adam's soliloquy links mortal terror and despair to the loss of Paradise, in which natural law had once – but would never again – confer personal and national election. But, on the other hand, this same despairing recognition of 'paradise lost', where 'God and Nature bid the same,' also forms the precondition for the sublime 'highth / Of happiness' (*PL*. 10.725–6), which Adam finally achieves, at great cost, in Books 11–12 upon the 'Hill / Of Paradise the highest' (11.377–8). It is at this highest 'highth' that Michael teaches Adam to divorce God and Nature by turning from birthright (the election accorded to 'the Sons of *Abraham's* Loins' [12.457], the biological progeny of Israel's first patriarch) to the 'merit' that specially marks not only the Son but also all 'the sons/Of Abraham's faith', who are the spiritual sons of the Son. Within this supersessionist progression from 'birthright' to 'merit', 'loins' to 'faith', dynasty's bloodline justifications of election and its 'natural' promise of endless progeny are mapped onto the outmoded Israel of Hebrew scripture, or 'carnal Israel' under the Law, and so relegated to a ruined, unreconstructable, and hence 'dead' past. By contrast, the 'unnatural' body politic of the sublime English republic, or new spiritual Israel, is projected onto a liberatory and spiritually regenerative Anglo-Protestant future.[13] Moving from soliloquized despair in Book 10 to the sublime 'joy broke forth' (11.869) that he expresses upon comprehending the typological significance of the olive leaf born by the ascending dove at the end of Book 11 (foreshadowing the end of the old Hebraic dispensation and the beginning of the New Covenant of the gospels), Adam models the ways in which the supersessional transformation of carnal into spiritual 'Israel' inwardly affects the postlapsarian subject – not to mention the aesthetic forms through which that exemplary affective transformation finds expression. But, we shall also see that, for Milton, Adam is a flawed model, an exemplar, finally, of psychic, social, and linguistic failure rather than of spiritual, political, and poetic sublimity; he never fully breaks free from loss, the body, tragedy, the past, and, he remains, as such, under the curse of death.

As the opening contradictions, 'O miserable of happy' (10.720) and 'Accurst of blessed' (10.723), in Adam's soliloquy make clear, mortal terrors and despair place Adam in a near-paralytic state of self-created intellectual and emotional bondage. After the Fall, his freedom to choose freely and spontaneously between contradictory ideas (especially 'obedience' and 'disobedience') is obstructed by the many intellectual roadblocks that his maze-like self-absorption in death puts before him. (It is this lost freedom of unmediated choice that the republican sublime restores.) The collapse of distinction between mourning and rejoicing signaled by Adam's self-definition as 'miserable of happy' is especially noteworthy in this context. Saul M. Olyan observes that 'mourning and cultic rejoicing are typically represented in biblical texts as antithetical and incompatible sets of ritual behaviors', but that in Jeremiah 41:5, in the face of the destroyed temple, these normally incompatible rites are uncharacteristically fused into a single ritual constellation (1).[14] Olyan argues this can 'only mean that the ritual order has collapsed [. . .]. There no longer exists a separate, sanctified cultic sphere with its distinct set of ritual requirements' (11). For Olyan, texts such as Jer 41:5 represent 'the way members of the community might speak about disaster *in the most profound and striking terms possible* [. . .]. the fusion of mourning and rejoicing not only marks loss poignantly; it implies that no return is possible to the ways things were' (17). Adam's lament recapitulates (with a difference) the discursive, ethical, and social concerns of Jer. 41:5. As in Jer. 41:5, Adam's fusion of misery and happiness articulates '*in the most profound and striking terms possible*' both the collapse of the 'separate, sanctified cultic sphere', which is Eden, and the tragedy of 'no return', of exile and diaspora.[15] At the same time, however, the radical Pauline vantage point that informs the latter part of Milton's epic provides a mechanism for converting catastrophic loss (and the radical break it creates from 'the way things were') into redemptive gain, more specifically, the free-and-clear 'new creation' of de-particularized unity celebrated in Galatians 3:28, which, as noted, finds expression in Milton's Samson-like, icon-smashing, poetic and national sublimity.

On the one hand, then, the fusion of rejoicing and mourning suggested by Adam's 'O miserable of happy!' poignantly marks the radical breakdown of Edenic nature and hence of ritual order as well, since in prelapsarian experience the natural order *is* the sanctified sphere of ritual order. With the Fall, the 'natural' nature of ritual, for example, Adam and Eve's unpremeditated prayers and the 'mysterious rites' of marriage, is made unnatural, and hence the death of nature means the death of ritual. On the other hand, the same de-naturalized and de-ritualized state of mourning/rejoicing also permits entry into the new 'sublime' unity of opposites, or the *discordia concors* that creates the sublime's form-and-ritual-breaking harmonies. In political terms, Adam's fusion of mourning and rejoicing translates the Fall into a conspicuously reformist and republican event, as an epoch-shifting, iconoclastic moment of 'unnatural' new union. The destruction of the old sanctified order becomes the governing principle of the new, which rises, phoenix-like, out of the ashes of ruins whose former integrity can never be recaptured. For Milton, social and historical transformation, like theological reformation, is simultaneously destructive and restorative, but not recuperative – a principle that informs Milton's republican revision of not only the Fall, or the beginning of history, but also its antitype, the Apocalypse, history's endpoint, which in Milton's utopian post-dynastic rendering is when 'thou thy regal Sceptre shalt lay by' (3.339).

It is precisely this new sublime epoch-shifting moment of 'unnatural' new union, that is, of mourning and rejoicing, death and/as life, (through which the 'happier' vision of Apocalypse and of the 'new creation' outlined in Galatians 3.28 finds expression), that Adam is unable to master in his soliloquy. Rather than emancipate him from a ruined world, the paradoxes that flood Adam's mind trap him within his damaged psyche, presenting him with the Reformation's crisis of mortality. Unmindful of Raphael's eschatological prediction in Book 5 that 'Your bodies may at last turn to spirit, / Improv'd by tract of time' (497–8), Adam is not ready to accept God's divorce from Nature. Deprived as yet of grace, he 'primitively' seeks resolution to the painful quandaries into which the unthinkable thought of death leads him by turning not to the transcendent paternal deity but to the earthy body of Nature, his once-nurturing 'mother', from whose 'clay' he was formed: 'How gladly would I lay me down / As in my Mother's lap! There I would rest / And sleep secure' (7.775–8). While this seductive fantasy of death as a form of natural maternal nurture offers Adam a moment of solace, another contradictory expression of mortal terror still troubles him, refusing him to let him rest in peace in his 'Mother's lap'. Adam knows that, though cursed with death, the spirit is immortal: 'the Spirit of Man / Which God inspir'd, cannot perish / Wit this corporeal Clod' (7.784–6). This 'thought / Horrid' brings Adam to the ultimate impasse, to the 'strange contradiction' that death might not represent a final rest.[16] Rather, death comes to seem to Adam as it does to Macbeth to be but a ceaseless and meaningless proliferation of empty tomorrows: 'Tomorrow and tomorrow and tomorrow'. 'Will he draw out,' Adam miserably wonders, 'For anger's sake, finite to infinite / In punisht Man' (10.801–3). The thought that this unthinkable state of never-ending negation – that 'death', is, in fact, the essential condition of postlapsarian 'life' – drives Adam into a self-made prison house of 'horrors', an 'Abyss of fears / And horrors [. . .] out of which / I find no way' (7. 7.842–40.) Just as the prospect of death forces Adam to understand the multiplying of tomorrows as eternal negation, so too do Adam's mortal terrors translate the multiplying of progeny in accordance with God's first law to be fruitful and multiply into a death sentence. Adam's lament, in short, brings him to the Damascan crossroads: having fallen from prelapsarian Hebraic monism to postlapsarian Pauline dualism, Adam (and we), like Saul/Paul, must 'freely' choose gospel over law, spirit over letter, God over Nature, life over death. Failing to make this emancipating decision, and hence unable to achieve a sublime 'soaring fancifully above due limits', Adam descends deeper into the hellish abyss created by – and that is – his soliloquy.

It is the life-or-death choice that Adam must make between God and fallen Nature that most concerns us at this juncture. While in the prelapsarian world 'God and Nature bid the same' (6.176), in the post-lapsarian world, in which Adam now finds himself, Mother Nature not only is divorced from God the Father, but, Medea-like, she gives birth to her offspring in the spring only in the end to kill them off in winter. This maternal allegory is worth briefly pausing over, since, as I have argued elsewhere, the figure of the nursing mother acquires new symbolic importance in the early decades of the seventeenth century, when it comes to emblematize the new nurturing Protestant family and nation that the Reformation hoped to usher in.[17] The cultural ascendancy of the nursing mother is paralleled by the cultural depreciation of the wet-nurse, who in Puritan domestic guidebooks, such as William Gouge's *Of Domesticall Duties* and Robert Cleaver and John Dod's *A Godly Form of Household Government*, is depicted as uncaring and indifferent to her charges, and is associated with the 'vulgar' superstitions of the old religion and state. By contrast, the figure of the nursing mother and the unstinting nurture she provides are deemed 'naturall' and hence subject to natural laws, and therefore 'scientifically' or rationally comprehensible and so able to serve and legitimate the new Protestant calculus of reformed experience.

The nexus Milton creates among nature, death, and kingship rules out any place for either Mother Nature or the 'naturall' mother in his 'sublime' Pauline narrative of reformation. (By contrast, as we shall see, the 'post-natural' mother, '*Mary*, second *Eve*' (5.387) has a foundational role to play in this same reformative tale.) Collapsing the categorical divide between the 'vulgar' nurse and the enlightened figure of the 'natural' mother, as carefully delineated in the aforementioned seventeenth-century guidebooks, Milton depicts Mother Nature as the 'nurse' of Death. Through the decay and corruption she breeds, Nature abundantly supplements the paltry nourishment that Death had hitherto received only from his mother/lover Sin's attenuated snake-like body. In the prelapsarian world, Death feeds exclusively on Sin's entrails; in the postlapsarian universe, however, Nature would appear to breed life for the sole purpose of supplying Death with a never-ebbing flow of corroding bodies and souls upon which to feast. While prelapsarian Eden had been 'a peaceable kingdom', in which all beings, including Adam and Eve, equitably feasted on fruit (with one notable exception) and 'dulcet cream', the natural scarcity that sets in after the Fall transforms the once fruitful and pastoral Eden into a bellicose realm of carnivorous hunters fighting over limited resources. We might recall here that the translation of the Garden into a hunting field is one of the first visible manifestations of the Fall: 'Beast now with Beast gan war, and Fowl with Fowl / And Fish with Fish; to graze the Herb all leaving, / Devour'd each other' (10.710–12). It is also this Hobbesian vision of Nature as a 'war of all against all' that prompts Adam's soliloquy on death. As the allusion to Nimrod in Book 12 makes clear, hunting is linked both to the Tower of Babel, 'whose top may reach to Heav'n' and to 'Empire tyrannous' (44, 32). As Death's 'nurse,' fallen Nature, in short, mandates meat eating, hunting, empire, tyranny, and the false epic or pseudosublime height and global prospect achieved by 'Authority usurped, from God not given'.

Hence, although the occasion for Adam's despairing soliloquy on death, the divorce of God from Nature after the Fall in fact clears the way for the truly sublime and redemptive modes of Reformation that *Paradise Lost* itself enacts. Rosenblatt, as noted, delineates the ways in which Pauline doctrine legitimates Milton's reformist theological arguments for splitting the natural from the divine order. In this Milton turns away from the Hebraic monism that dominates his thinking in the divorce tracts and the shapes the middle books of *Paradise Lost*. As Rosenblatt observes, this split is a consequence of the Fall: 'The disjunction [between God and Nature] began after Eve tasted the forbidden fruit, when Adam chose to disobey the divine law for the sake of the natural: "I feel / The Link of Nature draw me"' (9.913–14).[18] But, it is also important to see how Milton's 'sublime' Pauline justifications of a postlapsarian rupture between God and Nature allows him to rule out dynastic government as an antidote to mortal terror; Milton makes it impossible, in other words, for kingship to function as an 'immortality surrogate'.[19]

Risking some generalization, a very brief comparison to *Macbeth*, from which Milton directly quotes more than once in *Paradise Lost*, is useful here, since, as many readers have observed, Shakespeare's play illuminates with, literally, spectacular clarity, the ways in which dynasty relies on metaphors of 'natural' procreativity and continuity, on progeny as a hedge against death.[20] Time and again, the play proclaims that progeny and hence the possibility of a dynastic line and monarchical future are denied to Macbeth – that his bloody regicide and usurpation of the throne are literally sterile gestures. By contrast, Banquo remains a fertile and procreative father, the founder of a never-ending dynasty, as 'the mirror of kings' reveals, even after his horrible murder at the hands of Macbeth's henchmen. It is this open-ended dynastic future, cut off by the regicidal Macbeth, that Banquo's ghost comes to reclaim.

What makes for human tragedy in *Macbeth*, however, allows for divine comedy in *Paradise Lost*. Adam, who is made to share in Macbeth's vision of death as an eternally repeated act of negation – a vision in which there is no future, but rather an endless set of sterile tomorrows. Not unlike Macbeth, Adam can find neither strength nor solace in the future to be gained 'naturally' by procreation and progeny. Genealogy, for Adam, becomes an eternal curse. Having transmitted sin and death to his children, Adam believes that they will exist only to damn and disown him: 'for what can I increase / Or multiply, but curses on my head?' (10.729–30). But for Adam, unlike Macbeth, the fatal implications of God's first command to be fruitful and multiply, 'Now death to hear!' (10.731), in a post-natural universe also deliver the promise of salvific rebirth to fallen humanity. As Michael will instruct Adam in Books 11 and 12, postlapsarian victory over death can be obtained by embracing new non-procreative, non-genealogical alternatives to the promise of perpetual and 'natural' regeneration forever lost after the Fall. If before the Fall, 'natural' blood-and-soil measures (Adam's autochthonous birth, the sacred separateness of Eden, the natural fruitfulness of the land, the universal dispersion of progeny all linked by blood to the same original progenitors) had guaranteed election in prelapsarian Paradise, after the Fall, spiritual measures, that is, grace, baptism, free will, and conscience, which are indifferent to natural law, provide the reformed, 'sublime' way to salvation.[21]

It is for these death-defying reasons that, especially in Books 11 and 12, Milton's anti-dynastic epic strives to give manifest literary expression to new disembodied and internal forms of redemptive experience, 'the paradise within thee happier far' and 'inward consolations', through which the twinned curses of death and kingship, and the socially unproductive subjection and abjection that both inspire, can be overcome. In Book 5, Raphael tells Adam of the pleasures of disembodied or angelic 'sex'; not dissimilarly, in Books 11 and 12, Michael teaches Adam about how the pleasures of spiritual progeny, such as the 'seed' of Mary, can not only compensate for and but even improve upon – or are 'happier far' – than biological children, those endless generations of 'natural' offspring whom Adam fears will curse him.

The new post-natural child is 'the Son'. As Milton maintains: the Son is 'called God's own Son simply because he had no other Father but God'; he is born 'not from any natural necessity' but rather of God's 'own free will: a method more excellent and more in keeping with paternal dignity' (*CPW*, 6:208–9). Notably, the same postlapsarian distinction between generativity governed by 'free will' and procreation driven by 'natural necessity' enhances Adam's painful recognition of both the divine election that he himself has forfeited and the mortal curse he has forever inflicted upon his own future offspring: 'yet him [Adam's progeny] not thy election, / But Natural necessity begot / God made thee of choice his own' (10.764–6). Equally relevant here is that these 'more excellent' and more dignified forms of free-willed and anti-natural procreation and regeneration are associated with the Son's salvific, antidynastic kingship – the spiritual kingship that dismantles the temporal power of worldly kings. The sublime ascent of the Son by merit to God's 'throne hereditary' renders obsolete all 'natural' blood-line and birthright justifications of inherited sovereignty, including the law of primogeniture, and all other genealogical measures of procreative paternal power that support kingship's death-defying dynastic assertion of *imperium sine finum*. In defeating death by defying Nature and the body, the sublimity of the Son's spiritual reign spells the end of both 'carnal' kingship and physical fatherhood, allowing republican free will to triumph over monarchy's 'natural necessity'. Rather than our 'undignified' biological patriarch, Adam, it is 'our mother Eve', in her celebrated spiritualized role as '*Mary*, second *Eve*', who is given the last speech in Milton's epic, prophesying victory over death through 'this further consolation': 'By me the promised seed shall all restore' (12.623). We might recall that Eve's prophetic proclamation of her reformed, con-solatory role as an instrument of universal redemption, as the spiritual maternal vessel of the 'promised seed', is adumbrated when she tries to remedy Adam's melancholia in Book 10 by asking him for his forgive-ness, releasing him from the self-created bondage into which his soli-tary meditations on death, biological progeny, and 'natural necessity' have driven him.

The 'promised seed' in Eve's final speech clearly alludes to Jesus, the new-modelled nonbiological son, but the 'promise' in 'the promised seed' also evokes the Pauline notion of 'the children of the promise', those who, unlike biological progeny, alone can be 'reckoned as descen-dants' (Romans 9:6–8) in the new dispensation. These 'children' make up the 'Great numbers of each Nation' won by the apostles through 'their wondrous gifts' as they carry out their mission 'To evangelize the Nations' (12. 503, 500, 499). They are the new spiritual multitude that supersedes nature's deadly maternal bountifulness and regenerates Adam's prolific natural progeny – 'carnal Israel' – born under the curse of death. Adam rejoices at the good news of the restorative advent of the new kingdom of Christ, but he nevertheless clings to his 'natural' role as the Son's biological progenitor, 'Yet from my Loins / Thou shalt proceed' (12.380–1). Yet once more, Michael must teach Adam to exchange 'loins' for 'faith', 'natural' fatherhood for spiritual sonship, law for love, death for life. Unlike the newly awakened Eve at the end of Book 12, who (in Pauline fashion) instantaneously embraces her reformed, restorative role as spiritually fruitful mother, as 'second Eve', Adam is slow to relinquish his biological procreativity, thus insuring not only his own obsolescence as Hebraic patriarch but also that of all others who champion the once sacred but now cursed 'natural' imperative to be fruitful and multiply. If his prelapsarian qualities were expansiveness and prolificness, in the postlapsarian world, he can accomplish 'great things' only 'by small' and 'by simply meek'. By contrast, Eve is made full, and her role in the new narrative of reformation is enlarged by her spiritual maternity: 'though all by me is lost, [. . .]. By me the promised seed shall all restore.'

The final mark of his diminished stature in reformed history is made when Adam 'answer[s] not' (12.625) at the end of the epic – a silence that echoes his empty paternal future. As Book 12 makes clear, Adam's role as primordial father is drained of customary meaning, translated into spiritual terms, and assigned to the Abraham of Paul's epistles, 'the father of the promise'; Michael notes that 'all Nations of the Earth / Shall in [Abraham's] Seed be blessed' (12.147–8). As Michael reminds him, Adam's 'preeminence' as the world's 'great Progenitor [. . .] thou has lost'. Adam is 'Well pleas'd' (12.625) by Eve's hopeful prophesy of universal redemption and of her own central role in that salvific event, but he himself is granted no part in the revised, triumphant future. His concluding silence would seem then to confirm his historical obsolescence, in much the same way as his soliloquized lament in Book 10 intensifies rather than alleviates his grief: his 'answer[ing] not', in short, is but the flipside of his loquacious melancholic soliloquizing. To be sure, both Adam and Eve drop 'some natural tears' while 'looking back' to Paradise, 'so late their happy seat'; and both simultaneously then turn toward 'the World [that] was all before them' (12.645, 641, 646). But, Book 12 also implies that, if our first parents walk forward 'hand in hand' into the 'happier far', post-natural future, in which 'natural tears' shall no longer be shed, it is Adam, not Eve, who would seem to be contained by a ruined past that Milton's epic equates with death and which, as death, it attempts to disavow and negate.

Especially when read against the Book 12, Adam's lament thus helps us to see that, for Milton, death is the mark of historical obsolescence, stagnation, and redundancy; it also defines the psychic and social condition of those, not unlike Adam, who 'primitively' cling to nature, the body, the land, procreativity, progeny, history, the maternal 'lap', the paternal 'loins', and the Israel of Hebrew scripture. 'Both Death and I,' laments Adam, 'Am found Eternal and incorporate both' (10.815–16). Before the Fall, God and Nature, spirit and body, law and love 'bid the same', but the Fall insures that the monism that had defined paradisal experience can never be recuperated. The attempt to do so, for Milton, results in either the pagan 'cult of monarchy', restored by the Restoration, or the self-dramatizing and self-defeating postlapsarian melancholia exemplified by the soliloquizing Adam – and perhaps by many of Milton's fellow regicides undone and driven underground by the 'experience of defeat'. In keeping with the Pauline perspective that governs the latter part of Milton's epic, divorce, rupture, deracination, historical amnesia, and the repression of sexuality and procreation permit entry into the 'new creation' of disembodied social unity that is celebrated in Galatians 3:28 and which finds expression in Milton's poetic sublimity and his Samson-like, icon-smashing vision of national reunion and the true, hence non-dynastic, restoration. To this vision, the newly awakened Eve in Book 12 dedicates her reformed spiritually activated, future-directed, death-denying self. 'Now lead on,' she commands Adam; 'in me there is no delay.' By contrast, Adam, though 'Well pleas'd [. . .] answer'd not.' Adam's silence, like his lament, speaks volumes about Milton's, and his culture's, reformation of death. Milton's Pauline theology, his sublime, anti-theatrical poetics, and his post-dynastic, national vision require that death be pushed out of 'the perceptual world of the living', paving the way, as Benjamin so astutely observes, for the fateful advent of modernity.

## Notes

1. See Jonathan Dollimore *Death, Desire, and Loss in Western Culture* (59–118), Stephen Greenblatt, *Hamlet in Purgatory*, and Robert N. Watson, *The Rest is Silence: Death as Annihilation in the English Renaissance*.
2. On the 'male' coding of melancholia in Renaissance literature, see Juliana Schiesari's illuminating study, *The Gender of Melancholia: Feminism, Psychoanalysis, and the Symbolics of Loss in Renaissance Literature*.
3. Greenblatt sees the Protestant repudiation of the doctrine of Purgatory as central to the early modern reformation of death in his recent study, *Hamlet in Purgatory*.
4. All references to Milton's verse are taken from *The Complete Poems and Major Prose*, Don M. Wolfe, gen. ed. 8 vols (New Haven: Yale University Press, 1953–82), and noted in the text.
5. I would like to isolate in this context the specifically early modern implications of the sublime, while noting the importance of the sublime to theo-

ries of postmodernity; see Jean-Francois Lyotard, *The Postmodern Condition: A Report on Knowledge*. David Norbrook's observation is relevant here: 'It can be said that this early modern sublime needs to be distinguished from the version in postmodern theory, which involves a critique of Enlightenment models of representation, both in politics and language' (*Writing* 19).

6. See Chapter 3 of Sharon Achinstein, *Milton and the Revolutionary Reader*.

7. See Jason P. Rosenblatt's illuminating discussion of 'The Law in Adam's Soliloquy' (204–17) and his discussion of Adam after the Fall (ch. 7) in *Torah and Law in Paradise Lost*. 'Carnal Israel' is St. Augustine's term, formed in response to 1 Cor. 10:18, 'Behold Israel according to the flesh' in *Tractatus adversus Judaeos*, vii, 9. My understanding of this term is informed by Daniel Boyarin's important study, *Carnal Israel: Reading Sex in Talmudic Culture*, specifically, Boyarin's claim that 'one consequence of at least post-Pauline Christian adoption of dualist notions was to allegorize the reality of Israel quite out of corporeal existence.' Also pertinent to the larger argument of this essay is Boyarin's observation: 'The notion that the physical is just a sign or shadow of that which is really real allows for a disavowal of sexuality and procreation, of the importance of filiation and genealogy, and of the concrete, historical sense of scripture, of, indeed, historical memory itself' (6).

8. Norbrook astutely explores Milton's poetic sublimity in relation to his republican politics, but he does not read Milton's republican appropriation of Longinus and 'the sublime' in relation to the radical Paulinism that deeply informs especially his later writings. This essay, however, maintains not only that Milton's Paulinism informs his use of the Longinian 'sublime' but also that the close connection between the sublime and the Pauline in *Paradise Lost* is crucial to understanding the poetics and politics of death in Milton's epic.

9. See Raymond Williams, *The Year 2000* (New York: Pantheon, 1983), cited in Timothy Brennan, 'The National Longing for Form', *Nation and Narration*, ed. Homi K. Bhabha (London: Routledge, 1990) 45.

10. The verse echoes Genesis 1.27: those in Christ have entered a new creation where former distinctions are replaced by unity, a unity that, I argue, is, for Milton, reflected in the anticustomary harmonies, or *discordia concors*, achieved by the sublime. Pushing against the smooth language and balance that characterize Isocrates's eloquence, Longinus associates the sublime with asymmetrical harmonies: 'things . . . widely *different* are here by a strange *artifice* brought *together*'; 'the very *order* seems to be *disorderly*'.

11. See Thomas M. Corns (ed.). *The Royal Image: Representations of Charles I*.

12. The 'experience of defeat' is the central focus of *The Experience of Defeat: Milton and Some Contemporaries*, Christopher Hill's study of the lives of regicides and religious radicals after the Restoration.

13. These distinctions (between nature, kingship, bondage, the past, and death, on the one hand, and grace, republicanism, freedom, the future, and life, on the other) form a westering trajectory in *The Tenure of Kings and Magistrates*, where Milton associates the Jews, 'especially since the time they chose a King against the advice and counsel of God' with 'the people of Asia'. Both 'are noted by wise Authors much inclinable to slavery' (*CPW* III 202–3).

14. For Milton's interest in the Book of Jeremiah and his use of the jeremiad, see James Hulston, *A Rational Millenium: Puritan Utopias of Seventeenth-Century*

*England and America,* and Laura Knoppers, *Historicizing Milton: Spectacle, Power, and Poetry in Restoration England.*

15. I cite Olyan's fascinating paper, presented to the Religious Studies Seminar, University of New Hampshire, autumn 2001. On mourning and rejoicing in Hebrew scripture, see also G.A. Anderson, *A Time to Dance: The Expression of Grief and Joy in Israelite Religion.*

16. Of particular interest here, is Rosenblatt's cogent observation that the impasse Adam reaches in his soliloquy on death coincides exactly with the disintegration of the Hebraic monism (the unity between nature and ritual, between the body and spiritual devotion to God) that governs both the poem's central books and the prelapsarian world of Paradise: 'the various polarities Adam amasses here [...] are brought into focus by a law that promises life but threatens death: 'O voice once heard / Delightfully, *Increase and multiply,* / Now death to hear! (729–31).' Rosenblatt astutely untangles Adam's devaluation of the Hebraic principles of law and Torah's celebration of sexuality and progeny; he shows how, through Adam's example in Book 10, Milton, following establishes that 'Mosaic law is an instrument through which humankind recognizes its depravity Romans 7:10, ('the very commandment which promised life proved to be death in me').'

17. See my essay, 'Nourish Milk: Breast-Feeding and the Crisis of Englishness, 1600–1660.'

18. Rosenblatt argues that it is the Fall that translates proliferation into a curse: 'Adam and Eve, now "manifold in sin" (10.16), will multiply curses and evil by multiplying progeny.' Sinister associations with the propagation of 'multitudes' before the Fall suggest that the prelapsarian-postlapsarian divide may be a bit more fluid than Rosenblatt suggests. In Book 1, for instance, Milton compares the 'numberless' fallen angels that hover 'under the Cope of Hell' to a 'multitude, like which the populous North/ Pour'd never from her frozen loins' (351–2). Similarly, Sin tells the tale of her monstrous maternal prolificness in Book 2, 'These yelling Monsters with ceaseless cry / Surround me, as thou saw'st, hourly conceived / And hourly born' (796–8). Nature itself inherits the potential for sinister prolificness from her 'Ancestors': 'eldest *Night* and *Chaos'*; in their 'Eternal Anarchy', the 'embryo Atoms' of 'Hot, Cold, Moist, and Dry [...] Swarm populous, unnumber'd as the Sands of *Barca* or *Cyrene's* torrid soil' (895, 897, 903–4). Long before Book 10, then, the allusion to the Libyan desert in 'the Sands of *Barca* or *Cyrene's* torrid soil' associates death Nature's populousness, underscoring the elemental fruitlessness of natural fruitfulness: 'The Womb of nature and perhaps her Grave' (911).

19. Dollimore reads 9.911–16 as exemplifying the 'familiar misogynist strategy' of identifying mutability as 'an exclusively female attribute'. 'But such misogyny,' he adds, 'does not cancel sexual desire for women but remains an inextricable part of it' (97–9).

20. For example, the lines, '*Adam* could not, but wept, / Though not of Woman born; compassion quell'd / His best of Man' (11.495–9) allude to *Macbeth*, 5. 8.37–9 and 5. 8.23–4.

21. Both Watson (Chapter 4) and Norbrook (*Macbeth*) offer compelling, against-the-grain readings of 'nature' in *Macbeth*.

# 9
# Imagining the Death of the King: Milton, Charles I, and Anamorphic Art

*Laura L. Knoppers*

A little-known painting of King Charles I, now at Castle Gripsholm near Stockholm, presents an example of anamorphic art popular in sixteenth- and seventeenth-century Europe (Figure 9.1).[1] The observer first puzzles over a distorted and unsettling image, in which only a death's head on a circle is in focus. The solution is a cylindrical mirror, which, when placed over the death's head, reflects the corrected head-and-shoulders image of Charles with enhanced depth. As in earlier portraits by Sir Anthony Van Dyck, Charles is here shown with his characteristic left love-lock, wearing the 'George' medal, symbol of the Knights of the Garter, and dressed in sombre black, except for a white falling collar with laced edges.[2] The painting guides the viewer to look at Charles in and through death. Only from the perspective of death does the king's image gain coherence and meaning.

Anamorphic art plays an important and hitherto unrecognized role in the struggle over the meaning of the death of Charles I, who was beheaded outside of the Banqueting House at Whitehall on 30 January 1649.[3] *Eikon Basilike*, the king's book, draws upon optical and perspectival language to transform the meaning of the king's life – and death. The public trial and execution of the king, intended to be a display of just punishment for tyranny and treason, could be viewed instead as a spectacle of suffering and martyrdom. In *Eikonoklastes*, Milton in turn uses visual language and the techniques of anamorphosis to re-shape the king's book, but the distortion leads not to ultimate restoration but the tension of two contradictory images.[4] *Eikonoklastes* appears to subvert its own intentions by insisting upon a single perspective while at the same time, through its visual language and inclusion of the king's own words, making that perspective impossible. But in the opposed

*Figure 9.1*  Anamorphic Portrait of Charles I (ca. 1660).

interpretations – and imaginings – of the death of the king, things may not be as they first appear.

## Life and death in anamorphic art

Anamorphic art and the language and tools of perspective were one important means of representing and accommodating shifting views of death in the early modern period. Thanatologists such as Philippe Ariès have traced an increasing individualization of death in this period with the continuation of the late medieval *ars moriendi* and *danse macabre*, as well as a new emphasis on funerary rites, tombs, and other material memorials.[5] While the precise stages of Ariès's development scheme have been questioned, such work reminds us that 'death' is not (only) a natural, biological given but also constantly re-imagined through ritual and material object, visual and literary text.

The geometrically based art of anamorphoses, a term coming from the Greek and meaning to shape again, in particular captured the early modern sense of the intimacy of life and death, of death not only imagined as always present but defining and giving meaning (rather than opposed) to life. Anamorphic art was created with the help of a geometrical grid, by which linear frontal perspective was elongated or distorted: the undistorted image comes into focus when viewed from a particular angle or when reflected in a cylindrical mirror. Leonbattisti Alberti developed some early principles of anamorphic art in fifteenth-century Italy, and Leonardo Da Vinci experimented with the form, producing black and white sketches that were distorted from a frontal view, but formed human faces when viewed from an extreme edge. Texts explaining the principles of anamorphosis appeared in Italy, France, Germany, and England; by the seventeenth century optical illusions of various kinds had become widely popular.[6]

What is hidden in the anamorphic work of art could be secret, forbidden, or transgressive: some anamorphic images were erotic or obscene. Others, however, functioned as revelations of spiritual or higher realities: the proper perspective revealed the crucified Christ or the presence of death. Anamorphic art, with its revelatory or 'doubling' nature, particularly captured the intricacies of death in life, becoming a potent means of imagining death's perennial if uncanny presence.

Perhaps the best known anamorphic use of the skull or *memento mori* is a large-scale double portrait by Hans Holbein, now in the National Gallery, and known simply as *The Ambassadors* (Figure 9.2).[7] The painting is a virtuoso rendering of Jean de Dinteville, French ambassador to the court of Henry VIII, opulently attired in a pink and black lynx-lined satin gown, and his visiting friend, Georges de Selve, bishop of Lavaur, who wears an equally luxurious brown damask robe. The attention to texture and surfaces in the clothing and accoutrements of the sitters continues in the geometrical precision with which the objects and instruments in a double bookshelf are rendered. The globes of heaven and earth, astronomical tools, lute, flutes, and Lutheran hymnal, completing the panorama of the *trompe-l'oeil* image, represent the highest achievement of human learning and art. Yet across the lower foreground of this 'looking-glass' world is a distorted diagonal shape that shadows and threatens that achievement.

Viewed from the upper right, the slashing shape is revealed as a precisely delineated death's head (Figure 9.3): the distortion is also largely corrected by viewing the image in a cylindrical mirror (as with the Gripsholm portrait of Charles I).[8] Death is a mirror of the future for the viewer as well as subject of the painting, calling into question the worldly success signaled by the artifacts, splendid clothing, and other signs of prestige and wealth in the portrait. For Lacan, who commented

*Figure 9.2*   Hans Holbein, *The Ambassadors* (1533).

famously on this painting, Holbein's anamorphic technique is a kind of being-in-death, soliciting the gaze of the subject only to show him his own annihilation. The anamorphic text both positions the subject and shows its own lack – confronted with the phallic object that slashes the lower foreground and turns out to be the embodied image of castration or death.[9]

And yet the seeming polarities of life and death are not so much opposites as interwoven in the meaning of the portrait. If the death's head seems to undermine human achievement, it is, as has been pointed out, itself a virtuoso achievement of human art. Seemingly the ultimate disfigurement and effacement of human individuality, the skull may also be a pun on hollow bone, marking Holbein's own unique signature. And, despite the seeming oblivion of the sitters to the distorted

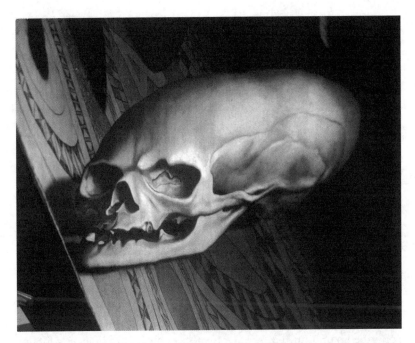

*Figure 9.3* Corrected image of anamorphic skull, Holbein, *The Ambassadors* (1533).

image in the foreground, the skull may also refer to Dinteville's own illness and melancholy in his years as ambassador, himself often not far from thoughts of morbidity and death; indeed, the skull has a tiny counterpart in a death's head worn on a brooch by Dinteville.[10] Further, the portrait reminds the viewer that death, seen from the perspective of religious belief, can also be a passage to life. Countering human death with a sacrificial, redemptive death, a tiny crucifix is revealed by the falling corner of the green damask curtain in the upper left hand of the painting.

Holbein's anamorphic art, then, reveals death not so much as the opposite as intricately interwoven in meaning and identity with life. The painting exemplifies not only the complexity and dual image of anamorphoses but also the constitutive role of the viewer.[11] Once put into play, the multiple perspectives – human achievement and death – do not cancel each other out, but oscillate and serve to define one another. Rather than a binary, either–or, the two perspectives exist together and one recent commentator has even argued that it is pos-

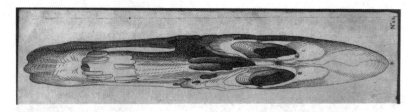

*Figure 9.4*   Anamorphosis of a Skull (1615) from Lucas Brunn, *Praxis Perspectivae* (Nürnberg, 1615).

sible to 'see' both the undistorted skull and the figures of the ambassadors – through visual compensation – at the same time.[12]

Such death's heads or *memento mori* were common in anamorphic art, reminding the early modern viewer of the presence of life in death and the need to prepare for one's end. In *La Perspective curieuse* (1638), J. F. Niceron writes of doubled pictures of life and death: 'seen from the front, they will represent a human face, and seen from the right, a death's head', adding that 'these drawings have become so common and trivial that they are seen everywhere'.[13] Similarly, the death's head alone could be anamorphized. A 1615 treatise published in Leipzig contains an elongated and distorted skull (Figure 9.4).[14] Ostensibly the ultimate sign of decay and mortality, the anamorphized skull is also an enduring mark of human artifice: the image comes into focus when viewed from a point, marked by an asterisk, on its upper edge (particularly when closing one eye). Life and death are intertwined, as the viewer brings the skull into proportion and focus: the skull or *memento mori* speaks to the viewer: *morieris*, you too shall die. And yet that message comes only as the viewer re-imagines its corrected shape and form.

Those anamorphic images not dealing directly with death could nonetheless reflect on the fleeting nature of life and the intertwining of life and death. A second anamorphic image of Charles I (Figure 9.5) shows an elongated and distorted image: when viewed from the lower edge – originally marked by the letter A – a corrected head and shoulders portrait of Charles I, derived from Van Dyck, comes into focus. While not containing the death's head of the Gripsholm portrait that we examined, this image – after 1649 at any rate – would have evinced a similar interplay, as the image of the dead king was brought to life through the constructing eye of the viewer.

It is the viewer, rather than the sitter, in these anamorphic images who grapples with the presence of death and its shadow over the living.

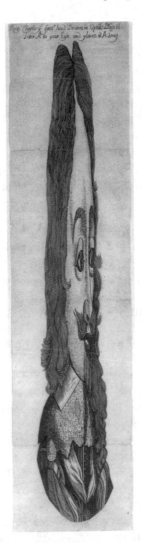

*Figure 9.5* Anamorphic Engraving of Charles I (ca. 1649).

But in more traditional *memento mori* images, the sitters themselves contemplate their own mortality, often signified by the presence of a skull. In *Eikon Basilike*, Charles examines the actions and events of his life and he meditates upon and prepares for death.[15] As he does so, Charles employs the language and techniques of perspective and vision to justify his own actions and overturn the verdict against him.

## 'Mortality crown'd with martyrdom': *Eikon Basilike* and the arts of perspective

In *Eikon Basilike* the defeated king – in captivity at Carisbroke Castle and fearing the worst – examines his life and envisions his approaching death. Using the language of optics, vision, and perspective, the 'death bed' meditations of *Eikon Basilike* position the reader to see through the disguises of Charles's enemies and into his own most secret thoughts. As in the reversals of anamorphic art, the designs of the king's enemies are viewed, then corrected by a second perspective. But, paradoxically, Charles's own innocence can only be demonstrated by the perfidy of his opponents, and the death of the king marks not the failure of Charles's claims but their ultimate proof.

The first English king to be put on trial by his own people, Charles was charged and tried by a High Court of Justice set up by the remnant of the House of Commons left after the military purge by Thomas Pride in December 1648.[16] By this time, the bloodshed of two civil wars and Charles's repeated double-dealing had convinced the Army that the king was not only untrustworthy but a 'man of blood' upon whom the blood-guilt of a nation lay.[17] The trial was perhaps not so much to convince the radicalized core who – out of the 59 commissioners named – actually participated in the proceedings, but rather it was to allow the nation as a whole to see Charles's intransigence and lack of repentance.[18]

Charged with 'a wicked design to erect and uphold in himself an unlimited and tyrannical power to rule according to his will, and to overthrow the rights and liberties of the people', Charles was impeached as 'a tyrant, traytor, murtherer, and a public and implacable enemy to the commonwealth of England'.[19] Yet for all the talk of justice and the impressive lists of crimes drawn up against the king, Charles indeed had history on his side when he objected that the House of Commons was never yet a Court of Judicature. Barred from the vote that had set up the Court by the relatively narrow margin of 26–20 were both the excluded Members of the Commons and the entire House of Lords.[20] Further, the charges turned on its head the traditional understanding of treason – codified in III Edward 25 – as 'imagining or compassing the death of the king'.[21] While the precedent for placing sovereignty in the people and not the king had been set in the trials and executions of two of Charles's closest advisors, Thomas Wentworth, Earl of Strafford and William Laud, Archbishop of Canterbury, the implications of the inversion of the traditional meaning of treason were now blatantly clear.[22]

Charles denied the authority of the court that tried him, insisting that no subject had power to judge his king. 'A subject and a soveraign', he would reiterate on the scaffold, 'are clean different things'.[23] Informed of the charges against him – treason, murder, and tyranny – Charles laughed in the face of the court.[24] But he also played a somber role that had been set out in *Eikon Basilike*, although that book appeared only after his death. Refusing to answer the charges against him, silent before his persecutors, Charles acted out the first act in a drama of Christ-like martyrdom, inverting the charges of treason and reversing for many the meaning of the spectacle of trial and punishment.[25]

The contours of the martyrology, as is well known, were laid out in *Eikon Basilike*, the king's book, apparently available in the streets on the day of the execution and in bookstalls by mid-February. Enormously popular and influential, the *Eikon Basilike* went through 35 editions in 1649 alone. Scholars have explored the work's appropriation of the Foxean tradition of martyrdom through biblical allusion and Christic language.[26] Much less explored, however, is the extent to which *Eikon Basilike* has recourse to language of sight and optics to show both the distortion of vision and the need for a new, corrected perspective. *Eikon Basilike* is replete with visual images of sight and blindness, disguise and illusion, clouds and sun, inner truth and external deception. By drawing upon the language of perspective, including instruments and techniques of vision, the text offers its readers a tool for seeing double, for discerning the Christic martyr in the public display of punishment, for imagining the piety and power of the king's death.

In face of military defeat, humiliation, and imprisonment, Charles (with his secret co-author John Gauden) appeals repeatedly in *Eikon Basilike* to this idea of second vision, most often located in the divine. Hence, defending his botched attempt to arrest five members of the House of Commons, the king evokes a deity who can see beyond false appearances to true reality: '*Thou that seest not as man seeth, but lookest beyond all popular appearances, searching the heart and trying the reins, and bringing to light the hidden things of darkness, show Thyself*' (13). Or, in commenting on his willingness to support the bill for triennial parliaments, he petitions a God '*Whose all-discerning justice sees through all the disguises of men's pretensions and deceitful darknesses of their hearts*' (23).

Other visual images in *Eikon Basilike* have to do with the dispelling of clouds or mists that obscure vision. Charles describes his early repulse at Hull by Sir John Hotham (who refused the king entry) as 'but the hand of that cloud which was soon after to overspread the whole kingdom and cast all into disorder and darkness' (34). Yet Hotham's betrayal of him (later repented – both Hotham and his son were ultimately executed as traitors by Parliament) also helped him to see more clearly: 'This gave me to see clearly through all the pious disguises and soft palliations of some men whose words were sometime smoother than oil, but now I saw they would prove very swords' (34). Charles equates disagreement and lack of loyalty to him with physical blindness, and he hopes for better sight on the part of his people. On the controversial publication of his apparently incriminating letters captured after the Battle of Naseby, he writes: 'I wish my subjects had yet a clearer sight into my most retired thoughts, where they might discover how they are divided between the love and care I have, not more to preserve my own rights than to procure their peace and happiness and that extreme grief to see them both deceived and destroyed' (130). 'Aftertimes may see', he later predicts, 'what the blindness of this age will not' (139).

*Eikon Basilike* thus draws upon traditional images of appearance versus reality, divine versus human sight; but it also employs more mechanical or optical figures of reflection and mirroring. Hence, commenting upon the 'Tumults' at London and Westminster that intimidated both the king and his supporters, Charles adduces the glass or mirror that reflects a true or corrected image: 'I believe the just avenger of all disorders will in time make those men and that city see their sin in the glass of their punishments' (18). Similarly, reflecting upon Queen Henrietta Maria's flight to France in 1644, Charles prays *'That in the glass of Thy truth she may see Thee in those mercies which Thou hast offered to us in Thy Son Jesus Christ, our only Saviour'* (33). And, defending himself against the charge of complicity in the Irish rebellion of October 1641 – in which Irish Catholics killed a considerable number of English and Scottish Protestant settlers – the king prays, *'Let not the miseries I and my kingdoms have hitherto suffered seem small to Thee, but make our sins appear to our consciences as they are represented in the glass of Thy judgments'* (67).

*Eikon Basilike* also uses language of sight, perspective, and vision as the king turns from examining his life in the face of death to envisioning that death itself. Charles writes that 'although my death at present may justly be represented to me with all those terrible aggravations which the policy of cruel and implacable enemies can put upon it ... yet, I bless God, I can look upon all those stings as unpoisonous, though sharp, since my Redeemer hath either pulled them out or given me the antidote of His death against them' (172).

With a stunning kind of rhetorical anamorphosis, Charles transforms his imagined death into imitation of Christ: 'I confess it is not easy for me to contend with those many horrors of death wherewith God suffers me to be tempted; which are equally horrid either in the suddenness of a barbarous assassination or in those greater formalities whereby my enemies (being more solemnly cruel) will it may be, seek to add (as those did who crucified Christ) the mockery of justice to the cruelty of malice' (174). The ordeal that he is about to undergo may have the appearance of justice, but a proper perspective, viewing, as it were from the margin – or in God's glass – shows not justice but cruelty and malice.

While the charges brought by his enemies may seem to 'obscure' the true picture, Charles strives to show underneath the image of Christ-like suffering for the sake of righteousness: 'My next comfort is that He gives me not only the honor to imitate His Example in suffering for righteousness' sake (though obscured by the foulest charges of tyranny and injustice), but also that charity which is the noblest revenge upon, and victory over, my destroyers' (176). Hence, while Charles may now appear humiliated and defeated, in his trial and death he will follow another script, that of martyrdom: 'If I must suffer a violent death with my Saviour, it is but mortality crowned with martyrdom' (179). As such, Charles paradoxically has the same goal as his most determined opponents during the trial: not to save his life, but to lose it.

## 'Which els no man could imagine': anamorphoses and Milton's *Eikonoklastes*

As Milton recognized in opening *Eikonoklastes*, there was no honour to be gained in debating a dead man, and particularly a dead king.[27] Nonetheless, using language of optics and perspective, he set out to correct the distortions of the king's book, in which the defeated party 'falsly or fallaciously representing the state of things' demanded a reply. Indeed, he need only clear their vision, 'by better information giv'n them, or, which is anough, by onely remembring them the truth of what they themselves know to be heer misaffirm'd' (338) regarding Charles's life – and his death.

Using visual and optical language, Milton contrasts the fair appearance with the far differing reality of the king's words and promises as he allegedly examines his life and prepares for death in *Eikon Basilike*. The 'gaudy name of Majesty' (338) serves in itself as a kind of disguise for the true contents of *Eikon Basilike*: 'containing little els but the

*Figure 9.6*   Charles I at prayer, frontispiece to *Eikon Basilike* (1649).

common grounds of tyranny and popery, drest up, the better to deceiv, in a new Protestant guise, and trimmly garnish'd over' (339). Such disguising has its model and source in the king himself, who – far from repenting – 'persists heer to maintain and justifie the most apparent of his evil doings, and washes over with a Court-fucus the worst and foulest of his actions' (347).

Milton particularly objects to the visual cozenage of the 'conceited portraiture' of the frontispiece of *Eikon Basilike*, 'drawn out to the full Measure of a Masking Scene, and sett there to catch fools and silly gazers' (342). For Milton, this image (Figure 9.6) – showing a kneeling Charles who spurns his earthly crown for a heavenly crown and evoking the passion of Christ himself in the garden of Gesthemane – is a 'Picture sett in Front [that] would Martyr him and Saint him to befool the people' (343). Yet the visual tricks of the frontispiece have an even more pervasive counterpart in the rhetorical tricks throughout. Milton focuses on the issue of martyrdom, insisting that Charles's method is not the revelation of anamorphosis but bad art badly explained: 'He who writes himself *Martyr* by his own inscription, is like an ill Painter who, by writing on the shapeless Picture which he hath drawn, is fain to tell passengers what shape it is; which els no man could imagine' (575).

Nonetheless Milton's own text will operate by a kind of a rhetorical anamorphosis, by which Charles's 'fair-spok'n words shall be heer fairly confronted and laid parallel to his far differing deeds, manifest and visible to the whole Nation' (347). Framed by and permeated with this language of false perspective and distorted or blinded vision, *Eikonoklastes* responds chapter by chapter to *Eikon Basilike*, quoting the king's own words and laying them aside his own actions and deeds. Milton continues with the contrast between the fair appearance and the false reality of the king's words, even in the face of death. In Charles's professed regard for parliament, '*To have always thought the right way [of Parliament], most safe for his Crown, and best pleasing to his People*' (356), Milton finds 'faire and specious promises . . . [which] contain nothing in them much different from his former practices, so cross, and so averse to all his Parlaments' (360). On the king's defense of his going to the House of Commons, including that his friends '*knew not the just motives and pregnant grounds with which I thought my selfe furnish'd*' to arrest the five suspected members, Milton writes: 'heer like a rott'n building newly trimm'd over he represents it speciously and fraudulently to impose upon the simple Reader' (377).

According to *Eikonoklastes*, Charles is a bad reader of signs, particularly in predicting the future. To Charles's declaration that '*He never thought any thing more to presage the mischiefes that ensu'd, then those Tumults*', Milton responds caustically: 'Then was his foresight but short, and much mistak' n' (388–9). When Charles comments on Sir John Hotham, that '*He could not but observe how God not long after pleaded and aveng'd his cause*' (428), Milton retorts: 'But how farr that King was deceav'd in his thought that God was favouring to his cause, that story unfolds; and how little reason this King had to impute the death of Hotham to Gods avengement of his repuls at *Hull*, may easily be seen' (429).

While the 'business of death is a plaine case, and admitts no controversie' (582), there too Milton must uncover the king's dissimulation. Since Charles in his 'few mortifying howrs' has taken the time 'to enveigh bitterly against that Justice which was don upon him' (582), Milton will show, in contrast, the intertwined truth and justice of the act of regicide: that 'god hath testif'd by all propitious, & the most evident signes, whereby in these latter times he is wont to testife what pleases him; that such a solemn, and for many Ages unexampl'd act of due punishment, was no *mockery of Justice*, but a most gratefull and well-pleasing Sacrifice' (596).

Milton insists that he is simply correcting distorted vision, allowing the truth to be 'not smother'd, but sent abroad, in the native confidence of her single self, to earn, how she can, her entertainment in the world, and to finde out her own readers' (339). He claims to write so that 'they that will, may now see at length how much they were deceiv'd in him, and were ever like to be hereafter' (364). Yet as Milton incorporates the king's words into his own text, *Eikonoklastes* contains two radically different but parallel discourses, the one the written words of the king (in fact his secret co-author) and the other the sharply critical and dissenting commentary, secondary in being derived from and dependent upon (even if in opposition to) the king's text.

As such, Milton neither disposes of the king's claim to our attention nor restores a unitary view of the truth – despite the overt intentions of the text to do so. Rather, the very coerciveness of the text is in tension with its claim to discover, reveal, disclose. The commentary, laid alongside Charles's own words, sets out to correct an initial misreading: that the king's words are trustworthy, genuine, and true. But the succeeding insight gained from Milton's commentary does not replace so much as exist in uneasy co-alliance with the king's word: as in an anamorphic picture. Milton's own text is at odds with his insistence on the self-evidence of the truth.

## 'Such a strooken blindness': the king's death and the English people

Has the tract then failed? Do the anamorphic techniques and the visual and optical language of *Eikonoklastes* undermine its own rhetorical ends? We recall, further, that the tract did not persuade its readers: the 35 editions of *Eikon Basilike* and the plethora of texts eulogizing the dead king as martyr served to underscore how few indeed were the readers of Milton's text. Yet a return to perspectival arts helps us to see that the 'failure' of *Eikonoklastes* proves its main points: the blindness and impenitence of king and people who idolize the dead king.

Although the king's tract and portrait have caught 'the worthles approbation of an inconstant, irrational, and Image-doting rabble [. . .] like a credulous and hapless herd, begott'n to servility, and inchanted with these popular institutes of Tyranny, subscrib'd with a new device of the Kings Picture at his praiers' (601), Milton claims to write so that 'the rest, whom perhaps ignorance without malice, or some error, less then fatal, hath for the time misledd, on this side Sorcery or obduration, may find the grace and good guidance to bethink themselves, and recover' (601). But how much hope for recovery does the tract hold out? Milton's own metaphors of sight and distortion point against such a recovery: the people, like the king, are not merely seeing ill but blind. Comparing Charles to Pharoah, Milton comments that 'whom God hard'ns, them also he blinds' (516) and he warns that they must not 'suffer one mans blind intentions to lead us all with our eyes op'n to manifest destruction' (416). When Charles prays regarding Queen Henrietta Maria *'That his constancy may be an antidote against the poyson of other mens example'* Milton scoffs: 'But what is it that the blindness of hypocrisy dares not doe? It dares pray, and thinks to hide that from the eyes of God, which it cannot hide from the op'n view of man' (422).

The people too are represented as blind. Milton writes not to convince so much as to hold them accountable, so that those 'so much affatuated, not with [King Charles's] person onely, but with his palpable faults, and [who] dote upon his deformities may have none to blame but thir own folly if they live and dye in such a strook'n blindness' (341–2). Those who fail to be convinced by what they see – 'who notwithstanding shall persist to give to bare words more credit then to op'n deeds', have a failure of vision that signifies a failure of knowledge: 'fatally stupifi'd and bewitch'd into such a blinde and obstinate beleef' (347).

Milton also uses more mechanical or optical images to predict that readers will not be convinced by his tract. *Eikonoklastes* is a kind of mirror held up to reflect the king's faults, but neither Charles nor his followers will see: 'But he who neither by his own Letters and Commissions under hand and Seale, nor by his own actions held as in a Mirror before his face, will be convinc'd to see his faults, can much less be won upon by any force of words, neither he, nor any that take after him' (547).

Milton needs to point to the words of the 'unrepentant' king as much as the king needs to point to his persecutors to construct himself as a martyr. As in an anamorphic image, two polarities form an interdependent – if unstable – whole. The king's book is viewed – then 'corrected' or 'erased' by a change of position, but it nonetheless remains visible. The meaning of *Eikonoklastes* comes from the distortion and the correction together: what seems to be a binary antithesis – the king's insistence upon his own martyrdom and Milton's counter-insistence on the death as an act of justice – are not so much opposed as two sides of the same image.

## The politics of dying: aftermath

Writing *Eikonoklastes*, Milton spoke on behalf of a regime that never had the consent or approval of the majority of the English. Milton made that minority support a positive, envisioning the supporters of the regicide as the remnant of Israel, even while he held the people and such erring groups as the Presbyterians accountable for their own blindness. The relation between *Eikon Basilike* and *Eikonoklastes* is not a simple matter of image making and image breaking. Rather, optical arts and the language and techniques of anamorphoses – seeing from different planes or perspectives – capture the rich complexity of the imaginings of death in each text. Charles constructs his own death as a martyr: drawing on and appropriating the arts of dying and the traditional *memento mori* for political ends. Milton views the king's meditation on his death as his own false imaginings. Rather than following the proper craft of dying – prayer and patience, examining one's life and repenting of sin, truly forgiving others, exhortation of family and friends, willingness to leave worldly things behind – Charles dissembles, plagiarizes, and makes public for political ends what should be between him and his God. Charles, according to Milton, gives up the world in a manner precisely calculated to retain it.

The cult of Charles the martyr, initiated by *Eikon Basilike* as well as by the king's courage and dignity during his trial and on the scaffold, did indeed keep the late king alive on earth.[28] In the absence of a funeral sermon or tomb, the elegies, tracts, and visual images, inspired by and modelled on *Eikon Basilike*, gained additional power in imagining and interpreting the king's death. *Eikon Basilike* and the other martyrologies were also an effective means of legitimating the rule of the late king's son, when, after the collapse of the republican regimes that succeeded the fall of Richard Cromwell's government, Charles II was restored to the English throne.

The anamorphic image of Charles I with which we began thus has another secret to reveal, another image that shows the true purpose and end of the king's death. On the reverse side of the painting is a second painting, this one showing from a frontal perspective the orb of sovereignty (Figure 9.7). As on the reverse side, the key is placing a cylindri-

*Figure 9.7*   Anamorphic Portrait of Charles II (ca. 1660).

cal mirror over the foregrounded orb. Reflected in the mirror is a corrected image of the martyr-king's son, Charles II, wearing rich ermine and scarlet that signify – although the crown is absent – his restored rule on earth. Like his father, Charles II endured seeming defeat after the battle of Worcester and years of exile, political intrigue, and near-penury. His restoration to the throne in 1660 offered a new perspective on the years of struggle: the regal image of the restored monarch. The late king himself could not have imagined a happier ending.

## Notes

1. I first came upon a copy of this portrait in the National Portrait Gallery Picture Library, London. The portrait has been reproduced, with brief commentary in Jurgis Baltrusaitis, *Anamorphic Art*, 106; and in Fred Leeman, *Hidden Images: Games of Perception, Anamorphic Art, Illusion*, fig. 131. Baltrusaitis's book, first published in French in 1969, was an important influence in rekindling modern interest in anamorphoses.
2. On Van Dyck portraiture, see Arthur Wheelock Jr, Susan J. Barnes and Julius

Held (eds), *Anthony van Dyck*, and John Peacock, 'The visual image of Charles I', in Corns, 176–239.

3. For an important article that demonstrates the relevance of optical figures and references in printed polemical tracts of the 1640s more broadly, see Sharon Achinstein, 'The Uses of Deception from Cromwell to Milton'.

4. *Eikonoklastes*, vol. 3 in *The Complete Prose Works of John Milton*, gen. ed. Douglas Bush (New Haven: Yale University Press, 1962) 335–601. Page numbers for quotations from this work will be given parenthetically in the text.

5. Philippe Ariès, *The Hour of our Death*, and Ariès, *Images of Man and Death*. Exploring cultural constructions of death in the early modern period, see Michael Neill, *Issues of Death: Mortality and Identity in English Renaissance Tragedy*; in his illuminating introduction (1–48), Neill sketches out the influence of Ariès, going on to argue that representations of death become increasingly secularized in the early modern period, in part through the genre of tragedy. Similarly, Robert Watson sees an erosion of belief and fear of annihilation prompting a crisis in English Renaissance culture in *The Rest Is Silence: Death as Annihilation in the English Renaissance*.

6. On the principles and history of anamorphic art, see especially Baltrusaitis, *Anamorphic Art*, and Leeman, *Hidden Images*. For more theoretical and literary considerations of anamorphoses, see Sylvia Söderlind, 'Illegitimate Perspectives and the Critical Unconscious: The Anamorphic Imagination'; Ned Lukacher, 'Anamorphic Stuff: Shakespeare, Catharsis, Lacan'; and Ernest Gilman, *The Curious Perspective: Literary and Pictorial Wit in the Seventeenth Century*.

7. On this portrait, see the comprehensive recent study by Susan Foister, Ashok Roy, and Martin Wyld, *Making and Meaning Holbein's Ambassadors*. On the portrait and anamorphoses, see Baltrusaitis, *Anamorphic Art*, 91–114; Leeman, *Hidden Images*, 13–14; and Stephen Greenblatt, *Renaissance Self-Fashioning: From More to Shakespeare*, ch. one.

8. E. R. Samuel, 'Death in the Glass: A New View of Holbein's Ambassadors'; Foister, Roy, and Wyld 53–5.

9. Jacques Lacan, *The Four Fundamental Concepts of Psycho-Analysis*, 79–90, esp. 88–90.

10. Foister, Roy, and Wyld, *Making and Meaning Holbein's Ambassadors*, 57.

11. For an emphasis on the viewer's active role in the creation of the anamorphic object, see Daniel Collins, 'Anamorphosis and the Eccentric Observer: Inverted Perspective and the Construction of the Gaze'.

12. See David Topper, 'On Anamorphosis: Setting Some Things Straight'.

13. J. F. Niceron, *La Perspective curieuse* (1638), 50 and 51; quoted and translated in Baltrusaitis, *Anamorphic Art*, 105.

14. Lucas Brunn, 55, plate 24.

15. On the arts of dying upon which Charles draws, see Phillipe Ariès, *The Hour of Our Death*, 107–10, and the comprehensive treatment in Mary Catherine O'Connor, *The Art of Dying Well: The Development of the Ars Moriendi*. For a treatment of the *ars moriendi* in *Eikon Basilike* and *Eikonoklastes*, linked brilliantly with the ambiguous death of Samson in *Samson Agonistes*, see Dennis Kezar, *Guilty Creatures: Renaissance Poetry and the Ethics of Authorship*.

16. For an extensive account of this military purge and surrounding events

and implications, see David Underdown, *Pride's Purge: Politics in the Puritan Revolution*.

17. See the important early article by Patricia Crawford, 'Charles Stuart: That Man of Blood'. More recently, David Scott looks at the motivations of regicides from a particular region, north-eastern and northwestern England, urging further study of the complex motives of those who sat on the High Court in 'Motives for King-Killing' in Peacey, 138–60.

18. So John Morrill and Philip Baker persuasively argue, with prime reference to Oliver Cromwell, in 'Oliver Cromwell, the Regicide and the sons of Zeruiah', in Peacey, *The Regicides*, 14–35. In the same volume, however, Sean Kelsey argues that the outcome of the trial was 'far from preordained'; Kelsey sees Charles as bringing on his own fatal end by his refusal to recognize the court and his intransigence in constructing himself as a martyr, See 'Staging the Trial of Charles I', in Peacey, *The Regicides*, 71–93.

19. *The Manner of the Tryall of Charles Stuart, King of England*, in J. G. Muddiman, *The Trial of Charles I* (London: W. Hodge and Co., 1928), 78–9. Contemporary printed versions of the events are also reproduced in Thomas Bayly Howell (ed), *A Complete Collection of State Trials*, Vol. IV, cols 1045–1135 and in C.V. Wedgwood, *The Trial of Charles I*.

20. See the re-examination of the circumstances surrounding the setting up of the High Court of Justice in S. M. Koenigsberg, 'The Vote to Create the High Court of Justice: 26 to 20?'.

21. *Statutes of the Realm*, vol. 1, 319–20. The definition of treason begins: 'When a Man doth compass or imagine the Death of our Lord the King, or of our Lady his [queen] or of their eldest Son and Heir'. The unusual use of the word *imagine* is taken from the original Law French ('compasser ou ymaginer la mort'), meaning to intend or plan. Originally intended to strengthen and centralize the powers of the monarchy, the treason laws were turned against the monarch in the mid-seventeenth century revolutionary crisis; the original meaning was reinstated with the Restoration and the execution of the regicides for 'imagining the death of the king'. See Lisa Steffen, *Defining a British State: Treason and National Identity, 1608–1820*, esp. ch. one.

22. See Steffen, 24–31.

23. King Charles, *His Speech Made Upon the Scaffold* (1649), reprinted in Muddiman, *The Trial of Charles*, 260–4, qtd 262.

24. Muddiman, *The Trial of Charles I*, 80.

25. The parallels between the trials of Charles and of Christ have been most extensively traced by Daniel P. Klein, who argues that in refusing to recognize the jurisdiction of the court, Charles acted not only on political or legal grounds, but – like the early martyrs – in conscious imitation of Christ at his trial and crucifixion (*Legal History* 18.1 (1997) 1–25).

26. On martyrdom and *Eikon Basilike*, see Florence Sandler, 'Icon and Iconoclast' as well as John Knott, '"Suffering for Truth's Sake": Milton and Martyrdom'; also Knoppers, *Historicizing Milton: Spectacle, Power, and Poetry in Restoration England*, ch. 1, and most recently, Robert Wilcher, *The Writing of Royalism, 1628–1660*.

27. Among the recent essays on *Eikonoklastes*, Elizabeth Skerpan Wheeler insightfully explores the composite construction of the king's book in '*Eikon*

*Basilike* and the Rhetoric of Self-Representation'. Jane Hiles addresses from a different perspective the 'failure' of argument that I explore in 'Milton's Royalist Reflex: the Failure of Argument and the Role of Dialogics in *Eikonoklastes*'. Achinstein comments briefly but perceptively on the uses of optical language in *Eikonoklastes*. With a focus on the *ars moriendi* in *Eikon Basilike* and *Eikonoklastes* as setting up a 'skeptical' reading of *Samson Agonistes*, see Dennis Kezar, *Guilty Creatures: Renaissance Poetry and the Ethics of Authorship* 152–71.

28. On the cult of Charles the martyr, in particular in relation to the Restoration, see Lois Potter, *Secret Rites and Secret Writing: Royalist Literature, 1641–1660*, especially chapter five; and Knoppers, *Historicizing Milton*, ch. one. Most recently, Robert Wilcher offers a rich and wide-ranging account of laments for the king and waiting for the restoration in *The Writing of Royalism*, chs 11 and 12. See also Andrew Lacey, 'Elegies and Commemorative Verse in Honour of Charles the Martyr, 1649–60', in Peacey, 225–46.

# 10
# Milton's Nationalism and the Rights of Memory

*Paul Stevens*

Like most of his contemporaries, Milton was more than familiar with death.[1] Unlike his own recently fallen Adam, not only had he seen death but he had seen it in many shapes. He knew that this world was a lot like a lazar-house wherein are 'laid / Numbers of all diseased, all maladies, / Of ghastly spasm, or racking torture, qualms / Of heart-sick agony' (*Paradise Lost* 11: 479–82). From early manhood, his life was punctuated by periods of intense grief following the death of family or friends. Between April 1637 and August 1638, for instance, his mother, his Cambridge contemporary Edward King, and his beloved friend Charles Diodati all died. In March 1647, his father died. Between May and June 1652, his first wife, Mary, and their baby son, John, died. Between February and March 1658, his second wife, Katherine, and their baby daughter, also named Katherine, died. The immediacy and power of death haunts Milton's works; it informs his most creative moments and gives *Paradise Lost*, his story of Christian regeneration, the ground of its authenticity. To a degree that is rarely emphasized, however, Milton was a patriot, an English nationalist, and the burden of imagining death and remembering the dead is strangely caught up with his sense of national election. In this essay, I want to suggest something of the modernity of Milton by drawing attention to what his work reveals about the relationship between the modern nation-states in which we live and what Stephen Greenblatt calls 'the rights of memory'. Let me begin with Greenblatt and his preoccupation with identity and memory.

## The rights of memory

Greenblatt's concern with identity and memory is a constant throughout his career from *Three Modern Satirists* through *Renaissance Self-*

*Fashioning* to his latest work, *Hamlet in Purgatory*. In this important book, the old existentialist agon between being and nothingness that animates all his work is reformulated in terms of remembering and forgetting, but specifically and emphatically remembering and forgetting the dead.[2] Anticipated and perhaps inspired by Antony Low's powerful *ELR* essay on 'Hamlet and the Ghost of Purgatory,' the first part of Greenblatt's book turns on a brilliant reversal. It begins with a story of liberation – of how the Protestant revolution in consciousness came to see the vast ideological system of oppression at whose centre was the doctrine of Purgatory as nothing more than 'a poet's fable', a fiction that need have no hold on us. The dark pit discovered by St. Patrick at Lough Derg through which the living might enter and experience the terrors of Purgatory turned out on Protestant inspection to be nothing but 'a poor beggarly hole [. . .] such as husbandmen make to keep a few Hogs from the rain' (qtd. 100). So it seems that contrary to the bleak Foucauldian argument of Greenblatt's new historicist classic, 'Invisible Bullets', there is hope and it is for us. But not quite. For, as Low points out, the demystification and destruction of Purgatory means condemning the dead to oblivion. This is a horror it takes some imagination for us in the present to see, and it is here that Greenblatt's notion of the scholar as magician comes into its own. Greenblatt conjures up the spirit of Thomas More to defamiliarize the present by allowing us to see the past in a new light. In More's 1529 *Supplication of Souls*, the purgatorial dead are made to speak and as we see the happiness of the living through their ghostly eyes we come to understand something of their right to be remembered:

> [R]emember how nature and Christendom bindeth you to remember us. . . . remember our thirst while ye sit and drink; our hunger while ye be feasting; our restless watch while ye be sleeping; our sore and grievous pain while ye be playing.                                   (qtd. 150)

Inspired by what becomes More's terrible vision of the indifference of the living to the dead, Greenblatt reminds us of the degree to which in destroying Purgatory liberation might mean its opposite, the erasure of our own humanity, our own being:

> Vows are broken, mourning is forgotten, life resumes its round of heedless pleasures, and even piety takes the form of cold lip service. The dead in their individuality, their intense suffering, their urgent claims on personal remembrance, are consigned to oblivion

or become at best an anonymous, generalized category, the 'all Christian souls' casually invoked in a ritual phrase by thoughtless children.

Against this terrible indifference the suffering souls in More's text cry out, passionately claiming *the right to be remembered and the rites of memory.* (146, my emphasis)

Greenblatt's much discussed return to his Jewish origins is governed by the same imperatives that move More – the humanity or identity implicit in the rights of memory. The bond of charity between the living and the dead so powerfully articulated in the rites of More's Purgatory are equally present in kaddish, the Jewish prayer for the dead Greenblatt says for his father (5–9). But in Greenblatt's work both these rites – purgatorial prayer for Hamlet and kaddish for Greenblatt himself – are perceived as being incapable of responding fully to the rights or imagined needs of the dead. Because of what has been lost neither son has a way of responding effectively to his dead father's command – 'Remember me'. The forgetting this incapacity brings about constitutes a new form of nothingness. Hamlet desperately tries to get his mother to remember and see the ghost: ' "Do you see nothing there?" "Nothing at all, yet all that is I see" ' (qtd. 225). What Greenblatt himself tries to see in his recent essay 'The Inevitable Pit' are the ghosts of his Jewish family.

In this very moving essay, Greenblatt raises the same issue of remembering and forgetting that he does in *Hamlet in Purgatory*, but specifically in terms of the Jewishness of his family. By emigrating to America in the 1890s, his Lithuanian Jewish family escaped the murderous pit that would be prepared for them by the Nazi authorities in 1943 only to consign their Jewish identity to the oblivion of Emerson's 'inevitable pit' – that is, the pit which 'the creation of new thought opens for all that is old' (qtd. 10), the pit into which 'traditional modes of living' are consigned 'in order to make way for new modes that will themselves soon be obsolete' (10), the pit of American cultural assimilation. The essay underlines this irony by ending with an impasse. While visiting the site of the Nazis' murder pits in the Ponary hills outside Vilna, Greenblatt's son sees a photograph in the museum and realizes that a Jewish man with one of Greenblatt's family names did escape: 'We would have made it after all,' he cries in triumph – glowing 'with absurd, precious American optimism', adds his father (12). The moment of liberation is thus confounded by the very Americanness of his son's optimism, for the act of identification behind the joy in the escape is paradoxically contingent on his son's Americanness, that is, the loss or diminution of his Jewish identity.

The impasse is false, however, for two interrelated reasons – one Greenblatt is aware of, but the other he seems blind to. First, as Greenblatt knows, liberation in its fullest sense lies not in escaping the pit but in entering it – just as one would enter the dark hole of Purgatory at Lough Derg or the nightmare chasm at Babi Yar. Liberation lies in responding to the rights of the dead by entering imaginatively into their lives and sufferings, by reading and writing stories about them, and so giving them identity by providing them with the answering voice of an informed audience. This is the substance of Greenblatt's individual, existentialist kaddish. The second reason why the impasse is false takes me to the heart of my argument. In the case of the Jewish dead murdered by the Nazis it is not Greenblatt alone or any individual who reads and tells the stories – the whole nation does. Their stories echo and re-echo throughout the nation's public sphere. The Holocaust or systematic murder of six million European Jews has been assimilated into the national imaginary not only of Israel but of many other nations, but none more so than Greenblatt's own nation, the United States. This does not mean, as Tim Cole claims, that the Holocaust has been Americanized simply in the sense of '"Hollywoodized," bought, packaged and sold' (xi); it means that it has become an integral, and specifically Jewish, part of the nation's narrative or self-representation. 'Where national memories are concerned,' says Ernest Renan, 'griefs are of more value than triumphs, for they impose duties, and require a common effort' (19). As Peter Novick has shown, the memory of those who died in the Holocaust has enormous force in *American* life: '[f]or the political center – on some level for all Americans – the Holocaust has become a moral reference point' (13).[3] However misunderstood or simplified, it shapes behaviour, imposes duties and demands effort. And whatever its faults, Washington's US Holocaust Memorial Museum standing in the midst of the nation's other monuments and explicitly reminding its citizens of their responsibilities bears eloquent witness to this new reality.[4] There at the end of the great Mall, as in Ezekiel's valley of dry bones, the dead that Greenblatt rightly wants to mourn are remembered in the life of the nation.

This is of immediate relevance to Milton's nationalism. What the writing of so many early modern English Protestants from John Foxe to John Milton makes clear is precisely the reverse of the claim implicit in Greenblatt and explicit in Low that '[a]fter the Reformation, few countries turned their backs more abruptly [than England] on Purgatory and, with it, on their own dead' (447). The English may have turned their backs on Purgatory, but not on their dead. Indeed, according to G. W. Pigman, Protestant England in the late sixteenth and early seventeenth centuries witnessed the emergence of a new sensitivity to the pain of the bereaved and the need to mourn the dead. He quotes, among many others, Bishop Jewel in his 1583 *Exposition* on the epistles to the Thessalonians:

> Our parentes, and our children are deare unto us. They are our fleshe and bloude, and the chiefe and principall partes of our bodie. Anye part of our bodie can not be cut off, but wee shall feele it. The father if he feele not the deathe of his sonne; or, the sonne if he feele not the death of his Father, and have not a deepe feeling of it, he is unnatural. (qtd. 34)

The dead were in fact remembered in innumerable memorials, monuments, endowments, histories, sermons, martyrologies, political pamphlets, churches and churchyards, all increasingly, to some extent or other, gathered into a new narrative of national election, a narrative that was felt to be far more real than any poet's fable. Linda Colley, focusing on the effect of the repeated editions of Foxe's 1563 *Acts and Monuments* or *Book of Martyrs*, puts it this way:

> [The agony of the martyrs] had been for a purpose, to demonstrate their own resolute faith and to bear witness to their countrymen's Protestant destiny. The weak and miscellaneous had gone through bitter trials to the stake and the torch, but out of the flames had come forth both a common steadfastness and triumphant confirmation that their land was blessed. (28)

What Milton in particular confirms is the degree to which this sense of national election or purpose could ease the personal grief of private citizens even for loved ones who had not been martyred or died public deaths. In what follows I want to suggest, first, how exactly this works, how personal grief in Milton gets acted out in the nation's story, and, second, how such mourning illuminates the present-day refusal of nation-states to disappear.

## Vesta's eternal flame

1658 opened tragically for Milton. On 3 February, his second wife Katherine died, and then just over a month later on 17 March, their baby daughter, also named Katherine, died. As Barbara Lewalski has recently emphasized, Milton's anguish is evident in one of the great love poems of the language, 'Methought I saw my late espoused saint':[5]

Methought I saw my late espoused saint
    Brought to me like Alcestis from the grave,
    Whom Jove's great son to her glad husband gave,
    Rescued from death by force though pale and faint.
Mine as whom washt from spot of child-bed taint,
    Purification in the old Law did save,
    And such, as yet once more I trust to have
Full sight of her in heaven without restraint,
Came vested all in white, pure as her mind:
    Her face was veiled, yet to my fancied sight,
    Love, sweetness, goodness, in her person shined
So clear, as in no face with more delight.
    But O as to embrace me she inclined
    I waked, she fled, and day brought back my night

What distinguishes the poem, what makes it so moving, is the degree to which the very powerful narratives of religious consolation Milton invokes all prove ineffective. At some level of consciousness, Milton's Protestant speaker is confident that his young wife, purified in mind by grace as she is in body after childbirth by the prescriptions of the old Law, is saved, a 'saint', and that he, who because of his blindness has never seen her in this life, will have 'Full sight of her in heaven without restraint'. The truth of this central story of Christian redemption is reinforced and dramatized by one of its shadowy classical types. The dream Milton's speaker has of his wife 'vested all in white', her face 'veiled', reminds him of the story of Alcestis brought back veiled from the grave and returned to her husband, Admetus, through the heroic agency of 'Jove's great son', Heracles. Although it is not clear whether this analogue occurs to the speaker in the dream or afterwards while recounting it, it is hard to imagine a narrative more carefully calculated to ameliorate suffering and produce hope. In his suffering, Euripides' Admetus speaks directly for John Milton in the winter of 1658:

What greater sorrow can a man have than the loss of his faithful wife? Would I had never married. . . . I envy the unmarried and childless. . . . For they have a single soul, and to feel its pain is only a moderate burden. But diseases of children and wives snatched by death from their marriage beds are unendurable.  (ll.879–88)

Similarly, in his hope, in his recognition of Alcestis redeemed, Admetus anticipates the joy of Milton's dream: 'O gods, what shall I say. Here is a wonder past all hoping' (l.1123). The difference is, of course, that the return of Admetus'wife is real, while that of Milton's wife turns out to be precisely the false hope, the vain 'delusive joy' that Admetus fears. 'But O,' when 'to embrace me she inclined,' Milton explains, 'I waked, she fled, and day brought back my night.' In this *volta* or reversal, both the religious narratives of comfort, the Christian and its classical type, are confounded in a renewed and intensified sense of loss, and Milton's blindness is made to figure the intractability of his grief.

Not all the narratives of consolation invoked in the poem are, however, religious. One of the strangest has an aggressively secular cast to it. 'Methought I saw my late espoused saint' almost inevitably brings to mind Sir Walter Raleigh's sonnet, 'Methought I saw the grave where Laura lay':

> Methought I saw the graue, where Laura lay,
> Within the Temple, where the vestall flame
> Was wont to burne, and passing by that way,
> To see the buried dust of liuing fame,
> Whose tumbe faire loue, and fairer vertue kept,
> All suddeinly I saw the Faery Queene:
> At whose approch the soule of Petrarke wept,
> And from thenceforth those graces were not seene.
> For they this Queene attended, in whose steed
> Obliuion laid him downe on Lauras herse:
> Hereat the hardest stones were seene to bleed,
> And grones of buried ghostes the heuens did perse.
>    Where Homers spright did tremble all for griefe,
>    And curst th'accesse of that celestiall theife.

Raleigh's narrative seems a strange one to invoke because the poem is not so much an act of mourning as a celebration of the prestige Spenser's *Faerie Queene* is likely to bring England and its verse. Raleigh's sonnet, 'A Vision upon this Conceipt of the Faery Queene', is the first of seven commendatory poems that introduce the 1590 edition of Spenser's great work. What at first appears to be an expression of personal grief, it soon becomes clear, is in fact an exclamation of national triumph. Whatever grief there is is not that of Raleigh's speaker or his beloved. In the fiction Raleigh creates, Spenser's dark conceit inspires in him a vision of England's poetic destiny. Laura is superseded by a new object of desire:

the graces that kept her tomb in the Temple of Vesta now desert her to attend England's faery queen and the power of the vestal flame that was 'wont to burne' there is implicitly transferred to Elizabeth as Gloriana. As Laura is cast into oblivion and the rights of memory are denied her, so stones bleed and the groans of ghosts pierce the heavens. Spenser's precursors in the creation of amorous and heroic poetry, Petrarch and Homer, are transumed; they weep and curse the Promethean success of England's Laureate. Their grief is inconsolable, but its very excess is the measure of Raleigh's joy because it is also the measure of the westward course of poetic empire. Finally, in the achievement of *The Faerie Queene*, England has a kingdom of its own language.[6]

It is central to my argument that the relationship between these two sonnets, Milton's act of mourning and Raleigh's exclamation of national triumph, is not quite as arbitrary as it might seem. The figure that renders the relationship substantial is that of Vesta, the ancient goddess of the hearth who in her chastity or purity, as A. D. Cousins has pointed out, gives the Roman *imperium* its moral force. In *The Aeneid* Vesta is chief among the household gods whom the ghost of Hector returns from the dead to command Aeneas to take with him on his journey to found the new nation: '[W]ith his own hands,' Aeneas explains, '[Hector] fetched out from the inner shrine the holy headbands, Vesta in whom dwells power, and her hearthfire which burns for ever [et manibus vittas Vestamque potentem / aeternumque adytis effert pene-tralibus ignem]' (II: 296–7).[7] The fire does, however, need protection, and as the young Milton remembers, it was the custom at Rome 'to guard the eternal fire most carefully and scrupulously, to secure the per-manence of the empire' (*CPW* I:279). No deity better exemplifies the public force of private virtue, for it is only the purity of Vesta and the virgins who attend the flame that ensure its permanence.[8] In the work of the nationalist poet, Raleigh, the power of the vestal flame or legacy of Vesta is transferred from Laura to the English Queen, Elizabeth. In the work of the mature republican poet, Milton, it is transferred from the Queen to the citizen's wife, Katherine, in such a way as to recover something of its original domestic authenticity. When Milton imitates Raleigh's nationalist poem, when Katherine, like the goddess, is 'vested all in white', she is implicitly re-membered as the new Vesta, the new Alcestis, the kind of faithful wife whose purity gives the English re-public its moral force. She is the antithesis of those wives who, like the biblical Delilah or the contemporary Queen Henrietta Maria, betray the hearth, undermine their husbands, and ruin the state.[9] Her memory shapes behaviour, imposes duties and demands effort. Milton's personal grief coincided with a period of heightened danger for the protectorate – the dual threat of a Royalist uprising in London and a Spanish invasion from Ostend. In this context, it seems more than an accident that Milton became once again increasingly active in the national war effort. Milton's grief is acted out in the writing of a great love poem, but as the nationalist undertow of that poem itself suggests, it may also be acted out in the renewed writing of government dispatches, dispatches written between March and June 1658 that echo the words of Milton's sonnet on the massacre of the Vaudois and rejoice in the Anglo-French victory over the Spanish at the battle of the Dunes.[10]

This pattern of fulfilling the rights of memory and remembering the dead by assimilating them into the story of the nation is at the heart of Lawrence Lipking's forcefully argued 1996 essay on *Lycidas* and the poetics of nationalism. 'Even as Milton was mourning a friend,' says Lipking, 'he also was forging a nation' (213). For Lipking, however, this pattern is seen as something entirely negative. Edward King is remembered but the drowned Lycidas is an agressively national spirit, the genius of a shore that has expanded to include Ireland – the protector of a 'Britannick Empire' threatened by Papists from without and prelates from within. For Lipking, there is a direct link between mourning and grievance. The memory of King, so he feels, is animated by an all-consuming sense of resentment whose only consolation is the unspoken prospect of conquest. The poem articulates grievances that will eventually bear fruit in the virulent ant-Irish sentiments of Milton's *Observations upon the Articles of Peace*, the 1649 tract that prepared the way for Cromwell's re-conquest of Ireland. What Lipking fails to acknowledge, however, is the degree to which modern nation-states are Janus-faced.[11] As they seek to define themselves, they are certainly capable of turning all that is outside or beyond the pale into the barbarous or polluted; as they seek to protect what they imagine to be their integrity and identity, they are capable of pursuing systematic exploitation and committing the most terrible atrocities – the names of Drogheda, My Lai, and Sabra and Shatila are not to be forgotten. But modern nation-states are more than the sum of their failures and the problem with Lipking's interpretation of *Lycidas* is that it depends on a pointed refusal to see anything but these negatives, to see only one face of Janus. His tone is polemical and his own resentment is focused on the extraordinary success of Benedict Anderson's book, *Imagined Communities*. '[G]rievances,' Lipking claims, 'are often the mark of the nation. Too many theories of nationhood prefer to forget this disturbing historical fact' (213). For Lipking, there is something self-indulgent

or weak-kneed about the widespread acceptance of Anderson: 'The imagined community united in bonds of sympathy and interest,' he says, 'makes a more satisfying picture than [what is so often the reality – ] people bound together by bitter memories and common hatreds' (213). The explanatory force of this view, specifically that Milton's nationalism is finally a matter of bitter memories and common hatreds, is then too limited; it is patently one-sided and ultimately no more compelling than his bathetic aside that Milton was probably not 'a very nice person' (219). Lipking's view does nothing to explain the complexity of a devotion to the nation which, as Milton's last pamphlet *Of True Religion* suggests, was lifelong.[12] Most important, it does nothing to explain the idealistic political vision of a text like *Areopagitica* where, in a way that bears immediately on Greenblatt's complaint, the imagined community includes not only the living but the dead.

## Conversation and living remembrance

In the fall of 1639, five years before Milton published *Areopagitica* and a year after *Lycidas*, at the end of another period marked by the death of various loved ones, Milton remembered his beloved friend, Charles Diodati, in the Latin poem *Epitaphium Damonis*. Milton speaks directly to Greenblatt's concern for the forgotten dead when he asks Diodati: 'Is this the way you leave me? Must your virtue vanish without trace and mingle with the nameless dead? [Siccine nos linquis, tua sic sine nomine virtus / Ibit, et obscuris numero sociabitur umbris?]' (21–2). Milton makes it clear that in a very practical way his own identity depends on remembering Diodati. The substance of their friendship, and indeed of Diodati's virtue, lies in their mutual ability to provide each other with the answering voice of an informed audience; that is, the ability to listen and respond to each other in such a way that each of them can best shape their most inventive utterances and so produce the kind of vitally interactive conversation that Milton felt himself denied in his relationship with his first wife, Mary Powell.[13] Bereft of Diodati, he laments the difficulty of finding 'one kindred spirit among thousands [parem de millibus . . . unum]' (108). The climax of the poem returns to the enabling power of their conversation, a conversation significantly rooted in the past and future of a British England. Milton relates how in Italy he dreamt of the two of them sequestered 'in the chequered shade beside the streams of the [river] Colne or among the acres of [the ancient British king] Cassivellaunus [in umbra, / Aut ad aquas Colni, aut ubi iugera Cassibelauni]' (148–9). There among the memories of the nation's past he would relish Diodati's laughter, charm, quick and piercing wit, and listen as *Diodati* told his stories, accounts of English plants and herbs. There, as it came to him only 'eleven nights and a day ago [ab undecima iam lux est altera nocte]' (156), he would reveal his most secret desire to re-tell in verse the matter of Britain – the stories of Brutus and Imogen, Arthur and Merlin. What is most remarkable, then, is that even though Diodati is dead he lives in Milton's mind as the enabling audience for his national epic. In a letter written two years before, Milton had explained to Diodati how even in absence 'living remembrance' animated friendship:

> For fostering such a friendship there is need not so much for writing as for a living remembrance of virtues on both sides. Even if you had not written, that obligation would not necessarily remain unfulfilled. Your worth writes to me instead and inscribes real letters on my inmost consciousness. (*CPW* I:326)

In making the nation, the dead impose duties and demand effort, but in what Milton calls 'living remembrance' they also create possibilities.

In terms of what exactly constitutes the nation, the difference between *Epitaphium Damonis* and *Areopagitica* could not, it seems, be greater. Legends and myths of national origin from Geoffrey of Monmouth reworked in Spenser – those 'lofty Fables and Romances' Milton alludes to in the 1642 *Apology* (*CPW* I:891) – give way to a mature political vision of great clarity. The difference is, however, largely superficial, for the England of *Areopagitica* is the public recreated in the image of the private, that is, the nation-state recreated in the image of the kind of dialogic creativity Milton experienced in his conversations with the sympathetic and quick-witted Diodati: 'Listen, Diodati, but in secret, lest I blush; and let me talk to you grandiloquently for a while. You ask what I am thinking of? So help me God, an immortality of fame' (*CPW* I:327). The bond of sympathy and interest, the dialogism that distinguishes their friendship, lives on after death – no longer private, it now animates the dynamism of the freshly imagined national community:

> Lords and Commons of England, [says Milton] consider what nation it is whereof ye are, and whereof ye are the governours: *a Nation not slow and dull, but of a quick, ingenious and piercing spirit, acute to invent, suttle and sinewy to discours, not beneath the reach of any point the highest human capacity can soar to.* . . . Behold now this vast City; a City of

refuge, the mansion house of liberty, encompast and surrounded with his protection; *the shop of warre hath not there more anvils and hammers waking*, to fashion out the plates and instruments of armed Justice in defence of beleaguer'd Truth, *then there be pens and heads there, sitting by their studious lamps, musing, searching, revolving new notions and idea's wherewith to present, as with their homage and fealty the approaching Reformation: as others as fast reading, trying all things, assenting to the force of reason and convincement.* What could a man require more from a Nation so pliant and so prone to seek after knowledge.

(CPW II:551, 553–4, my emphasis)

What adds a crucial dimension to this vision of the nation as a dialogic society is that, as David Norbrook has recently pointed out (129–30), the passage is heavily indebted to Pericles' funeral oration. Here in Athens, says Pericles:

> each individual is interested not only in his own affairs but in the affairs of the state as well. . . . We Athenians, in our own persons, take our decisions on policy or submit them to proper discussions: for we do not think that there is an incompatibility between words and deeds; the worst thing is to rush to action before the consequences have been properly debated. (Thucydides II:40 [p.147])

Most important, the supremely creative dialogism of Athenian democracy is represented as the great memorial of the state's ancestors and the principal reason for its citizens to defend it with their lives:

> They gave their lives [says Pericles] to her [Athens] and to all of us, and for their own selves they won praises that never grow old, the most splendid of sepulchres – not the sepulchre in which their bodies are laid, but where their glory remains eternal in men's minds, always there on the right occasion to stir others to speech or to action. (Thucydides II:43 [p.149])

*Areopagitica* is resonant with the memory of the dead stirring the living to speech and action. Towards the end of the tract, for instance, Milton remembers the recently slain Lord Brooke's plea for tolerance and inclusion: 'both for his life and for his death,' says Milton, '[Lord Brooke] deserves, that what advice he left be not laid by' (*CPW* II:561). Unlike the dead in the rites of Purgatory, in making the nation the dead in Milton appear to be in active dialogue with the living. Not only are they remembered but through the agency of Milton's stories Katherine Milton, Edward King, Charles Diodati, and Lord Brooke all help to shape what the nation will be. This is Milton's dialogic, republican kaddish. If Pericles'civic nationalism responds directly to Lipking's polemic and offers us a view of the positive face of Janus even at the height of a terrible war, so, despite its well-known limitations, does *Areopagitica*. As Milton responds to the dead, as he is stirred by the language of his ancestors, the 'language of men ever famous, and formost in the acthievements of liberty' (*CPW* II:505), so – long after his own death – his vision of the nation as the polity where the desire for both individual self-realization and interactive creation may best be fulfilled is assimilated into the national imaginary of England and many other modern nations.

In the introduction to the new multi-volume Oxford *Rethinking Literary History*, Linda Hutcheon, in her characteristically generous desire for inclusivity, wonders why exclusive and single narratives of identity such as national literary histories and, implicitly, the nation-states that foster them continue to persist. The answer is manifold, but part of it lies in her own awareness that '[m]ore than perhaps any other form of collective life, the nation possesses immense imaginative power' (5). As Milton makes clear, one of the ways in which this imaginative power manifests itself is in the nation's extraordinary ability to respond to the rights of memory and the needs of the dead. The power of nations – what Benedict Anderson would call the 'goodness' of nations (360–8) – lies in their formidable ability to re-imagine death, to transform 'fatality into continuity' and 'contingency into meaning' (*Imagined Communities* 11) – so much so that even for those of us who most want to transcend the nation turning one's back on it still feels so much like turning one's back on the dead.

## Notes

1. Compare Lawrence Stone: 'The most striking feature which distinguished the Early Modern family from that of today does not concern either marriage or birth; it was the constant presence of death' (*The Family, Sex and Marriage in England, 1500–1800*, 54).
2. For more on Greenblatt's debt to popular existentialism, see Stevens, 'Pretending to be Real'.
3. Like Cole, Peter Novick is highly critical of the Americanization of the Holocaust: 'So, in the end, it seems to me that the pretense that the Holocaust is an American memory [. . .] works to devalue the notion of historical responsibility' (*The Holocaust in American Life* 15). While full of admiration for the work of both Cole and Novick, I think they underestimate the degree to

which the Americanization of the Holocaust, whether rightly or wrongly, constitutes the production of a new layer of the national imaginary in which Jewish identity is being valorized.

4. 'The Museum's primary mission,' according to the USHMM's *Visitors Guide*, 'is to advance and disseminate knowledge about this unprecedented tragedy, to preserve the memory of those who suffered, and to encourage its visitors to reflect upon the moral and spiritual questions raised by the events of the Holocaust *as well as their own responsibilities as citizens of a democracy*' (my emphasis).

5. See Barbara K. Lewalski 350–1, 355–6.

6. Richard Helgerson 21–62 and James P. Bednarz.

7. *The Aeneid* is quoted from Fairclough and the translation from Jackson Knight.

8. For more on Vesta, see Bednarz; Cousins 14–16; Frazer, *The* Fasti *of Ovid* IV:188–271; Richard Gordon, 'Vesta', *Oxford Classical Dictionary*, 1591, and Geraldine Herbert-Brown, *Ovid and the* Fasti: *An Historical Study* 66–81.

9. See Milton's representation of the relationship between Charles I and his wife, Henrietta Maria, in *Eikonoklastes*: 'He ascribes [. . .] *all vertue* to his Wife, in straines that come almost to Sonnetting: How fitt to govern men, under-valuing and aspersing the great Counsel of his Kingdom, in comparison of one Woman. Examples are not farr to seek, how great mischeif and dishon-our hath befall'n to Nations under the Government of effeminate and Uxorious Magistrates. Who being themselves govern'd and overswaid at home under a Female usurpation, cannot but be far short of spirit and authority without dores, to govern a whole Nation' (*CPW* III:420–1).

10. For more on Milton's involvement in the war effort of spring and early summer 1658, see Stevens, 'Milton's "Renunciation" of Cromwell', esp. pp. 373–82.

11. See Tom Nairn, *The Break-Up of Britain: Crisis and Neo-Nationalism*, 348–9 and Stevens, 'Milton's Janus-faced Nationalism'.

12. Milton is a Protestant nationalist to the end. Even in 1673, 13 years after the trauma of the final collapse of the republic, England is still seen as the nation that first shook off the Pope's '*Babylonish* Yoke' in the struggle for civil and religious freedom. Despite its failures, it is still a nation worth fighting for: 'I thought it no less then a common duty to lend my hand, how unable soever, to so good a Purpose [to protect England from Catholicism]' (*CPW* VIII:430, 417–18).

13. As John Rumrich has thoughtfully argued, there may have been a homo-erotic element in Milton's relationship with Diodati, but the critical factor is conversation. Milton's letters to Diodati routinely emphasize their mutual delight in conversation: 'Are there in those parts any fairly learned people with whom you can associate pleasantly and with whom you can talk, as we have been used to talking?' (*CPW* I:324). At the same time, Milton's princi-pal complaint against Mary Powell is her refusal or inability to join him in conversation: in Mary, it is clear, he felt that he had met 'if not with a body impenetrable' then certainly 'with a minde to all other due conversation inaccessible, and to all the more estimable and superior purposes of matrimony uselesse and almost livelesse' (*CPW* II:250). Also see Lewalski, esp. 163–5.

# 11
## Death's Afterword

*David Lee Miller*

Spenser died in 1599. Ten years later, the printer Matthew Lownes brought out a folio edition of Spenser's collected poetry containing a previously unpublished work under the title 'Two Cantos of Mutabilitie: Which, both for Forme and Matter, appeare to be parcel of some following Booke of the *Faerie Queene*, under the legend of Constancie'. The cantos, numbered VI and VII, end with two additional stanzas under the heading 'The VIII. Canto, unperfite'.

In the poem, the Titaness Mutability challenges Jove's sovereignty over the created universe. Her claim is referred to the Goddess Nature for judgment. Mutability's evidence includes an allegorical pageant of the seasons, the months, day and night, and the hours:

> And after all came *Life*, and lastly *Death*,
> *Death* with most grim and grisly visage seene,
> Yet is he nought but parting of the breath;
> Ne ought to see, but like a shade to weene,
> Vnbodied, vnsoul'd, vnheard, vnseene.
> But *Life* was like a faire young lusty boy,
> Such as they faine *Dan Cupid* to haue beene,
> Full of delightfull health and liuely ioy,
> Deckt all with flowers, and wings of gold fit to employ.

> (*Mutabilitie Cantos*, vii.46)

Spenser cannot have known, can he, that the *Mutabilitie Cantos* would be his final poem? As Marshall Grossman observes in his essay for this collection, we have learned to say that *The Faerie Queene* is intrinsically, not just circumstantially, incomplete, and we therefore read both its romance narrative and its allegorical design as a prolonged endgame that never ends, although it must eventually break off.[1] With the *Muta-bilitie Cantos* Spenser appears to play even more deviously with the sense of an ending. Do the *Cantos* belong to *The Faerie Queene*? Are they finished? The poet – or his death – suspends us in a distinctively Spenserian uncertainty, unable to say whether we are reading one poem or two, unable to say where, let alone how, *The Faerie Queene* ends. And of course the *Mutabilitie Cantos* are about this problem. Who will have the last word, the Titaness Mutabilitie or the Goddess Nature? In fact, who *does*? Nature speaks last, but then the narrator's voice returns to question the finality of her verdict. He does so, inevitably, in stanzas that seem at once to end the poem and to begin a new canto.

These questions about finality, raised in the poem's narrative and explored in its philosophical themes, are embodied in the movements of its verse. How does the great cyclic procession staged by Mutabilitie end? 'And after all came *Life*, and lastly *Death*.' So Life comes last – except for Death, which comes last. Death is 'with most grim and grisly visage seene' – except that there is 'Ne ought to see', and he is there-fore 'vnseene'. A graduate seminar I recently taught designated this pervasive quality of the poem 'the Spenser two-step', in honour of the goddess Ate.[2] As readers of *The Faerie Queene* may recall, Ate appears in the first canto of Book IV – just after the poet has withdrawn-and-rewritten his original ending to Book III. She embodies (with sublime redundancy) the principle of division: her eyes point in different direc-tions, she speaks with forkéd tongue, her heart is 'discided' (a homonym that divides the word 'decided' against itself), her ears don't match, 'And as her eares so eke her feet were odde, / And much vnlike, th'one long, the other short, / And both misplact; that when th'one forward yode, / The other backe retired, and contrarie trode' (IV.1.28.6–9). How char-acteristic of Spenser's extraordinarily self-conscious craftsmanship, and of his extraordinarily poker-faced wit, that he should embed a parody of his own verse footwork in the exuberantly perverse *blazon* of Ate.

Spenser calls Ate 'mother of debate', which Hamilton glosses as 'strife'. We might also call her the death wish, for Spenser's allegory is capa-cious enough to absorb *Beyond the Pleasure Principle*. Ate's vocation cor-responds to Freud's vision of death as a drive, a *work*, lodged in the heart of life. It is just this insight that Spenser expresses in the distinctive movements of his verse two-step:

> Right in the midst the Goddesse selfe did stand
> Vpon an altar of some costly masse,
> Whose substance was vneath to vnderstand:

> For neither pretious stone, nor durefull brasse,
> Nor shining gold, nor mouldring clay it was;
> But much more rare and pretious to esteeme,
> Pure in aspect, and like to christall glasse,
> Yet glasse was not, if one did righty deeme,
> But being faire and brickle, likest glasse did seeme.

> (IV.x.39)

We will learn in stanza 41 that this goddess, like Nature in the *Mutabilitie Cantos*, is veiled, and that the doubleness of her appearance (seen but unrevealed) *may* reflect a doubleness in her essence, said to comprehend both sexual kinds in one. 'They say' she is purely originary and autonomous, like the spherical universe in Plato's *Timaeus*.

Gordon Teskey has well described the aporia within Platonic metaphysics which deifies form by reducing materiality to matter, an abstract and featureless 'substance' on which ideal form must then be re-imprinted.[3] Spenser, in his description of the statue's 'altar', or pedestal, is flaunting the aporia that Teskey describes. He puns on both 'substance' and 'under-stand', lest we should miss the point that it's hard to tell (metaphysically speaking) what *grounds* transcendent being. The stuff of Venus's pedestal, says the Spenserian narrator, is not gemstone, brass, gold, or clay, but something rarer and more strange – something like glass, but not glass; but more like glass than anything else. This is the Spenser two-step.

As the goddess of love, life, and procreation, Venus is Ate's counterpart, Eros to her Thanatos. She represents coupling, not 'discision'. Her feet, therefore, are not mismatched. In fact, they are barely separate at all, bound *so* closely together that we may wonder how she remains standing: 'both her feete and legs together twyned / Were with a snake, whose head and tail were fast combined' (40.8–9). Eternity seems to have Venus immobilized. And how securely is she placed? The goddess stands on a mystery, but when Spenser describes it his own feet dance the two-step. Teskey would remind us here that, as the patroness of the *copula*, Venus signifies the very aporia on which she stands: the trope of coupling is used in Plato and the allegorical tradition at once to signify and to conceal the logical impossibility of understanding substance, or of rejoining transcendent form to featureless matter.[4] 'Vneath to understand' indeed: the idol of Venus, propped up by her own mystery, is in every sense a figure of speech.

At stake in these ambiguities is the *difference* between life and death. Our usual ways of thinking about death – as the event that terminates life, or as the state of nonbeing opposed to life – are deconstructed by the poetic thinking that unfolds in the movements of Spenser's verse. 'To be, or not to be' is indeed the question. Death, writes Spenser, is 'nought but parting of the breath', but is that 'parting' a *de*parting, a final separation, or is it a pause – the point of rest that punctuates the rhythms of respiration, music, and speech, the still point that measures the movement of verse? Hamlet fears that death may *not* be terminal, but he remains in doubt, and it is this doubt, as he says with amazing precision, that 'must give us pause'. Spenser locates this dubious pause within death as he locates death within life:

> And after all came *Life*, and lastly *Death*,
> *Death* with most grim and grisly visage seene,
> Yet is he nought but parting of the breath;
> Ne ought to see, but like a shade to weene,
> Vnbodied, vnsoul'd, vnheard, vnseene.
> But *Life* was like a faire young lusty boy. . . .

'Death' here assumes the verbal form of anadiplosis, the repetition of a key word from the *end* of one clause or phrase at the *beginning* of the next. Spenser locates this turn within the larger pattern of chiasmus, the cross-coupler, so that his two-step comes back around to life 'after all'. Death is nothing, neither body nor soul, neither visible nor audible. Is it, then, *nothingness*, or is it nothing but *spacing* – the cesura, the pause in which an end becomes a beginning?

Look again at the fifth line of the stanza. Empson remarks in *Seven Types of Ambiguity* that fifth lines are the pivot point on which the movement of the Spenserian stanza turns (33–4). Here, line 5, with its three hard stops, acts almost like a stanzaic cesura. These emphatic pauses set off the pounding repetition of the negative particle, *un*. They provide, so to speak, the neutral background against which the line's negations start forth, parting the breath harshly with glottal stops. In this way the line's form distinguishes sharply between the alternatives of negation and spacing. Its halting series is then followed by the chiasmic return of life, and with it of unchecked breath, as the movement of the stanza quickens with two unimpeded lines: 'But Life was like a faire young lusty boy, / Such as they faine Dan Cupide to haue beene.'

Is death negation, nonbeing? That is the question. It is a question that Spenser, like Shakespeare, has the artistry to ask and the honesty not to answer. Shakespeare raises it again – in strikingly Spenserian terms – when Leontes, marvelling at the resurrection of Hermione in *The Winter's Tale*, asks 'What fine chisel / Could ever yet cut breath?'

(V.iii.78–9). The answer to this rhetorical question is, literally, the *space*, the line-break, that follows the word 'chisel' and is represented typographically by a forward-slash. This space may be inflected as life or death, but Shakespeare, like Spenser, makes it both: it is the 13-year hiatus that stretches from Hermione's last gasp in Act III of *The Winter's Tale* to her miraculous resuscitation in Act V, during which (a bit like Spenser's Guyon in his mysterious swoon) she is apparently dead, except that she is apparently still alive. We may rationalize her suspended animation, assuming, for example, that she remains sequestered under Paulina's protection for 13 years, awaiting the fulfilment of the oracle. But Shakespeare, although he might easily have produced this information – as he does for Hero in *Much Ado About Nothing* – conspicuously leaves the question open.

This figurative use of the cesura is not uncommon among Renaissance poets. Ben Jonson carries it off with his usual air of deceptive simplicity in the third stanza of the song 'Queen and Huntress':

> Lay thy bow of pearl apart,
> And thy crystal-shining quiver;
> Give unto the flying hart
> Space to breathe, how short soever.
> Thou that mak'st a day of night,
> Goddess excellently bright.

> (Maclean 90)

The one strong cesura in these lines follows immediately after the prayer for 'space to breathe'. Implicitly, this prayer aligns the singer with the 'flying hart' hunted by the queen. Is she, thus magnified – 'Queen *and* huntress, chaste *and* fair' – a figure of immortality ('Thou that mak'st a day of night') or, with her bow and quiver, an avatar of death? The lyric does not resolve these ambiguities but cross-couples them in the pause figured by its beginning and ending cesuras – the pause it prays to the goddess to grant, but creates for itself in the act of prayer.

These formal devices – the cesura, the line-break, the tropes of anadiplosis and chiasmus, the Spenser two-step, and others, if we wanted to extend the list – work to express a poetic notion of death as unrepresentable because intrinsic to life. Milton's celebrated portrait of death in Book II of *Paradise Lost* stands directly in this poetic 'line'. The Spenserianism of the episode has long been noted. But along with its clunky allegory, its flaunted debt to the 'Errour's den' episode of *The Faerie Queene*, and its recollection of death as vacancy in the *Mutability*

*Cantos* ('Vnbodied, vnsoul'd, vnheard, vnseene'), we may also detect a more subtle borrowing in the re-emergence of the Spenser two-step:

> The other shape,
> If shape it might be called that shape had none
> Distinguishable in member, joint, or limb,
> Or substance might be called that shadow seemed,
> For each seemed either; black it stood as Night,
> Fierce as ten Furies, terrible as Hell,
> And shook a dreadful dart; what seemed his head
> The likeness of a kingly crown had on.

(II.666–73)

Samuel Johnson lamented the machinery of the whole episode as a grievous fault, while Edmund Burke praised the last line and a half of the quoted passage as a touchstone of the sublime; both form part of Milton's *homage* to Spenser as a poet who declines to reify death.

On this point only would I revise Marshall Grossman's lucid assessment of the literary–historical relation between these two poets, for Spenser's sense of death is best described not as pre-emptive deferral or hysterical denial, but as a refusal to reify. Death in Spenser, as Linda Gregerson aptly puts it, forms 'the ground rhythm of cognitive method and aesthetic apprehension'. Milton learns from Spenser that Death's personification can only be sheer contradiction, the presence of an absence that must be *dis*-scribed through the fancy footwork of the two-step.[5] Death is not *there* in his own allegorical personification because 'he' (it) cannot be named, described, or gathered into a presence. It is never *there* because it is always *here*: not beyond or against life, but within it; not in the future, nor even quite in the present, but *between* present moments.

Gordon Teskey, in his contribution to the present collection, identifies death in allegory with fixity of meaning, which he opposes to the existential vitality of agents in narrative. But it seems to me that Spenser also associates death with what Teskey calls 'the rift within each character between the living and the significant'. This rift is itself opposed to the life-giving copula figured by Venus, who infuses substance with form figuratively, if not metaphysically, through the act of generation. As Teskey's reading of Book II, canto viii so suggestively argues, Guyon's paradoxical swoon, hovering between life and death, is an ingenious allegorical strategy for manifesting this rift in his being. It figures the rift as a condition in which life and death are indistinguishable. It is this blurring of distinction, I want to suggest, that gives rise to 'the uneasy suspicion that death is mysteriously, imperceptibly, disturbingly present in the working of the poetry itself'.

Theresa Krier locates this disturbing presence in specific ways that the poetry of the Mammon episode works to block 'linking'. This concept, adapted from the analyst Wilfred Bion, traces back to the link between parent and child the psyche's ability 'to create generative, mobile, ongoing meanings'. Bion proposed that the psyche's openness to associative thinking derives from parental nurture, while the failure of this primary relation leads to 'psychic deadness', expressed in various forms of resistance to, or aggressive attacks upon, 'the mobility of interpretive thought'. Krier develops her reading of the Mammon's cave episode in partial response to Teskey's theory of allegory, so perhaps it is not surprising that her essay both complements and qualifies Teskey's account of Guyon's faint. What Teskey sees as the 'rift' between meaning and being appears from Krier's perspective as an attack on linking. The universe itself, as Plato imagines it in the *Timaeus*, is formed in the image of an eternal and unchanging deity, wholly self-sufficient and inclusive and therefore not connected to anything outside itself. In Teskey's genealogy of allegory, this refusal of organic dependency and exchange is the primal fantasy that gives rise to the world of metaphysics. Krier, on the other hand, has recourse not to the *Timaeus* but to the *Symposium*; where Teskey locates the 'rift' intrinsic to allegorical discourse, she finds the daimonic power of Cupid, who 'interprets' in the root sense of passing back and forth between gods and humans, crossing and recrossing the rift that separates the transcendent from the mundane. In the episode of Guyon's faint, Krier finds this erotic daimon figured in the guardian angel that attends the fallen knight – brooding, as it were, over the abyss that Teskey has located within Guyon's prostrate form.

The differences between these two conceptions of allegory are instructive, but both see it as a form of thinking, concrete rather than abstract, and both apprehend death in Spenser's text as kind of internal resistance to the movements of allegorical thought. On this level, I want to suggest, both critics are reading Spenser in the way that Anne Prescott and Roger Kuin think Milton read him: 'What we want to attend to,' they write, 'is Milton's rapt listening to his predecessor's "sage and solemn tunes," the seriousness of his ear, the concentration and focus of his inward I. In his poetical filiation Milton was a fine and most individual apprentice; in the depth of his attention he was an exemplary reader.' It is clear that Milton listened attentively to the way death hovers in the pauses of Spenser's verse, but it is equally clear that his own verse appropriates this sense of death in order to transform it. We see the difference in his appropriation of the two-step, for in place of Spenser's wavering assertion, withdrawal, and tentative re-proffering of a denied similitude, Milton's negation of his own language is pointed, compressed, and irreversible. He needs to transform Spenser's sense of death in order to write what Leslie Brisman calls the 'poetry of choice', in which life and death are not suspended and cross-coupled but separated by a decisive turn.[6] This turn, as Grossman points out, depends on a radically different formal relation between narrative and closure: choice is always decisive in *Paradise Lost* because 'each narrated episode we encounter is (re)read according to its anticipated consequence, even as it unfolds'. Hamlet shows us the consequences of a Spenserian dilation of choice, transposed into tragic form; Milton, however, incorporates tragedy into the structure of *Paradise Lost* in order to transcend it. The first cesura in the poem follows the first disobedience as inevitably as death. In effect, it brings death into the poem ahead of itself, two lines before the poem brings death into the world:

> Of man's first disobedience, and the fruit
> Of that forbidden tree, whose mortal taste
> Brought death into the world, and all our woe,
> With loss of Eden, till one greater man
> Restore us, and regain the blissful seat . . .

> (I.1–5)

Historical time itself is constructed in these lines as an interval, a 'mortal' pause between loss and restoration. In this pause we are suspended between death and life (the first man and the greater man). But we are suspended there in order to choose.

Milton's interval therefore *contrasts* the breach through which death entered the world with the decisive turning-point through which immortality will be regained. In 1674, when Milton divided the tenth book of his first edition to create Books XI and XII, he chose the moment after the flood, a moment that prefigures the final destruction by fire. At the newly created beginning of Book XII, 'betwixt the world destroyed and world restored', he inserted five new lines:

> As one who in his journey baits at noon
> Though bent on speed, so here the Archangel paused
> Betwixt the world destroyed and world restored,

> If Adam aught perhaps might interpose;
> Then with transition sweet new speech resumes.

These lines are at once a magnified cesura and a miniature Incarnation: space to breathe, how short soever (since 'objects divine / Must needs impair and weary human sense', ll. 9–10); but also a moment suspended between the destruction and restoration of the world, a divine accommodation that creates the freedom and possibility of human choice.[7] Adam, we are told, *might* interpose. As it happens he doesn't, but he might have. Milton, however, does. The moment seems trivial – a pause in which nothing happens – but its 'aught' stands poised momentously against an implicit Spenserian 'nought'. It therefore answers with some precision to the far more melodramatic intervention that the narrator fantasized, but could not stage, at the beginning of Book IV:

> O for that warning voice, which he who saw
> Th'Apocalypse, heard cry in Heavn' aloud,
> Then when the Dragon, put to second rout,
> Came furious down to be revenged on men,
> *Woe to the inhabitants on earth!* That now,
> While time was, our first parents had been warned
> The coming of their secret foe, and scap'd
> Haply so scap'd his mortal snare; for now
> Satan, now first inflam'd with rage, came down . . .
>
> (1–9)

The jarring tenses of this passage reflect the co-presence to eternity of all historical times. Without this super-temporal perspective it would not be possible for John to have seen and heard, in the distant past, events that belong to the distant future, nor for past and future events to correspond as antitype and type. But these jarring tenses also reflect the human and historical impossibility of such a perspective. There is no voice that can reach from the seventeenth century back to the moment before the fall, no narrative in which 'time was' can equal 'now'. The 'haply' of these lines thus stands in pointed contrast to the 'perhaps might' of their counterpart in Book XII, for it can evoke only a might-have-been that never could be. The intervention possible to historical agents is humbler and more mundane: it is the one that Milton himself performs in creating Book XII, as he aligns the moment of composition with that of narrative action in order set his own poetic utterance against Adam's pointed silence.

For Spenser the choice between life and death is never so clearly distributed. His poem opens with the Redcrosse knight:

> But on his brest a bloudie Crosse he bore,
> The deare remembrance of his dying Lord,
> For whose sweet sake that glorious badge he wore,
> And dead as liuing euer him ador'd.
>
> (I.i.2.1–4)

Christ is remembered here as a 'dying Lord', and the knight's adoration of him is compromised accordingly. What does 'dead as liuing' mean? Does it mean that Redcrosse adores the saviour equally whether he (the savior) is living or dead? That Redcrosse forever adores the dead saviour *as if* he were living? Or that Redcrosse adores the dead savior *as he once did* adore him living? Could it even imply that he adores the living savior *as if* he were still dead? As a member of Christ, the knight should be incorporate in a mystical body, but these lines imply that he has, rather, incorporated a dead body in the manner of Freudian melancholy (we learn in line 8 that the knight 'of his cheere did seeme too solemne sad'). Moreover, Book I will play out the terms of this confusion in episode after episode. Abandoning Una, Redcrosse dallies with 'Fidessa', who claims to seek the stolen corpse of her slain beloved (she does not understand the Resurrection). In Orgoglio's dungeon the knight will *become* the corpse he has incorporated, as if painfully extruding the form of his melancholy identification by literalizing it in the flesh of his body.[8]

The turning point in this progress comes, or seems to come, in canto ix when Redcrosse confronts Despair, a dissociated reflection of himself as the body of death. By separating (dis-pairing) law from grace, Despair produces a vision of death as 'eternall rest' (I.ix.40.1) – a consummation devoutly to be wished.[9] In this respect as in others, then, he is the consummate anti-Spenserian poet: his rhetoric reifies death. Contemplation appears within the allegorical scheme as Despair's opposite, the custodian of a vision of eternal life rather than one of eternal death. Accordingly, Redcrosse can reach this figure only after Fidelia has first re-established the reciprocity of life and death – 'For she was able, with her words to kill, / And raise again to life the hart, that she did thrill' (I.x.19.8–9) – and only after she has then handed the knight off to Speranza, re-establishing the link bween faith and hope. Yet the very words that celebrate the power at work in Fidelia are shadowed by the dark opposite Redcrosse still harbors within himself: 'And when she list poure out her larger spright, / She would commaund the hastie Sunne to stay, / Or backward turn his course from heauens hight' (I.x.20.1–3). When the 'corse' of the Son turns backward from heaven's hight, the Resurrection is undone, and Fidelia has become her own opposite, 'Fidessa' – otherwise known as Duessa, daughter to the emperor of the west. It was she who told Redcrosse at their first meeting about her 'backward' quest for the 'corse' to which she was betrothed: 'Then forth I went his woefull corse to find, / And many yeares throughout the world I straid, / A virgin widow' (I.ii.24.6–8).

In much the same way Contemplation (as Gegerson nicely observes) seems uncomfortably similar to Despair. He may dwell on a mountain-top, not in a cave, but he looks like a living skeleton, and his mixed message to Redcrosse (blood yields 'nought but sin'; now back to the battlefield with you, young man!) seems to echo the counsel of Despair: 'All those great battles, which thou boasts to win, / Through strife, and bloud-shed, and auengement, / Now praysd, hereafter deare thou shalt repent' (I.x.60.9, 63.6–9; I.ix.43.3–5). Most tellingly, perhaps, Redcrosse responds to the vision of hope, the New Jerusalem, with the very impulse provoked by Despair and his tables of the damned: 'let me,' he beseeches, 'straight way on that last long voyage fare, / That nothing may my present hope empare' (I.x.63.3–5). The difference between this hope and despair is a matter of life and death, to be sure. But that is the distinction Spenser's verse calls into question.

In the peroration to their essay, Prescott and Kuin call on Spenseri-ans to read their author's texts 'with a seriousness which, though it can never be Milton's, would nevertheless be equivalent in its scrupulous and affectionate attention to the text's moral aesthetic, in its rapt absorption of Spenser's serious and allegorical game'. This New Milton-ism, they suggest, will require a 'complex exercise of *un-distancing*', an effort to integrate the skills and canons of professional scholarship into 'a new simplicity'. Underlying their call is a belief that the edifice of modern scholarship and criticism too often serve to defer our encounter with the text itself – and that this evasion is symptomatic of a deeper denial, a refusal to integrate our own deaths into the rhythms and pur-poses of our work.

This is a serious argument, close in spirit to Grossman's emphasis on 'the ethics of enjoyment':

> The ethics of enjoyment lie in the alternative pleasures offered by these two texts and the modes of narrative they represent, for each fosters a different relation toward death, silence and closure. Doubt-less there are historical determinants at work in the appearance of one or the other mode of narration in a given time and place.

However, my interest here has been the implications of reading in the present. It strikes me that a reader's choice of the infinite unfolding of contiguity offered by Spenser or the dialectics of metaphoric totalization offered by Milton can profoundly affect the way he or she lives in the world. The ethics of reading inheres in its ability to put the choice before us.

The essays in this volume put the choice before us in many ways, not least in the differences – methodological, but also ethical – between formalist and historicist modes of argument. I raise this issue not to create a false dichotomy, since ultimately neither of these modes can work independently of the other, but because I want to ask whether death, and especially the question of its reification, may not be a fundamental point of difference between overlapping critical practices.

If we equate death with closure, then Spenser's deferral of closure may appear to be an evasion. I have tried to show on the contrary that what we call deferral in Spenser isn't really a putting off but a taking on of death, a deconstruction that redistributes the promised end throughout every dimension of life. From this point of view, evasion may just as easily lie in the effort to concentrate death into definite form, to treat it as spectacular, or to isolate it as the event that terminates life. These terrible shapes have immense power, and the greater our proximity to their historical referents the greater the power they have over us. The dimension of proximity may be temporal or spatial, since we are most affected by recent and nearby calamities, but ultimately it is always imaginative and even aesthetic. If it were not, Spenser's description of the Munster famine would not retain the power it has to horrify us even now, while the children outside the window are laughing and dancing to a nursery rhyme about the bubonic plague: *ashes, ashes, all fall down*.

The impulse to reify death is not a casual error, or a correctable mistake. The personal deaths of those closest to us are shattering, their long aftermath a terrible struggle between our compulsion to isolate the event, insisting on it as an absolute end, and the need to reintegrate it (and ourselves) back into a life that is shared and ongoing. That shared life, the public or communal aspect of our existence, depends on death to form and reform the ties that bind: religious ties, based on great public images of death such as the Crucifixion, and political ties, based on ceremonies and images such as funerals, executions, martyrdoms, and military sacrifices. Representations of death that achieve both intense proximity and wide circulation do so because they invest symbols of collective identity with intimately personal fears and sorrows. Because they serve to negotiate and inflect the terms of our loyalty to church and state, their function is profoundly ideological.

Laura Knoppers locates the deep paradox of Charles I's death precisely in the power of its representations. The king's *Eikon Basilike* and Milton's *Eikonoklastes* lock horns over the ideological import of the king's execution. Charles seeks to cast himself in the martyr's role, but unfortunately for the king, this strategy succeeds best if his persecutors do indeed put him to death: 'Charles's own innocence can only be demonstrated by the perfidy of his opponents, and the death of the king marks not the failure of Charles's claims but their ultimate proof.' Similarly, Milton's rhetorical success in portraying the popular readership of the king's book as 'a credulous and hapless herd' requires, by implication, the failure of his own persuasive project: the very obduracy of that 'inconstant, irrational, and Image-doting rabble' serves to vindicate the truth they disavow. The language of perspectival optics in both works calls attention to the rivalry of their projects, which seize on the king's death in order to shape political consensus in opposed ways; but the logic of martyrdom that governs the self-image of each text tends to confound the difference between failure and success.

Assessing the ethical, historical, and political dimensions of death's presence in literary texts requires critical tact because, as Prescott and Kuin indicate, we are negotiating our own loyalties and resistances even as we contemplate those of the text. Andrew Hadfield's wide-ranging discussion of *The Faerie Queene*'s narrative as 'framed by two deaths, neither of which actually appears in the poem', perceptively describes Spenser's sustained engagement with the issue of the royal succession. In doing so, Hadfield brings modern readers into renewed proximity with the context of royalist and reformist politics in which Spenser wrote. At the same time, I wonder whether Hadfield does not at times undervalue the very *distancing* that keeps the deaths of Elizabeth I and Mary Queen of Scots external to the narrative. To call Arthur's union with Gloriana 'barren' is to repudiate a whole layer of figuration in the text that represents Arthur's noble deeds as the offspring, gestated and brought to parturition, of his spiritual insemination by a vision of glory. The point is not to accept such textual figures uncritically, but to *read* them. Too peremptory a sense of death as topical may blind us to more subtle layers of the text, as it does when Hadfield concludes his discussion of Arthur's dream by asserting, 'An encounter that looks as though it promises union and procreation *only* serves to remind readers of the missed opportunities of the past and the impending death of both queen and regime' (emphasis added). As Theresa Krier reminds us, Chaucer in the 'Pardoner's Tale' long ago skewered the impulse to reify allegorical death: charging off to lay hands on its literal body, we are all too liable to encounter it in forms we fail to recognize.

Hadfield is right, of course, to emphasize the sixteenth-century monarch's equivocal role as the privileged bearer of both life and death. By the mid-seventeenth century, however, Milton and other reformist writers were fully engaged in a struggle to destroy the royalist iconography of death. Along with the essay by Laura Knoppers, those of Paul Stevens and Rachel Trubowitz describe a series of radical transformations in the way representations of death invest forms of collective identity with intense personal emotions. Like Teskey and Krier, Stevens and Trubowitz develop arguments that both complement and qualify one another. Trubowitz provides a complex account of the 'mortality-crisis' of the seventeenth century, Stevens a subtle exploration of ways in which poetic commemoration of the dead continues both to inflect private loves with the presence of 'imagined communities' and to re-imagine public life 'in the image of the private'. Trubowitz makes a strong case for the convergence of Pauline theology and Longinian poetics in Milton's re-writing of the nation – and with it, of death – but I wonder whether she may not be overstating the extent to which Milton's 'post-apocalyptic ideal of antidynastic community' negates all natural relations, bringing forth the elect nation in a movement that is 'simultaneously destructive and restorative, but not recuperative'. Such a utopian state would have an unmediated relation to the individual ('for you are all one in the Elect Nation'); Stevens, by contrast, argues that death continues to function as a point of cross-coupling between the public and private domains.

Underlying this divergence is Benjamin's argument about the disappearance of death from 'the perceptual world of the living'. Trubowitz takes this argument a step further, equating the disappearance of death from 'the public stage of modernity' with denial, denegation, and 'unthinking the unthinkable'. This equation, I want to suggest, loses track of the possibility that death's withdrawal from 'the perceptual world' does not *necessarily* entail its complete absence, or even its unqualified denial. To foreclose the Spenserian sense of death as an ambiguous interval known also by the alias 'life' may itself be a form of denial. The ethics of reading are enlarged if we prolong the moment of doubt that Spenser and Hamlet share, working to diffuse the powerful and recurring reifications that death is heir to – including, I would say, the reification of its absence. In this respect, to borrow a slip of rhetoric from Milton, I dare be known to think Spenser a better teacher than Benjamin.

## Notes

1. Grossman cites Jonathan Goldberg's seminal *Endlesse Worke: Spenser and the Structures of Discourse* (Baltimore: Johns Hopkins University Press, 1981); I would add Patricia Parker, *Inescapable Romance: Studies in the Poetics of a Mode* (Princeton, NJ: Princeton University Press, 1979).
2. Thanks to Steve Hopkins for the term.
3. Here I refer less to Teskey's essay for the present collection, which does not emphasize the problem of the *materia*, than to such previous works as 'Mutability, Genealogy, and the Authority of Forms', *Representations* 41 (1993): 104–22; 'Allegory, Materialism, and Violence', in *The Production of English Renaissance Culture*, eds David Lee Miller, Sharon O'Dair and Harold Weber (Ithaca: Cornell University Press, 1994), 293–318; and *Allegory and Violence* (Ithaca: Cornell University Press, 1996).
4. In a similar vein Gregerson, noting the dark undertow that flows 'against' the wedding day in Spenser's 'Epithalamion', reads the problematic allusion to Jove's rape of Leda as a comment on the separation of the transcendent from the mundane: 'only by an act of violence can godhead be thought to enter the human directly'.
5. For this reason I have reservations about Gregerson's assertion that 'the recurrent imperative in Spenser's writings is to insist that death *has* a body, that it is legible', or, again, that 'Spenser habitually renders death by means of fixed anatomy and sharpness of outline; Milton renders death by means of formlessness'. Gregerson's argument stresses the discursive function of 'anatomy', where mine emphasizes what I am calling *dis*cription, or the Spenser two-step; where she sees death's formlessness in Milton as opposed to its Spenserian anatomy, I discern a genealogy in which this formlessness, construed as a resistance to the powers of representation, comes to Milton *from* Spenser.
6. Leslie Brisman, *Milton's Poetry of Choice and Its Romantic Heirs* (Ithaca: Cornell University Press, 1973).
7. These lines also mark the transition from vision to discourse in Michael's presentation, accommodating the weakness of Adam's powers.
8. See Judith Butler, *Gender Trouble: Feminism and the Subversion of Identity* (New York: Routledge, 1990), for an account of melancholy incorporation as literalizing parental identification in the flesh of the body.
9. On the significance of the pun in Despair's name, see Maureen Quilligan, *The Language of Allegory: Defining the Genre* (Ithaca: Cornell University Press, 1979), 36–7.

# Bibliography

Achinstein, Sharon. 'The Uses of Deception from Cromwell to Milton', *The Witness of Times: Manifestations of Ideology in Seventeenth Century England*, eds Katherine Z. Keller and Gerald J. Schiffhorst (Pittsburgh: Duquesne University Press, 1993) 174–200.

——. *Milton and the Revolutionary Reader* (Princeton: Princeton University Press, 1994).

Adams, Mary. 'Fallen Wombs: The Origin of Death in Miltonic Sexuality', *Milton Studies* 29 (1993) 165–79.

Anderson, Benedict. *Imagined Communities: Reflections on the Origin and Spread of Nationalism*, rev. edn (London: Verso, 1992).

——. 'The Goodness of Nations', *The Spectre of Comparisons: Nationalism, Southeast Asia and the World* (London: Verso, 1998) 360–8.

Anderson, G. A. *A Time to Dance: The Expression of Grief and Joy in Israelite Religion* (University Park, PA: Pennsylvania State University, 1991).

Ariès, Philippe. *Western Attitudes Toward Death: From the Middle Ages to the Present*, trans. Patricia Ranum (Baltimore: Johns Hopkins University Press, 1974).

——. *The Hour of Our Death*, trans. Helen Weaver (London: Allen Lane, 1981).

——. *Images of Man and Death*, trans. Janet Lloyd (Cambridge: Harvard University Press, 1985).

Ariosto, Ludovico. *'Orlando Furioso': Translated into English Heroical Verse*, trans. Sir John Harington (Oxford: Oxford University Press, 1972).

Aristotle. *Nicomachean Ethics*, trans. David Ross, Rev. J. L. Ackrill and J. O. Urmson (Oxford: Oxford University Press, 1980).

Arnold, Matthew. 'The Study of Poetry', *Essays on English Literature*, ed. F. W. Bateson (London: University of London Press, 1965).

Axton, Marie. *The Queen's Two Bodies: Drama and the Elizabethan Succession* (London: Royal Historical Society, 1977).

Baltrusaitis, Jurgis. *Anamorphic Art* (New York: Harry Abrams, 1977).

Barthes, Roland. 'Introduction to the Structural Analysis of Narratives', *Image, Music, Text*, trans. Stephen Heath (New York: Hill and Wang, 1977) 97–104.

Bate, Jonathan. *Shakespeare and Ovid* (Oxford: Clarendon Press, 1993).

Bednarz, James P. 'Raleigh in Spenser's Historical Allegory', *Spenser Studies* 4 (1983) 49–70.

——. 'The Collaborator as Thief: Ralegh's (Re)vision of *The Faerie Queene*,' *ELH* 63 (1996) 279–307.

Bellamy, Elizabeth J. *Translations of Power: Narcissism and the Unconscious in Epic History* (Ithaca: Cornell University Press, 1992).

Bellamy, John. *The Tudor Law of Treason: An Introduction* (London: Routledge, 1979).

Benjamin, Walter. *Illuminations*, ed. and Intro. Hannah Arendt, trans. Harry Zohn (New Schocken Books, 1969).

Berger, Harry. *Revisionary Play: Studies in the Spenserian Dynamics*, intro. Louis Montrose (Berkeley and Los Angeles: University of California Press, 1988).

Bernheimer, Richard. *Wild Men in the Middle Ages: A Study in Art, Sentiment and Demonology* (Cambridge: Harvard University Press, 1952).

Bion, Wilfred. 'Attacks on Linking', *Second Thoughts: Selected Papers on Psycho-Analysis* (London: William Heinemann Medical Books, 1967) 93–109.

——. 'On Arrogance' (1957), *Second Thoughts: Selected Papers on Psycho-Analysis* (London: William Heinemann Medical Books, 1967) 86–92.

——. 'A Theory of Thinking' (1962), *Second Thoughts: Selected Papers on Psycho-Analysis* (London: William Heinemann Medical Books, 1967) 110–19.

Blanchot, Maurice. 'L'œuvre et l'espace de la mort', *L'espace littéraire* (Paris: NRF Gallimard, 1955).

——. *Le livre à venir* (Paris: Gallimard, 1959).

Boris, Harold. *Sleights of Mind: One and Multiples of One* (Northvale, NJ: Jason Aronson, 1994).

Boyarin, Daniel. *Carnal Israel: Reading Sex in Talmudic Culture* (Berkeley: University of California Press, 1993).

Brisman, Leslie. *Milton's Poetry of Choice and Its Romantic Heirs* (Ithaca: Cornell University Press, 1973).

Brooks, Peter. 'Freud's Masterplot', *Literature and Psychoanalysis: The Question of Reading: Otherwise*, ed. Shoshana Felman (Baltimore: Johns Hopkins University Press, 1982).

Brunn, Lucas. *Praxis perspectivae. Das ist: von Verzeichnungen ein aüszfuhrlicher Bericht* (Leipzig, 1615).

Bunyan, John. *The Pilgrim's Progress from This World to That Which Is to Come*, 2nd edn, eds James Blanton Wharey and Roger Sharrock (Oxford: Clarendon Press, 1960).

Burke, Edmund. *A Philosophical Enquiry into the Origin of Our Ideas of the Sublime and the Beautiful*, ed. James T. Boulton (Oxford: Oxford University Press, 1987).

Burns, J. H. *The True Law of Kingship: Concepts of Monarchy in Early Modern Scotland* (Oxford: Clarendon Press, 1996).

Burrow, Colin. *Epic Romance: Homer to Milton* (Oxford: Clarendon Press, 1993).

Butler, Judith. *Gender Trouble: Feminism and the Subversion of Identity* (New York: Routledge, 1990).

*Calendar of State Papers relating to Scotland, 1589–1603*, ed. Markham John Thorpe (London: Longman, 1858).

Campbell, Lily B. (ed.). *Tottel's Miscellany* (Cambridge, Mass.: Harvard University Press, 1965).

Carroll, Clare. 'The Construction of Gender and the Cultural and Political Order in *The Faerie Queene* 5 and *A View of the Present State of Ireland*: The Critics, the Context' and the Case of Radigund, *Criticism* 32: 2 (1990) 163–92.

Cavanagh, Sheila T. *Wanton Eyes and Chaste Desires: Female Sexuality in The Faerie Queene* (Bloomington and Indianapolis: Indiana University Press, 1994).

Chaucer, Geoffrey. *The Riverside Chaucer*, 3rd edn, eds Larry D. Benson *et al.* (New York: Houghton Mifflin, 1987).

Cheney, Patrick. *Marlowe's Counterfeit Profession: Ovid, Spenser, Counter-Nationhood* (Toronto: University of Toronto Press, 1997).

Claudian. *De raptu proserpinae*, trans. Maurice Platnaur. *Claudian*, vol. 2 (Cambridge: Harvard University Press, 1972).

Cleaver, Robert and John Dod. *A Godly Form of Household Government: For the Ordering of Private Families, According to the Direction of God* (London, 1621).

Coldiron, E.B. 'Milton in parvo: Mortalism and Genre Transformation in "Sonnet 14"', *Milton Quarterly* 28.1 (1994) 2–9.

Cole, Tim. *Selling the Holocaust: From Auschwitz to Schindler: How History Is Bought, Packaged and Sold*, 1999; rpt. (London: Routledge, 2000).

Colley, Linda. *Britons: Forging the Nation 1707–1837*. 1992; rpt. (London: Vintage, 1994).

Collins, Daniel. 'Anamorphosis and the Eccentric Observer: Inverted Perspective and the Construction of the Gaze', *Leonardo* 25.1 (1992) 73–82.

Corns, Thomas M. (ed.). *The Royal Image: Representations of Charles I* (Cambridge: Cambridge University Press, 1999).

Cousins, A.D. 'Ralegh's *A Vision upon this Conceipt of the Faery Queene*', *Explicator* 41:3 (1983) 14–16.

Crawford, Patricia. 'Charles Stuart: That Man of Blood', *Journal of British Studies* 16 (1977) 41–61.

Cressy, David. *Birth, Marriage, and Death: Ritual, Religion, and the Life-Cycle in Tudor and Stuart England* (Oxford: Oxford University Press, 1997).

Cullen, Patrick. *Infernal Triad: The Flesh, the World, and the Devil in Spenser and Milton* (Princeton: Princeton University Press, 1974).

Culler, Jonathan. 'Fabula and Sjuzhet in the Analysis of Narrative: Some American Discussions', *Poetics Today* 1 (1980) 27–37.

Daniel, Clay. *Death in Milton's Poetry* (Lewisburg: Bucknell University Press, 1994).

Deleuze, Gilles and Félix Guattari. 'Bilan-programme pour machines désirantes', *Minuit* no. 2 (January 1973), trans. Robert Hurley as 'Balance-sheet Programme for Desiring Machines' in *Semiotext(e)* 2:3 (1977) 117–135.

Derrida, Jacques. 'La différance', *Marges de la philosophie* (Paris: Minuit, 1972).

*A detection of the Actions of Mary Queen of Scots* (1721).

De Troyes, Chrétien. *The Knight of the Cart (Lancelot) in Arthurian Romances*. Trans. William W. Kibler and Carleton W. Carroll (Harmondsworth: Penguin, 1991) 207–94.

Doebler, Bettie Anne. *Rooted Sorrow: Dying in Early Modern England* (Rutherford, NJ: Fairleigh Dickinson University Press, 1994).

Dollimore, Jonathan. *Death, Desire, and Loss in Western Culture* (New York: Routledge, 1998).

Doran, Susan. *Monarchy and Matrimony: The Courtships of Elizabeth I* (London: Routledge, 1996).

——. 'Revenge her Foul and Most Unnatural Murder? The Impact of Mary Stewart's Execution on Anglo-Scottish Relations', *History* 85 (2000) 589–612.

Dryden, John. *Essays*, 2 vols (1900), ed. W. P. Ker (New York: Russell and Russell, 1961).

Eccles, Audrey. *Obstetrics and Gynaecology in Tudor and Stuart England* (London; Croom Helm, 1982).

Eigen, Michael. *Psychic Deadness* (London: Jason Aronson, 1996).

*Eikon Basilike: The Portraiture of His Sacred Majesty in His Solitudes and Sufferings*, ed. Philip Knachel (Ithaca, NY: Cornell University Press for the Folger Shakespeare Library, 1966).

Eliot, T. S. *Collected Poems 1909–1962* (New York: Harcourt Brace, 1963).

Empson, William. *Seven Types of Ambiguity* (London: Chatto & Windus, 1947).

Erasmus. *The Enchiridion of Erasmus*, trans. and ed. Raymond Himelick (Bloomington: University of Indiana Press, 1963).

Erskine-Hill, Howard. *Poetry and the Realm of Politics: Shakespeare to Dryden* (Oxford: Clarendon Press, 1996).

Euripides. *Cyclops, Alcestis, Mediea*, ed. and trans. David Kovacs, Loeb Classical Library (Cambridge, Mass.: Harvard University Press, 1994).

Fichter, Andrew. *Poets Historical: Dynastic Epic in the Renaissance* (New Haven, CT: Yale University Press, 1982).

Fletcher, Angus. *Allegory: The Theory of a Symbolic Mode* (Ithaca: Cornell University Press, 1964).

——. *The Prophetic Moment: An Essay on Spenser* (Chicago: University of Chicago Press, 1971).

——. *The Transcendental Masque: An Essay on Milton's 'Comus'* (Ithaca: Cornell University Press, 1971).

Foister, Susan, Ashok Roy and Martin Wyld. *Making and Meaning Holbein's Ambassadors* (London: Yale University Press for the National Gallery, 1998).

Foucault, Michel. *Discipline and Punish: The Birth of the Prison*, trans. Alan Sheridan (Harmondsworth: Penguin, 1977).

Fowler, Elizabeth. 'The Failure of Moral Philosophy in the Work of Edmund Spenser', *Representations* 51 (1995) 47–76.

Fraser, Antonia. *Mary Queen of Scots* (London: Weidenfeld and Nicolson, 1969).

Frazer, Sir James George (ed.). *The* Fasti *of Ovid*, 5 vols. (London: Macmillan – now Palgrave Macmillan, 1929).

Freud, Sigmund. *Beyond the Pleasure Principle. The Standard Edition of the Complete Psychological Works of Sigmund Freud*, 24 vols, ed. James Strachey *et al.* (London: Hogarth Press and Institute of Psycho-Analysis, 1953–73).

Frye, Northrop. *Secular Scripture: A Study of the Structure of Romance* (Cambridge: Harvard University Press, 1976).

Frye, Roland Mushat. *Milton's Imagery and the Visual Arts: Iconographic Tradition in the Epic Poems* (Princeton: Princeton University Press, 1978).

Gilman, Ernest. *The Curious Perspective: Literary and Pictorial Wit in the Seventeenth Century* (New Haven and London: Yale University Press, 1978).

Gittings, Clare. *Death, Burial and the Individual in Early Modern England* (London: Croom Helm, 1984).

Gittings, Clare and Peter Jupp (eds). *Death in England: An Illustrated History* (New Brunswick: Rutgers University Press, 2000).

Goldberg, Jonathan. *Endlesse* Worke*: Spenser and the Structures of Discourse* (Baltimore: Johns Hopkins University Press, 1981).

Gordon, Bruce and Peter Marshall. *The Place of the Dead: Death and Remembrance in Late Medieval and Early Modern Europe* (Cambridge: Cambridge University Press, 2000).

Gordon, Richard. 'Vesta', *Oxford Classical Dictionary*, eds Simon Hornblower and Anthony Spawforth (New York: Oxford University Press, 1996).

Gouge, William. *Of Domesticall Duties: Eight Treatises* (London, 1622).

Greenblatt, Stephen. *Renaissance Self-Fashioning: From More to Shakespeare* (Chicago: University of Chicago Press, 1980).

——. 'Invisible Bullets: Renaissance Authority and its Subversion', *Glyph* 8 (1981) 40–61.

——. Gen. Ed. *The Norton Shakespeare* (New York: W.W. Norton, 1997).

——. 'The Inevitable Pit', *London Review of Books* (21 September 2000) 8–12.

——. 'Racial Memory and Literary History', *PMLA* 116:1 (2001) 48–63.

——. *Hamlet in Purgatory* (Princeton: Princeton University Press, 2002).

'Greenblatt Named University Professor', *Harvard College Gazette* (November 2000) 2.

Gregerson, Linda. *The Reformation of the Subject: Spenser, Milton, and the English Protestant Epic* (Cambridge: Cambridge University Press, 1995).

Gross, Kenneth. ' "Each Heav'nly Close": Mythologies and Metrics in Spenser and the Early Poetry of Milton', *PMLA* 98 (1983) 21–36.

——. 'The Postures of Allegory', *Edmund Spenser: Essays on Culture and Allegory*, eds Jennifer Klein Morrison and Matthew Greenfield (Aldershot, England: Ashgate, 2000) 167–79.

Grossman, Marshall. *'Authors to themselves': Milton and the Revelation of History* (Cambridge: Cambridge University Press, 1987).

——. *The Story of All Things: Writing the Self in Renaissance English Narrative Poetry* (Durham: Duke University Press, 1998).

Guilfoyle, Cherrell. ' "If Shape It Might Be Call'd That Shape Had None": Aspects of Death in Milton', *Milton Studies* 13 (1978) 35–58.

Guillory, John. *Poetic Authority: Spenser, Milton, and Literary History* (New York: Columbia University Press, 1983).

Guy, John. *Tudor England* (Oxford: Oxford University Press, 1988).

——. 'The 1590s: The Second Reign of Elizabeth I?' *The Reign of Elizabeth I: Court and Culture in the Last Decade*, ed. John Guy (Cambridge: Cambridge University Press, 1995) 1–19.

——. 'Tudor monarchy and its critiques', *The Tudor Monarchy*, ed. John Guy (London: Arnold, 1997) 78–109.

Hackett, Helen. *Virgin Mother, Maiden Queen: Elizabeth I and the Cult of the Virgin Mary* (Basingstoke: Macmillan – now Palgrave Macmillan, 1995).

Hadfield, Andrew. *Spenser's Irish Experience: Wilde Fruit and Salvage Soyl* (Oxford: Clarendon Press, 1997).

Hamilton, A. C. (ed.). *The Structure of Allegory in 'The Faerie Queene'* (Oxford: Clarendon Press, 1961).

——. *The Spenser Encyclopedia* (London, Toronto and Buffalo: Routledge/Toronto University Press, 1990) 680–2.

Heidegger, Martin. *Being and Time*, trans. John Macquarrie and Edward Robinson (New York: Basic Books, 1962).

Helgerson, Richard. *Forms of Nationhood: The Elizabethan Writing of England* (Chicago: University of Chicago Press, 1992).

Herbert, George. *The English Poems of George Herbert*, ed. C. A. Patrides (London: J. M. Dent, 1974).

Herbert-Brown, Geraldine. *Ovid and the Fasti: An Historical Study* (Oxford: Clarendon Press, 1994).

Hieatt, A. Kent. 'Three Fearful Symmetries and the Meaning of *Faerie Queene* II', *A Theatre for Spenserians*. Eds Judith M. Kennedy and James A. Reither (Toronto: University of Toronto Press, 1973) 19–52.

——. *Chaucer, Spenser, Milton* (Montreal: McGill-Queen's University Press, 1975).

Hiles, Jane. 'Milton's Royalist Reflex: The Failure of Argument and the Role of Dialogics in *Eikonoklastes*', *Spokesperson Milton: Voices in Contemporary Criticism*, eds Charles W. Durham and Kristin Pruitt McColgan (Cranbury, NJ: Susquehanna University Press, 1994) 87–100.

Hill, Christopher. *The Experience of Defeat: Milton and Some Contemporaries* (New York: Viking, 1984).

*The History of Scotland written in Latin by George Buchanan; faithfully rendered into English* (J. Fraser) (1690).

Holahan, Michael. '*Imque opus exegi*: Ovid's Changes and Spenser's Brief Epic of Mutability', *ELR* 6 (1976) 244–70.

Howell, Thomas Bayly (ed.). *A Complete Collection of State Trials*, Vol. IV (London: T.C. Hansard, 1816) cols. 1045–1135.

Hughes, Merritt Y. (ed.). *John Milton: The Complete Poems and Major Prose* (New York: Odyssey, 1957).

Hulston, James. *A Rational Millenium: Puritan Utopias of Seventeenth-Century England and America* (New York: Oxford University Press, 1987).

Hutcheon, Linda. 'Rethinking the National Model', *Rethinking Literary History* (New York: Oxford University Press, forthcoming).

Kay, Dennis. *Melodious Tears: The English Funeral Elegy from Spenser to Milton* (Oxford: Clarendon, 1990).

Keller, Katherine Z. and Gerald J. Schiffhorst (eds). *The Witness of Times: Manifestations of Ideology in Seventeenth Century England* (Pittsburgh: Duquesne University Press, 1993).

Kelsey, Sean. 'Staging the Trial of Charles I', *The Regicides and the Execution of Charles*, ed. Jason Peacey (Basingstoke: Palgrave – now Palgrave Macmillan, 2001) 71–93.

Kernan, Alvin. *Shakespeare, the King's Playwright: Theater in the Stuart Court, 1603–1613* (Princeton: Princeton University Press, 1995).

Kezar, Dennis. *Guilty Creatures: Renaissance Poetry and the Ethics of Authorship* (Oxford: Oxford University Press, 2001).

King, John N. *Spenser's Poetry and the Reformation Tradition* (Princeton: Princeton University Press, 1990).

——. *Milton and Religious Controversy: Satire and Polemic in Paradise Lost* (Cambridge: Cambridge University Press, 2000).

Klein, Daniel P. *Legal History* 18.1 (1997) 1–25.

Klein, Melanie. *Love, Guilt and Reparation and Other Works 1921–1945: The Writings of Melanie Klein*, vol. I (New York: Free Press, 1975).

——. *Envy and Gratitude and Other Works 1946–1963: The Writings of Melanie Klein*, vol. III (New York: Free Press, 1975).

Knoppers, Laura Lunger. *Historicizing Milton: Spectacle, Power, and Poetry in Restoration England* (Athens: University of Georgia Press, 1994).

Knott, John. ' "Suffering for Truth's Sake": Milton and Martyrdom', *Politics, Poetics, and Hermeneutics in Milton's Prose*, eds David Loewenstein and James Turner (Cambridge: Cambridge University Press, 1990) 153–70.

Koenigsberg, S. M. 'The Vote to Create the High Court of Justice: 26 to 20?', *Parliamentary History*, XII (1993) 281–6.

Kolbrener, William. *Milton's Warring Angels: A Study of Critical Engagements* (Cambridge: Cambridge University Press, 1997).

Koller, Kathrine. 'Art, Rhetoric, and Holy Dying in the *Faerie Queene* with Special Reference to the Despair Canto', *SP* 61 (1964) 128–39.

Krier, Theresa. *Birth Passages: Maternity and Nostalgia, Antiquity to Shakespeare.* (Ithaca: Cornell University Press, 2001).

——. 'Mother's Sorrow, Mother's Joy: Mourning Birth in Edmund Spenser's Garden of Adonis', *Grief and Gender, 700–1700*, eds. Jennifer Vaught and Lynne Dickson Bruckner (New York: Palgrave Macmillan, forthcoming).

Kuin, Roger. *Chamber Music: Elizabethan Sonnet Sequences and the Pleasure of Criticism* (Toronto: University of Toronto Press, 1998).

Lacan, Jacques. *The Four Fundamental Concepts of Psycho-Analysis (Seminar Book XI)*, ed Jacques-Alain Miller, trans. Alan Sheridan (New York: Norton, 1973, 1978).

——. *The Seminar of Jacques Lacan Book VII: The Ethics of Psychoanalysis 1959–1960*, ed. Jacques-Alain Miller, trans. Dennis Porter (New York: Norton, 1992).

Lacey, Andrew. 'Elegies and Commemorative Verse in Honour of Charles the Martyr, 1649–60', *The Regicides and the Execution of Charles*, ed. Jason Peacey (Basingstoke: Palgrave – now Palgrave Macmillan, 2001) 225–46.

Leeman, Fred. *Hidden Images: Games of Perception, Anamorphic Art, Illusion* (New York: Harry Abrams, 1976).

Lewalski, Barbara K. *The Life, of John Milton* (Oxford: Blackwell, 2000).

Lewis, C. S. *Spenser's Images of Life*, ed. Alastair Fowler (Cambridge: Cambridge University Press, 1967).

Lewis, Jayne Elizabeth. *Mary Queen of Scots: Romance and Nation* (London: Routledge, 1998).

Litten, Julian. *The English Way of Death: The Common Funeral since 1450* (London: R. Hale, 1991).

Lipking, Lawrence. 'The Genius of the Shore: Lycidas, Adamastor, and the Poetics of Nationalism', *PMLA* 111:2 (1996) 205–21.

Llewellyn, Nigel. *The Art of Death: Visual Culture in the English Death Ritual C. 1500–C. 1800* (London: Reaktion, 1991).

Low, Anthony. *The Reinvention of Love: Poetry, Politics and Culture from Sidney to Milton* (Cambridge: Cambridge University Press, 1993).

——. '*Hamlet* and the Ghost of Purgatory: Intimations of Killing the Father', *ELR* 29 (1999) 443–67.

Lukacher, Ned. 'Anamorphic Stuff: Shakespeare, Catharsis, Lacan', *Rereadings in the Freudian Field*, ed. A. Leigh De Neef, *The South Atlantic Quarterly* 88 (1989) 863–98.

Lyotard, Jean-François. *The Differend: Phrases in Dispute*, trans. Georges Van Den Abbeele (Minneapolis: University of Minnesota Press, 1988).

McCabe, Richard A. 'The Masks of Duessa: Spenser, Mary Queen of Scots, and James I', *ELR* 17 (1987) 224–42.

MacCaffrey, Isabel G. *Spenser's Allegory: The Anatomy of Imagination* (Princeton: Princeton University Press, 1976).

McCoy, Richard C. *The Rites of Knighthood: The Literature and Politics of Elizabethan Chivalry* (Berkeley: University of California Press, 1989).

MacDonald, Michael and Terence R. Murphy. *Sleepless Souls: Suicide in Early Modern England* (Oxford: Clarendon, 1990).

Maclean, Hugh (ed.). *Ben Jonson and the Cavalier Poets* (New York: Norton, 1974).

Maley, Willy. *A Spenser Chronology* (Basingstoke: Macmillan – now Palgrave Macmillan, 1994).

Malory, Sir Thomas. *Le Morte D'Arthur*, 2 vols, ed. Janet Cowen (Harmondsworth: Penguin, 1969).

Marotti, Arthur F. ' "Love is not Love": Elizabethan Sonnet Sequences and the Social Order', *ELH* 49 (1982) 396–428.

Mason, Roger A. 'George Buchanan, James VI and the Presbyterians', *Scots and Britons: Scottish Political Thought and the Union of 1603*, ed. Roger A. Mason (Cambridge: Cambridge University Press, 1994) 112–37.

Mendelson, Sara and Patricia Crawford. *Women in Early Modern England* (Oxford: Clarendon Press, 1998).

Miller, David Lee. Opening Round Table, '*The Faerie Queene* and the World, 1596–1996, Edmund Spenser among the Disciplines', Yale Center for British Art, New Haven, Conn. (6 September, 1996).

Milton, John. *Areopagitica. Complete Prose Works of John Milton*, eds. Don M. Wolfe *et al.*, 8 vols (New Haven: Yale University Press, 1953–82).

——. *Eikonoklastes, The Complete Prose Works of John Milton*, vol. 3, ed. Douglas Bush (New Haven: Yale University Press, 1962).

——. *The Poems of John Milton*, eds John Carey and Alastair Fowler. 1968; rpt. (Norton: New York, 1972).

——. *The Complete Poems*, ed. John Leonard (London: Penguin, 1998).

Morrill, John and Philip Baker. 'Oliver Cromwell, the Regicide and the sons of Zeruiah', *The Regicides and the Execution of Charles*, ed. Jason Peacey (Basingstoke: Palgrave – now Palgrave Macmillan, 2001) 14–35.

Muddiman, J. G. *The Trial of Charles I* (London: W. Hodge, 1928).

Nairn, Tom. *The Break-Up of Britain: Crisis and Neo-Nationalism*, 2nd edn (London: Verso, 1981).

Neill, Michael. *Issues of Death: Mortality and Identity in English Tragedy* (Oxford: Clarendon Press, 1997).

Neuse, Richard. 'The Virgilian Triad Revisited', *ELH* 45 (1978) 606–39.

Nohrnberg, James. *The Analogy of 'The Faerie Queene'* (Princeton: Princeton University Press, 1976).

Norbrook, David. *Poetry and Politics in the English Renaissance* (London: Routledge, 1984).

——. '*Macbeth* and the Politics of Historiography', *Politics of Discourse: The Literature and History of Seventeenth-Century England*, eds Kevin Sharpe and Steven N. Zwicker (Berkeley: University of California Press, 1987) 78–116.

——. *Writing the English Republic: Poetry, Rhetoric and Politics, 1627–1660* (Cambridge: Cambridge University Press, 1999–2000).

Novick, Peter. *The Holocaust in American Life* (New York: Houghton Mifflin, 1999).

Oakeshott, Walter. *The Queen and the Poet* (London: Faber, 1961).

O'Connell, Michael. *Mirror and Veil: The Historical Dimension of Spenser's Faerie Queene* (Chapel Hill: University of North Carolina Press, 1977).

O'Connor, Mary Catherine. *The Art of Dying Well: The Development of the Ars Moriendi* (New York: Columbia University Press, 1942).

Olyan, Saul. ' "They Shall Wail the Songs of the Temple": Sanctioned Mourning in Biblical Cultic Settings.' Religious Studies Seminar, University of New Hampshire, autumn, 2001.

Parker, Patricia. *Inescapable Romance: Studies in the Poetics of a Mode* (Princeton: Princeton University Press, 1978).

Peacock, John. 'The visual image of Charles I', *The Royal Image: Representations of Charles I*, ed. Thomas N. Corns (Cambridge: Cambridge University Press, 1999) 176–239.

Phillips, James Emerson. *Images of a Queen: Mary Stuart in Sixteenth-Century Literature* (Berkeley: University of California Press, 1964).

Pigman III, G. W. *Grief and English Renaissance Elegy* (Cambridge: Cambridge University Press, 1985).

Plato. *Symposium*. Trans. Michael Joyce. *The Collected Dialogues*, eds Edith H. Hamilton and Huntington Cairns (Princeton: Princeton University Press, 1961).

Potter, Lois. *Secret Rites and Secret Writing: Royalist Literature, 1641–1660* (Cambridge: Cambridge University Press, 1989).

Prudentius, Aurelius Clemens. *Psychomachia*, Vol. 3 of *Prudence*, ed. M. Lavarenne (Paris: Belles Lettres, 1948).

Quilligan, Maureen. *Milton's Spenser: The Politics of Reading* (Ithaca: Cornell University Press, 1983).

Quint, David. 'The Figure of Atlante: Ariosto and Boiardo's Poem', *Modern Language Notes* 94:1 (1979), 77–91.

——. *Epic and Empire: Politics and Generic Form from Virgil to Milton* (Princeton: Princeton University Press, 1993).

Raleigh, Sir Walter. *The Poems of Sir Walter Ralegh*, ed. Agnes M. C. Latham. (London: Constable, 1929).

Renan, Ernest. 'What is a Nation?' ['Qu'est-ce qu'une nation?' (1882)] *Nation and Narration*, ed. Homi K. Bhabha (London: Routledge, 1990) 8–22.

Ricks, Christopher. *Milton's Grand Style* (Oxford: Clarendon Press, 1963).

Riffaterre, Michael. *Semiotics of Poetry* (Bloomington: Indiana University Press, 1978).

Roche, Thomas P. 'The Menace of Despair and Arthur's Vision, *Faerie Queene* I.9', *SpStud* 4 (1983) 71–92.

Rosenblatt, Jason P. *Torah and Law in* Paradise Lost (Princeton: Princeton University Press, 1993).

Rovang, Paul R. *Refashioning "Knights and Ladies Gentle Deeds": The Intertextuality of Spenser's Faerie Queene and Malory's Morte D'arthur* (London: Associated Universities Press, 1996).

Rumrich, John P. 'The Erotic Milton', *Texas Studies in Language and Literature* 41:2 (1999) 128–41.

Sacks, Peter. *The English Elegy: Studies in the Genre from Spenser to Yeats* (Baltimore: Johns Hopkins University Press, 1985).

Sallenave, Danièle. *Le Don des morts* (Paris: NRF Gallimard, 1991).

Samuel, E. R. 'Death in the Glass: A New View of Holbein's Ambassadors', *Burlington Magazine* 105 (October 1963): 436–41.

Sandler, Florence. 'Icon and Iconoclast', *Achievements of the Left Hand: Essays on the Prose of John Milton*, eds Michael Lieb and John Shawcross (Amherst: University of Massachusetts Press, 1974) 160–84.

Schiesari, Juliana. *The Gendering of Melancholia: Feminism, Psychoanalysis, and the Symbolics of Loss in Renaissance Literature* (Ithaca: Cornell University Press, 1992).

Schroeder, J. W. 'Spenser's Erotic Drama: the Orgoglio Episode', *ELH* 29 (1962) 140–59.

Schoenfeldt, Michael C. *Bodies and Selves in Early Modern England: Physiology and Inwardness in Spenser, Shakespeare, Herbert, and Milton* (Cambridge: Cambridge University Press, 1999).

Scott, David. 'Motives for King-Killing', *The Regicides and the Execution of Charles,* ed. Jason Peacey (Basingstoke: Palgrave – now Palgrave Macmillan, 2001) 138–60.

Shakespeare, William. *The Riverside Shakespeare*, eds G. Blakemore Evans *et al.* (Boston: Houghton Mifflin, 1974).

Sidney, Sir Philip. *A Defence of Poesy*, in *Miscellaneous Prose*, eds Jan van Dorsten and Katherine Duncan-Jones (Oxford: Clarendon Press, 1973).

Silberman, Lauren. *Transforming Desire; Erotic Knowledge in Books III and IV of* The Faerie Queene (Berkeley: University of California Press, 1995).

Skulsky, Harold. 'Spenser's Despair Episode and the Theology of Doubt,' *MP* 78 (1981) 227–42.

Snyder, Susan. 'The Left Hand of God: Despair in Renaissance Tradition', *StudRen* 12 (1965) 18–59.

Söderlind, Sylvia. 'Illegitimate Perspectives and the Critical Unconscious: The Anamorphic Imagination', *Canadian Review of Comparative Literature* (1990) 213–26.

Spence, Joseph. *Observations, Anecdotes and Characters of Books and Men*, ed. J. M. Osborn (New Haven: Yale University Press, 1966).

Spenser, Edmund. *The Variorum Edition of the Works of Edmund Spenser*, eds Edwin Greenlaw, Charles Osgood, and Frederick Morgan Padelford (Baltimore: Johns Hopkins University Press, 1947).

——. *The Faerie Queene*, ed. A. C. Hamilton (London: Longman, 1977).

——. *The Faerie Queene*, ed. Thomas P. Roche, Jr, with the assistance of C. Patrick O'Donnell, Jr (Harmondsworth, Middlesex: Penguin, 1978).

——. *A View of the State of Ireland*, eds Andrew Hadfield and Willy Maley (Oxford: Blackwell, 1997).

——. *The Faerie Queene*, ed. A. C. Hamilton (London: Longman, 2001, rev. edn).

——. *The Yale Edition of the Shorter Poems of Edmund Spenser*, eds William A. Oram, Einar Bjorvand, Ronald Bond, Thomas H. Cain, Alexander Dunlop, and Richard Schell (New Haven: Yale University Press, 1989).

Stackhouse, Amy Dunham. 'Disseminating the Author: Milton and the Trope of Collaboration', unpublished dissertation, University of Maryland, 1998.

*Statutes of the Realm*, vol. 1 (London: Pall Mall, 1819; rpt 1963).

Steffen, Lisa. *Defining a British State: Treason and National Identity, 1608–1820* (Basingstoke: Palgrave – now Palgrave Macmillan, 2001).

Stein, Arnold. 'Imagining Death: The Ways of Milton', *Milton Studies* 29 (1993) 105–20.

Steiner, Franz Baermann. *Selected Writings*, vol. 1, *Taboo, Truth and Religion*, eds Jeremy Adler, and Richard Fardon Berghahn (2001): cited in *TLS* 2 March 2001, in a review by Henning Ritter 31.

Stevens, Paul. 'Milton's Janus-faced Nationalism: Subject, Soliloquy, and the Modern Nation-State', *JEGP* 100:2 (2001) 247–68.

——. 'Milton's 'Renunciation'of Cromwell: The Problem of Raleigh's Cabinet-Council', *Modern Philology* 98:3 (2001) 363–92.

——.'Pretending to be Real: Stephen Greenblatt and the Legacy of Popular Existentialism', *New Literary History*, forthcoming.

Stevens, Wallace. *The Collected Poems of Wallace Stevens* (New York: Alfred A. Knopf, 1968).

Stone, Lawrence. *The Family, Sex and Marriage in England, 1500–1800*, abridged edn 1979; rpt (Harmondsworth: Penguin, 1988).

Strong, Roy. *The Cult of Elizabeth: Elizabethan Portraiture and Pageantry* (London: Thames and Hudson, 1977).

Teskey, Gordon. 'From Allegory to Dialectic: Imagining Error in Spenser and Milton', *PMLA*, 101:1 (1986) 9–23.

——. 'Milton's Choice of Subject in the Context of Renaissance Critical Theory', *ELH* 53 (1986) 53–72.

——. 'Mutability, Genealogy, and the Authority of Forms', *Representations* 41 (1993) 104–22.

——. 'Allegory, Materialism, and Violence', *The Production of English Renaissance Culture*, eds David Lee Miller, Sharon O'Dair and Harold Weber (Ithaca: Cornell University Press, 1994) 293–318

——. *Allegory and Violence* (Ithaca: Cornell University Press, 1996).

Thucydides. *History of the Peloponnesian War*, trans. Rex Warner, intro. M. I. Finlay (Harmondsworth: Penguin, 1972).

Topper, David. 'On Anamorphosis: Setting Some Things Straight', *Leonardo* 33.2 (2000) 115–24.

Trubowitz, Rachel. ' "Nourish-Milke": Breast-Feeding and the Crisis of Englishness, 1600–1660', *Journal of English and German Philology* 99.1 (2000) 29–49.

Tuve, Rosemond. *Allegorical Imagery: Some Mediaeval Books and Their Posterity*. (Princeton: Princeton University Press, 1966).

Underdown, David. *Pride's Purge: Politics in the Puritan Revolution* (Oxford: Oxford University Press, 1971).

Van Dyke, Carolynn. *The Fiction of Truth: Structures of Meaning in Narrative and Dramatic Allegory* (Ithaca: Cornell University Press, 1985).

Vicari, Patricia. 'The Triumph of Art, the Triumph of Death: Orpheus in Spenser and Milton', *Orpheus: The Metamorphoses of a Myth*, ed. John Warden (Toronto: University of Toronto Press, 1982) 207–30.

Virgil. *The Aeneid*, trans. H. Rushton Fairclough. Loeb Classical Library, rev. edn. (Cambridge: Harvard University Press, 1934).

——. *Eclogues, Georgics, Aeneid, and Minor Porms*, ed. and trans. H. Rushton Fairclough, 2 vols, Loeb Classical Library (Cambridge: Harvard University Press, 1947).

——. *The Aeneid*, trans. W. F. Jackson Knight. 1956; rpt (Harmondsworth: Penguin, 1958).

*Visitor's Guide*. US Holocaust Memorial Museum, Washington DC, 2002.

Watson, Robert N. *The Rest Is Silence: Death as Annihilation in the English Renaissance* (Berkeley and Los Angeles: University of California Press, 1994).

Wedgwood, C. V. *The Trial of Charles I* (London: Collins, 1964).

Wheeler, Elizabeth Skerpan. '*Eikon Basilike* and the Rhetoric of Self-Representation', *The King's Image: Representations of Charles I*, ed. Thomas Corns (Cambridge: Cambridge University Press, 1999) 122–40.

Wheelock Arthur Jr, Susan J. Barnes, and Julius Held (eds), *Anthony van Dyck* (New York: Harry N. Abrams, 1990).

White, Robert B. 'Milton's Allegory of Sin and Death: A Commentary on Backgrounds', *Modern Philology* 70 (1972–3): 337–41.

White, T. H. *The Once and Future King* (London: Collins, 1958).

Wilcher, Robert *The Writing of Royalism, 1628–1660* (Cambridge: Cambridge University Press, 2001) 276–86.

Williams, Kathleen. 'Milton, Greatest Spenserian', *Milton and the Line of Vision*, ed. J. A. Wittreich, Jr (Madison: University of Wisconsin Press, 1975) 25–55.

Williamson, Arthur. 'Patterns of British Identity: "Britain" and its Rivals in the Sixteenth and Seventeenth Centuries', *The New British History: Founding a Modern State, 1603–1715*, ed. Glenn Burgess (London: Taurus, 1999) 138–73.

Wilson, D. Harris. *King James VI and I* (London: Jonathan Cape, 1956).

Wittreich, Joseph A. Jr, *Visionary Poetics: Milton's Tradition and His Legacy* (San Marino, CA: Huntington Library, 1979).

Wollebius, John. *The Abridgement of Christian Divinitie* (London, 1650).

# Index

*Abridgement of Christian Divinitie* (Wollebius), 135
*Acts and Monuments* (Foxe), 175
Addison, Joseph, 4
*Aeneid* (Virgil), 9, 116, 178
Alberti, Leonbattisti, 153
*Ambassadors, The* (Holbein) (painting), 153–6
anamorphosis, 151
  content of, 153
  examples of, 153–6
  literary, 151–2, 158–61, 166
  mechanism of, 153
Anderson, Benedict, 179, 183
Anderson, Judith, 34
*Apology* (Milton), 181
*Areopagitica* (Milton), 7, 125–6, 180
  allegory in, 126
  importance of time in, 128–9
  memory and, 182–3
  portrayal of sin in, 122, 123
  republican sentiments in, 137, 181
  Spenserian influence on, 127
Ariès, Philippe, 1, 2, 152
Ariosto, Ludovico, 10–12, 29, 33
Aristotle, 31
Augustine, saint, 118

Barthes, Roland, 124
*Basilikon Doron* (James I), 134
Bataille, Georges, 91
Benjamin, Walter, 131, 132, 134, 198
Bion, Wilfred, 49–52, 191
Blanchot, Maurice, 87, 88, 90, 91
Boiardo, Matteo, 68
*Book of Martyrs* (Foxe), 175
Boris, Harold, 52
Bothwell, James, earl of, 37
Bowes, Robert, 37–8
Bresson, Robert, 124
Brisman, Leslie, 192
Brooks, Peter, 9

Brunn, Lucas, 156
Buchanan, George, 39
Bunyan, John, 66, 67
Burghley, William, 79
Burke, Edmund, 134, 190

Catherine of Aragon, 42
Caxton, William, 30
Charles I
  execution of, 134, 135, 138–9
  portraiture of, 151, 152, 157, 162, 166–7
  trial of, 158
  writings of, 151, 157–61, 166
Charles II, 166, 167
Chaucer, Henry, 46, 198
Cleaver, Robert, 143
Cole, Tim, 174
Colley, Linda, 175
commiseration, as aspect of sorrow, 95
*Confessions* (Augustine), 118
Cousins, A. D., 178
Cromwell, Oliver, 179
Cromwell, Richard, 166

Da Vinci, Leonardo, 153
Dante, 48
Darnley, Henry Lord, 37
dearth, 97
death
  in allegory, 65–77
  in anamorphic art, 153–7
  attitudes toward, 196–7
  evolution of attitudes toward, 1, 133–8
  and generation, 107–12
  and kingship, 143
  vs. life, 187–8
  modern view of, 131, 174
  and nature, 143–4
  Pauline view of, 136–8
  and poetic form, 102–7

death – *continued*
  tragedy and, 3
  virginity and, 34–5
Derrida, Jacques, 87–8, 91, 92
*Detection of the Actions of Mary Queen
  of Scots* (Buchanan), 39
Dinteville, Jean de, 153, 155
Diodati, Charles, 171, 180–1, 183
Dod, John, 143
Donne, John, 65
Dryden, John, 78

eating
  and Fall, 101
  violence of, 49, 99
*Eikon Basilike* (Charles I), 151, 157, 197
  imagery of, 158–61
  influence of, 166
*Eikonoklastes* (Milton), 139
  anamorphosis in, 151–2, 163
  imagery of, 161–4
  as response to *Eikon Basilike*, 163–4,
    166, 197
  rhetoric of, 164–6
Eliot, T. S., 111
Elizabeth I, 178
  death of, 29
  as Faerie Queene, 30–1
  plots against, 37
  royal claim of, 42
  sexual repression of, 35
Empson, William, 188
'Epitaph on the Marchioness of
  Winchester' (Milton), 21
*Epitaphium Damonis* (Milton), 22,
  180–1
*Epithalamion* (*Spenser*)
  death in, 112
  outlook of, 114
  setting of, 107
  syntax of, 112–14
*Everyman*, 65
*Exposition* (Jewel), 175

*Faerie Queene, The* (Spenser)
  allegory in, 8–9, 54–6, 116
  Aristotelian philosophy in, 32
  attacks on linking in, 49–50, 60–2
  contemporary adulation for, 177–8

deep structure of, 9–10
epic prophecy in, 9–10
narrative style of, 120
nonfinality of death in, 8–9, 36,
  67–77, 80–7, 188, 194–6
parallels with Classical literature,
  187
poetic form in, 189
portrayal of death in, 5–6, 14, 78,
  117, 118, 119, 124
portrayal of despair in, 100
portrayal of error in, 4–5, 6–7, 121,
  122–3
portrayal of greed in, 46–9, 52–62
portrayal of Mary, Queen of Scots
  in, 38–43
relationships in, 29–30
semiological investigation of, 87–92
sources and precursors of, 7–8,
  10–12, 33, 178, 181
structure of, 119–20, 127–8
syntax of, 106–7
tone of, 13–14
varieties of death experience in, 28
virginity in, 32–6
Foxe, John, 174, 175
Frye, Northrop, 4

Gauden, John, 159
Geoffrey of Monmouth, 181
*Gerusalemme Liberata* (Tasso), 116
*Godly Form of Household Government,
  A* (Cleaver and Dod), 143
Gouge, William, 143
Greenblatt, Stephen, 24, 133, 135,
  138, 171–4, 180
Gregerson, Linda, 2, 23, 190, 195
Greville, Fulke Lord Brooke, 182, 183
Grossman, Marshall, 2, 23, 185, 190,
  192, 195

Hadfield, Andrew, 22, 197–8
Hall, John, 137
Hamilton, A. C., 71, 75, 92, 186
*Hamlet* (Shakespeare), 3, 109, 133
*Hamlet in Purgatory* (Greenblatt), 172,
  173
Henri II (France), 42
Henrietta Maria, queen, 160, 165, 178

Henry VII, 42
Henry VIII, 42
*Hero and Leander* (Marlowe), 33
Hesiod, 120
Hieatt, A. Kent, 55, 56
Hill, Christopher, 139
*History of Scotland* (Buchanan), 39
Holbein, Hans, 153
*Holy War* (Bunyan), 66
Homer, 178
Hotham, Sir John, 159–60, 163
Hutcheon, Linda, 183

*Imagined Communities* (Anderson),
   179, 183
*Inferno* (Dante), allegory in, 48
*Issues of Death* (Neill), 3

Jacobean drama, view of death in,
   133–4
James I, writings of, 134
James VI, 37
   and Spenser, 37–8
Jewel, John, bishop, 175
Johnson, Samuel, 4, 190

Keats, John, 66, 80
King, Edward, 171, 179, 183
King, John, 4
Klein, Melanie, 51–2
Knoppers, Laura, 24, 197, 198
Kolbrener, William, 126–7
Krier, Theresa, 22, 191, 198
Kuin, Roger, 23, 191, 195, 197

*Lancelot du lac* (Bresson) (film), 124
Laud, William, 158
*Le Don des morts*, 79
*Letter to Raleigh* (Spenser), 32, 41, 128
Lewalski, Barbara, 175
Lewis, C. S., 31
Lipking, Lawrence, 179–80, 183
Longinus, 136–7
Low, Anthony, 172, 174
Lownes, Matthew, 185
*Lycidas* (Milton), 22, 179

*Macbeth* (Shakespeare), 134, 144–5
Malory, Thomas, 30

Marlowe, Christopher, 33
Mary, Queen of Scots
   death of, 36
   life of, 37
   portrayal by Spenser, 38–43
Mary I, 37
Mary Tudor, 42
Medici, Catherine de, 37
Meditation XVII (Donne), 65
memento mori, 156
   anamorphic, 156–7
memory
   as commemoration of death,
      174–5
   as counter to death, 180–3
   responsibilities of, 172–4
   rights of, 171–2
   as spur to action, 182–3
'Methought I saw my late espoused
   saint' (Milton), 22, 176, 177
'Methought I saw the grave where
   Laura lay' (Raleigh), 177
Miller, David, 118
Milton, John
   influence of death on oeuvre of,
      21–2, 175–7, 179
   influence on modern view of
      death, 131–3
   influence of Spenser on, 2, 3–6,
      78–80, 189–90, 192
   nationalism of, 174–5, 179–80
   personal loss in life of, 171, 175–6
   prosody of, 102, 103–6
   republicanism of, 138–44, 178, 198
   view of death of, 102, 136–8
Milton, Katherine, 171, 175, 183
*Milton's Spenser* (Quilligan), 3
*Monty Python and the Holy Grail* (film),
   124
More, Sir Thomas, 172, 173
*Morte d'Arthur, Le* (Malory), 29, 35
*Much Ado About Nothing*
   (Shakespeare), 189
Munster famine, 95–6
'Mutabilitie Cantos' (Spenser), 15
   literary place of, 186
   portrayal of death in, 31, 78
   portrayal of royalty in, 41–2
   publication of, 185

'Nativity Ode, The' (Milton), 132
nature, and death, 143–4
Neill, Michael, 3
Neoplatonism, 76
Niceron, J. F., 156
*Nichomachean Ethics* (Aristotle), 31
Nicolson, George, 38
Nohrnberg, James, 8, 57
Norbrook, David, 134, 136, 137, 182
Novick, Peter, 174

O'Brien, Murrogh, execution of, 96
*Observations upon the Articles of Peace* (Milton), 179
*Of Domesticall Duties* (Gouge), 143
*Of Education* (Milton), 136
*Of True Religion* (Milton), 180
Olyan, Saul, 140, 141
'On the Death of the Beadle of the University of Cambridge' (Milton), 21
'On the death of the Bishop of Ely' (Milton), 22
'On the Death of the Bishop of Winchester' (Milton), 21
'On the Death of a Fair Infant dying of a Cough' (Milton), 22
'On the death of Vice-Chancellor, a physician' (Milton), 22
'On the Late Massacher in Piemont' (Milton), 22
'On Shakespeare' (Milton), 21
'On the University Carrier' (Milton), 21
*Orlando Furioso* (Ariosto), 10–12, 28, 33
*Orlando Innamorato* (Boiardo), 68

*Paradise Lost* (Milton)
  allegory of death in, 5, 134–5
  consequences of Fall in, 98–9
  contradictory emotions in, 139–42
  denial of death in, 131–48
  evolution of death in, 21
  Fall as suicide in, 101
  historical context of, 135–7
  imitation of Spenser in, 23, 121–2
  introduction of death in, 124–5

and modern view of death, 132–3
narrative style of, 116, 120
poetic form in, 189–90, 192–3
political view of, 139–44
portrayal of death in, 14–16, 17–21, 22, 97–8, 117, 118–19, 124
portrayal of sin in, 16, 120–1, 123
syntax of, 103–6
*Paradise Regained* (Milton), 131
  style of, 120
*Pardoner's Tale* (Chaucer), 46–7, 198
'Passion, The' (Milton), 22, 131
*Peri Hypsous, On the Sublime* (Longinus), 136–7
Pericles, funeral oration of, 182, 183
*Perspective curieuse, La* (Niceron), 156
Petrarch, 178
Philip II, 37
Pigman, G. W., 175
*Pilgrim's Progress* (Bunyan), 67
pity, as aspect of sorrow, 95
Plato, 187, 191
Powell, Mary, 171, 180
*Praxis Perspectivae* (Brunn), 156
*Preface to Fables Ancient and Modern* (Dryden), 1
Prescott, Anne Lake, 23, 191, 195, 197
Pride, Thomas, 158
*Prothalamion* (Spenser)
  mortality in, 111–12
  setting of, 107
  syntax of, 108–11
Prudentius, 66
*Psychomachia* (Prudentius), 66–7

Quilligan, Maureen, 3, 4
Quinn, Walter, 38

Raleigh, Sir Walter, 34, 177–8
*Renaissance Self-Fashioning* (Greenblatt), 172
Renan, Ernest, 174
*Rest is Silence, The* (Watson), 1
*Rethinking Literary History* (Hutcheon), 183
Riffaterre, Michael, 89
Rosenblatt, Jason, 136, 144

St Bartholomew's Day Massacre, 37

Sallenave, Danièle, 79

*Samson Agonistes* (Milton), 131–2

Saussure, Ferdinand de, 87

*Secular Scripture* (Frye), 4

Selve, Georges de, 153

*Seven Types of Ambiguity* (Empson), 188

Shakespeare, 3, 109, 133, 134, 144–5, 188–9

Sidney, Sir Philip, 83, 85

Sonnet 19 (Milton), 102

sorrow, aspects of, 95

Spenser, Edmund
  influence on Milton, 2, 3–6, 78–80, 189–90, 192
  royal disfavor on, 37–8
  view of death of, 66, 102, 117

*Spenser Encyclopedia, The* (Hamilton), 78, 80, 91

Steiner, Franz Baermann, 22

Stevens, Paul, 24–5, 198

suicide
  in *The Faerie Queene*, 100
  Fall as, 102

*Supplication of Souls* (More), 172

*Symposium* (Plato), 191

Tasso, Torquato, 116

Tennyson, Alfred Lord, 80

*Tenure of Kings and Magistrates* (Milton), 139

Teskey, Gordon, 2, 4, 6, 23, 48, 120, 187, 190, 191

*Three Modern Satirists* (Greenblatt), 171

Throckmorton, Elizabeth, 34

*Timaeus* (Plato), 187, 191

*Tourneiment Antichrist*, 66

tragedy, social importance of, 3

Trapnel, Anna, 136

Trubowitz, Rachel, 24, 198

Tuve, Rosemond, 47

'Upon the Circumcision' (Milton), 132

Van Dyck, Sir Anthony, 151, 156

Van Dyke, Carolynn, 66

*View of the Present State of Ireland, A* (Spenser), 39, 95–7

Virgil, 9, 116, 178

virginity, 32–4
  and death, 34–5

'Vision upon this Conceipt of the Faery Queene, A' (Raleigh), 177

*Waste Land, The* (Eliot), 111

Watson, Robert, 1, 135

Wentworth, Thomas, 158

White, T. H., 86

Willoughby, Francis Lord, 85

Winnicott, D. W., 49

*Winter's Tale, The* (Shakespeare), 189

Wollebius, John, 135